Nine Principal Upanishads

With kind regards, ॐ and prem

Swami Niranjan

Nine Principal Upanishads

Text, Transliteration, Translation and Notes

from the teachings of

Swami Satyananda Saraswati

Yoga Publications Trust, Munger, Bihar, India

Published by Bihar School of Yoga
    First edition 1975
    Reprinted 1985

Published by Yoga Publications Trust
    Second edition 2004
    Reprinted 2007

ISBN: 81-85787-34-4

Publisher and distributor: Yoga Publications Trust, Ganga Darshan, Munger, Bihar, India.

Website: www.yogavision.net

Printed at Thomson Press (India) Limited, New Delhi, 110001

Dedication

*In humility we offer this dedication to
Swami Sivananda Saraswati, who initiated
Swami Satyananda Saraswati into the secrets of yoga.*

Dedication

Contents

Phonetic Pronunciation Guide

अ	a	*as in* mica		ट्	t	true
आ T	aa	far		ठ्	th	anthill
इ ि	i	hill		ड्	d	do
ई ी	ee	fleet		ढ्	dh	redhead
उ ु	u	pull		ण्	n	gong
ऊ ू	oo	mood		त्	t	water (*dental*)
ऋ ृ	ri	clarity		थ्	th	nuthook
ॠ ॄ	ree	marine		द्	d	bud
लृ ॢ	lri	rivalry		ध्	dh	adhere (*more*
ल ॣ	lree	coral reef				*dental*)
ए े	e	prey		न्	n	not
ऐ ै	ai	aisle		प्	p	pay
ओ ो	o	go		फ्	ph	photo
औ ौ	au	cow		ब्	b	rub
ं	m	rum		भ्	bh	abhor
ँ	m	rum		म्	m	map
:	h	bah		य्	y	yoga
क्	k	meek		र्	r	red
ख्	kh	inkhorn		ल्	l	bull
ग्	g	go		व्	v	vice
घ्	gh	yoghurt		श्	sh	shield
ङ्	n	sing		ष्	sh	assure
च्	ch	check		स्	s	sit
छ्	chh	churchhill		ह्	h	hit
ज्	j	jab		क्ष्	ksh	kshatriya
झ्	jh	hedgehog		त्र्	tr	track (*dental*)
ञ्	n	canyon		ज्ञ्	jn	jnana

The Essence of the Upanishads

The Glory of the Upanishads

1. Salutations to all Brahma Vidya Gurus, or the preceptors of knowledge of Brahman.
2. Prostrations to Satchidananda Para Brahma, who is the prop, basis and source of everything.
3. The acme of wisdom of the sages is to be found in the Upanishads.
4. The Upanishads teach the philosophy of absolute unity.
5. Knowledge of the Upanishads destroys ignorance, the seed of samsara.
6. Behind the names and forms of the world dwells the eternal, infinite Satchidananda Brahman.
7. This world is indwelt by Para Brahman or the Absolute.
8. Renounce all desires. Renounce egoism, selfishness and identification with the body. Then alone will you attain moksha or liberation.
9. The desire for liberation will destroy all worldly desires.
10. Do your religious rites and daily duties without expectation of the fruits of your actions.
11. Constantly do selfless service for the benefit of humanity with Atma bhava, or devotion to God. You will purify your heart in this way. Then realization will dawn.

Excerpt from *Essence of The Principal Upanishads* by Swami Sivananda Saraswati, 1st edn, published in 1959 by the Divine Life Society, Rishikesh.

12. Your work and actions will not bind you if you perform them without egoism and without expectations.

The Nature of Atman

13. This Atman is motionless yet at the same time swifter than the mind. Why? Because it is all-pervading and complete in itself, without any limitation.
14. The Atman is already at all planes the mind can reach, because it is everywhere and infinite.
15. The Atman is distant yet it is near. It is within all this and yet it is also outside all this.
16. For the ignorant and those people who are totally immersed in worldliness, it is far away. For the enquirer and for one who is equipped with purity of mind, it is very near.
17. The Atman is infinitely subtle. It is the inner Self of all beings. It fills and encompasses everything in the universe.
18. The Atman is the substratum or basis of all beings.
19. Sages see all beings in Atman, and Atman in all beings.
20. One who sees that the Atman pervades everything fears nothing.
21. A sage who has realized the Atman beholds that all objects and all beings are not really distant from his own Self, and that his Atman is the very same Atman of all.
22. The Atman is the same consciousness that is shared by all beings.
23. The Atman is the same in a king and a peasant, a saint and a sinner, a cobbler and a barber, an ant and an elephant, a tree and a stone; it is the same Atman.
24. How can a liberated soul who is resting in his own Atman and who has an exalted cosmic consciousness shrink from any being or object with a feeling of repulsion? How can he dislike anything? How can he hate anything?
25. Mere intellectual knowledge that the one Self abides in all beings is not enough. Aparoksha anubhava, direct perception or actual Self-realization, is the only way.

26. The knower of Brahman becomes fearless and transcends delusion and sorrow.
27. The three knots of the heart: avidya (ignorance), kama (desire) and karma (action), are annihilated by the knowledge of Brahman.
28. The realized man always rejoices in the bliss of Atman. Even the heaviest sorrow cannot shake or disturb him.
29. The Atman is all-pervading, bright, bodiless, pure, untouched by sin or evil action, omniscient, transcendental and self-existent. He is scatheless and without muscles.
30. This Atman is without a physical body, without an astral body and without a causal body.
31. The Atman is totally independent and it never depends on anything else.
32. The Atman is beyond the reach of the senses and the mind.
33. The Atman is the mind of the mind, the ear of the ears, the eye of the eyes and the life of the lives.
34. Behind the breath, the senses and the mind is the supreme Brahman or the Absolute.
35. The mind, the senses and the breath function only by the light of Brahman.

Knowledge of Brahman

36. When karma (work and action) is done without expectations of the fruits, the mind is purified and the spiritual aspirant experiences a strong desire for final emancipation.
37. The need to know Brahman and to attain liberation from the endless cycle of births and deaths can only arise in a person who is endowed with a pure and calm mind, who is desireless in the world of forms and names and who is disgusted with the sensual objects of this illusory, material world.
38. Realization of Brahman cannot be attained by logical discussions.

3

39. It is said in the scriptures that in order to know Brahman, the spiritual aspirant has to approach a preceptor who is well versed in the Vedas and who is centred in the light of Brahman.
40. The scriptures also say that one who has studied under a teacher knows the Truth.
41. Only that knowledge that is acquired by studying under a teacher or guru is of use.
42. Knowledge of Brahman totally destroys ignorance, which is the cause of bondage and the driving force behind actions performed for the attainment of objects of desire.
43. The scriptures say, "There is neither sorrow nor delusion for the knower of the Self, who beholds the one Atman everywhere. He who knows the Atman goes beyond sorrow."
44. Moksha (liberation) cannot be attained by karma (actions) alone or karma combined with intellectual knowledge. Moksha can only come from jnana (spiritual wisdom). Karma purifies the mind and helps the aspirant to attain knowledge.
45. The performance of karma will take one only to the world of manas or pitraloka, the world of the ancestors. It cannot make one immortal.
46. Brahman, the only real entity, cannot be attained by any other means than removal of ignorance through knowledge of the Self.
47. One who attains the supreme Brahman, the unborn, unchangeable, birthless, undecaying, immortal, fearless, eternal, self-luminous, all-blissful and all-pervading, is freed from the wheel of births and deaths.
48. Para Brahman, the Absolute, controls and guides the mind, life and the senses.
49. Having abandoned the idea and feeling of I-ness and rising above the life of the senses, the wise become immortal.

Prashnopanishad

In this Upanishad, six seekers after Truth come to Rishi Pippalada, and each one asks him a question. The answers are very clear and carefully explained, and range from the gross to the subtlest principles of life.

The first question concerns the origin of living beings. It is explained how the Lord, the Creator, created prana, the sun (energy) and rayi, the moon (matter). Without the sun, there is no time, no seasons, no day or night, no life and no creation. Without the moon, there is no matter, no food to sustain life. Matter, energy, food, etc. are related and have a common link

The second question relates to the deities who are the helpers of living beings, who are manifest in the senses and who are the substance of the body. These represent the five gross elements, the organs of knowledge and the five organs of action. Prana is the chief among them. Whatever is within or beyond this world is controlled by prana. Here the powers, glory and grandeur of prana are acclaimed.

The third question refers to the nature and origin of the transcendental prana. Prana comes from the Self (Atman) and is always with Him, just as a man and his shadow are inseparable. Prana sees to it that the organs of the body carry out all their different activities separately and smoothly with the help of the sub-divisions of energy. When a man dies the thought within his mind enters into prana, and prana, along with other companions of the soul, guides him back to the world according to where his desires lie. He who knows the origin, the place of entrance, the location, the fivefold divisions of prana and its identity within the body attains immortality. These first three questions are concerned with Apara Vidya (the lower or gross knowledge).

The fourth question refers to sleep and dreams. Just as the rays of the sun between setting and rising are absorbed into the shining disc of the sun, similarly, in deep sleep the senses become absorbed in the mind. All activity ceases, except for that of the five pranas, which remain active and vigilant in the body. In the dreaming state the mind creates a fantasy world made up of the impressions received in the waking state and thereby derives enjoyment. The mind sees both the seen and the unseen, hears the heard and the unheard, experiences the experienced and the unexperienced, the true and the untrue, and sometimes a mixture of experiences from past births as well as the present birth. But the mind becomes dreamless when it is overpowered by illumination, and then it enjoys bliss.

The fifth question concerns Om or Pranava. Om is both the higher and the lower Brahman. Those who know this truth will attain one of them. He who meditates on Om, the supreme Self residing in the hearts of all, becomes immortal.

The sixth and last question relates to Purusha, who exists in the body in sixteen forms (kalaas). Purusha created prana; from prana He created desire; from desire He created ether, air, fire, water, earth, the senses, mind, food; and from food He created vitality (seed), rites (karma), the worlds, and the names within the worlds. Supreme Purusha is the goal of the sixteen kalaa, as the ocean is to rivers. He who knows Purusha gains immortality.

These last three questions are related to Para Vidya or Brahma Vidya (the superior or transcendental knowledge).

SHANTI PATH

ॐ भद्रं कर्णेभिः शृणुयाम देवा भद्रं पश्येमाक्षभिर्यजत्राः।
स्थिरैरंगैस्तुष्टुवाꣳसस्तनूभिर्व्यशेम देवहितं यदायुः ॥ स्वस्ति न इन्द्रो
वृद्धश्रवाः स्वस्ति नः पूषा विश्ववेदाः। स्वस्ति नस्ताक्ष्यों अरिष्टनेमिः
स्वस्ति नो बृहस्पतिर्दधातु ॥

ॐ शान्तिः शान्तिः शान्तिः

*Om Bhadram Karnebhih Shrinuyaama Devaah Bhadram
Pashyemaakshabhiryajatraah; Sthirai Rangaih Tushtuvaam
Sastanoobhirvyashema Devahitam Yadaayuh. Svasti Na Indro
Vriddhashravaa Svasti Na Pooshaa Vishvavedaah; Svasti
Nastaarkshyo Arishtanemih Svasti No Brihaspatirdadhaatu.*

Om Shaantih Shaantih Shaantih.

Om. O ye Gods. May we hear auspicious words and see
auspicious sights while worshipping you. May we be blessed
in life with perfect health and vigour while singing your
praise. May the Lord Indra, the loved one of old, be well-
inclined towards us. May He, in his kindness, be watchful
for our prosperity. May He, the nourisher and possessor of
all wealth, give us what is good for us. May the Lord, the
destroyer of evil and the protector of the great ones, protect
us too.

Om peace, peace, peace.

FIRST QUESTION

ॐ सुकेशा च भारद्वाज: शैव्यश्च सत्यकाम: सौर्यायणी च गार्ग्य:
कौसल्यश्चाश्वलायनो भार्गवो वैदर्भि: कबन्धी कात्यायनस्ते हैते ब्रह्मपरा
ब्रह्मनिष्ठा: परं ब्रह्मान्वेषमाणा एष ह वै तत्सर्वं वक्ष्यतीति ते ह समित्पाणयो
भगवन्तं पिप्पलादमुपसन्ना: ॥ 1 ॥

*Om Sukeshaa Cha Bhaaradvaajah Shaibyashcha Satyakaamah
Sauryaayanee Cha Gaargyah Kausalyashchaashvalaayano
Bhaargavo Vaidarbhih Kabandhee Kaatyaayanaste Haite
Brahmaparaa Brahmanishthaah Param Brahmaanveshamaanaa
Esha Ha Vai Tatsarvam Vakshyateeti Te Ha Samitpaanayo
Bhagavantam Pippalaadamupasannaah. (1)*

Sukesha, the son of Bharadvaja, Satyakama, the son of Sibi,
Gargya, the grandson of Surya, Kausalya, the son of Ashvala,
Bharadvaja, the son of Vidarbhi, and Kabandhi, the son of
Katya, all bore great love for Brahman and had pledged
themselves to him. Intent on discovering the Supreme
Brahman, they went to the saintly Pippalada in the hope
that he would enlighten them, and they took with them
sacrificial fuel (samit) as an offering.

तान्ह स ऋषिरुवाच भूय एव तपसा ब्रह्मचर्येण श्रद्धया संवत्सरं संवत्स्यथ
यथाकामं प्रश्नान्पृच्छत यदि विज्ञास्याम: सर्वं ह वो वक्ष्याम इति ॥ 2 ॥

*Taanha Sa Rishiruvaacha Bhooya Eva Tapasaa Brahmacharyena
Shraddhayaa Samvatsaram Samvatsyatha Yathaakaamam
Prashnaan Prichchhata Yadi Vijnaasyaamah Sarvam Ha Vo
Vakshyaama Iti. (2)*

And Pippalada said to them: Remain with me for one year,
observing austerity, celibacy and faith, and after that put to
me whatever questions you wish. To the best of my ability I
will solve your difficulties, and give you full satisfaction in
my explanations.

8

अथ कबन्धी कात्यायन उपेत्य पप्रच्छ। भगवान् कुतो ह वा इमा: प्रजा:
प्रजायन्त इति ॥ 3 ॥

Atha Kabandhee Kaatyaayana Upetya Paprachchha; Bhagavan Kuto Ha Vaa Imaah Prajaah Prajaayanta Iti. (3)

When the first year was completed, Kabandhi came to Pippalada and asked this question: O Venerable One, how was it that animate things came into being?

तस्मै स होवाच प्रजाकामो वै प्रजापति: स तपोऽतप्यत स तपस्तप्त्वा स
मिथुनमुत्पादयते। रयिं च प्राणं चेत्येतौ मे बहुधा प्रजा: करिष्यत इति ॥ 4 ॥

Tasmai Sa Hovaacha Prajaakaamo Vai Prajaapatih Sa Tapo Atapyata Sa Tapastaptvaa Sa Mithunamutpaadayate; Rayim Cha Praanam Chetyetau Me Bahudhaa Prajaah Karishyata Iti. (4)

And Pippalada made the following reply: The Lord of life had the wish to create. He meditated and brought forth food and prana (matter and life), who were to create manifold creatures for him.

आदित्यो ह वै प्राणो रयिरेव चन्द्रमा रयिर्वा एतत् सर्वं यन्मूर्तं चामूर्तं च
तस्मान्मूर्तिरेव रयि: ॥ 5 ॥

Aadityo Ha Vai Praano Rayireva Chandramaa Rayirvaa Etat Sarvam Yanmoortam Chaamoortam Cha Tasmaanmoortireva Rayih. (5)

The sun is prana (life) and the moon is food (matter). All that which possesses form (like earth, water and fire) or lacks form (like air and ether) is food. therefore, all form is rayi, food, indeed.

अथादित्य उदयन्यत्प्राचीं दिशं प्रविशति तेन प्राच्यान् प्राणान् रश्मिषु
संनिधत्ते। यद्दक्षिणां यत्प्रतीचीं यदुदीचीं यदधो यदूर्ध्वं यदन्तरा दिशो
यत्सर्वं प्रकाशयति तेन सर्वान् प्राणान् रश्मिषु संनिधत्ते ॥ 6 ॥

*Athaaditya Udayanyatpraacheem Disham Pravishati Tena
Praachyaan Praanaan Rashmishu Samnidhatte; Yaddakshinaam
Yatprateecheem Yadudeecheem Yadadho Yadoordhvam Yadantaraa
Disho Yatsarvam Prakaashayati Tena Sarvaan Praanaan
Rashmishu Samnidhatte. (6)*

When the sun rises in the east, he sends out life-giving rays
to all creatures there. Similarly, in the northern, southern,
western, upper and lower regions, he fills all creatures with
his energy. Thus all creatures depend on him for life.

स एष वैश्वानरो विश्वरूप: प्राणोऽग्निरुदयते । तदेतदृचाभ्युक्तम् ॥ 7 ॥

*Sa Esha Vaishvaanaro Vishvaroopah Praanoagnirudayate;
Tadetarichaabyuktam. (7)*

The sun which rises every day, which is life (prana) and fire
(agni), is Him, who assumes all forms and is all living beings.

विश्वरूपं हरिणं जातवेदसं परायणं ज्योतिरेकं तपन्तम् । सहस्ररश्मि:
शतधा वर्तमान: प्राण: प्रजानामुदयत्येष सूर्य: ॥ 8 ॥

*Vishvaroopam Harinam Jaatavedasam Paraayanam Jyotirekam
Tapantam; Sahasrarashmih Shatadhaa Vartamaanah Praanah
Prajaanaamudayatyesha Sooryah. (8)*

The form of all forms, the lustrous, all-knowing, the ultimate
goal, the light from whence all lights spring, the giver of
heat, possessor of a thousand rays and a hundred forms, the
life of all life, this is the rising sun.

संवत्सरो वै प्रजापतिस्तस्यायने दक्षिणं चोत्तरं च। तद्ये ह वै तदिष्टापूर्ते कृतमित्युपासते ते चान्द्रमसमेव लोकमभिजयन्ते। त एव पुनरावर्तन्ते तस्मादेत ऋषय: प्रजाकामा दक्षिणं प्रतिपद्यन्ते। एष ह वै रयिर्य: पितृयाण: ॥ 9 ॥

Samvatsaro Vai Prajaapatistasyaayane Dakshinam Chottaram Cha; Tadye Ha Vai Tadishtaapoorte Kritamityupaasate Te Chaandramasameva Lokamabhijayante; Ta Eva Punaraavartante Tasmaadeta Rishayah Prajaakaamaa Dakshinam Pratipadyante; Esha Ha Vai Rayiryah Pitriyaanah. (9)

The southern and the northern are the two paths of the Lord of creation, who is also known as the year (time). Those who follow the path of karma, and only perform pious actions and sacrifices, go to the world of the moon, and later return again to this world. It is this southern path which those desirous of progeny take, and which is the path of our ancestors.

अथोत्तरेण तपसा ब्रह्मचर्येण श्रद्धया विद्ययाऽऽत्मानमन्विष्यादित्यमभिजयन्ते। एतद्वै प्राणानामायतनमेतदमृतमभयमेतत्परायणमेतस्मान्न पुनरावर्तन्त इत्येष निरोधस्तदेष श्लोक: ॥ 10 ॥

Athottarena Tapasaa Brahmacharyena Shraddhayaa Vidyayaatmaanamanvishyaadityamabhijayante; Etadvai Praanaanaamaayatanametadamritamabhayametat Paraayanametasmaanna Punaraavartanta Ityesha Nirodhastadesha Shlokah. (10)

But those who seek the Self (Atman) through control of the senses, celibacy, faith and meditation go by the northern path to the sun. Here lies the home of all living beings, the immortal highest goal, beyond fear. From here none return; it is the Ultimate.

पंचपादं पितरं द्वादशाकृतिं दिव आहुः परे अर्धे पुरीषिणम् । अथेमे अन्य उ परे विचक्षणं सप्तचक्रे षडर आहुरर्पितमिति ॥ 11 ॥

Panchapaadam Pitaram Dvaadashaakritim Diva Aahuh Pare Ardhe Pureeshinam; Atheme Anya U Pare Vichakshanam Saptachakre Shadara Aahurarpitamiti. (11)

Sages say that the sun, the father of all, has five feet (the five seasons); and twelve forms (the twelve months); and that he is the rain giver sitting in the sky. They say he is the omniscient seated in a chariot with seven wheels, each with six spokes. In this way the whole universe is established.

मासो वै प्रजापतिस्तस्य कृष्णपक्ष एव रयिः शुक्लः प्राणस्तस्मादेत ऋषयः शुक्ल इष्टं कुर्वन्तीतर इतरस्मिन् ॥ 12 ॥

Maaso Vai Prajaapatistasya Krishnapaksha Eva Rayih Shuklah Praanastasmaadeta Rishayah Shukla Ishtam Kurvanteetara Itarasmin. (12)

The month is Prajapati, the Lord of life. Its dark fortnight is matter, food, and its bright fortnight is prana, sun. The wise perform sacrifices during the latter fortnight, the unwise during the former.

अहोरात्रो वै प्रजापतिस्तस्याहरेव प्राणो रात्रिरेव रयिः प्राणं वा एते प्रस्कन्दन्ति ये दिवा रत्या संयुज्यन्ते ब्रह्मचर्यमेव तद्यद्रात्रौ रत्या संयुज्यन्ते ॥ 13 ॥

Ahoraatro Vai Prajaapatistasyaahareva Praano Raatrireva Rayih. Praanam Vaa Ete Praskandanti Ye Divaa Ratyaa Samyujyante Brahmacharyameva Tadyadraatrau Ratyaa Samyujyante. (13)

The Lord is also the day and night; the day is prana and the night is food. Those who unite in passion in the daytime waste their prana, but those who unite in passion at night are considered celibate (brahmacharis).

अन्नं वै प्रजापतिस्ततो ह वै तद्रेतस्तस्मादिमा: प्रजा: प्रजायन्त इति ॥ 14 ॥

Annam Vai Prajaapatistato Ha Vai Tadretastasmaadimaah Prajaah Prajaayanta Iti. (14)

Food (matter) is none other than the Lord of creation (Prajapati). For from food is created semen, and from semen all living things.

तद्ये ह वै तत्प्रजापतिव्रतं चरन्ति ते मिथुनमुत्पादयन्ते। तेषामेवैष ब्रह्मलोको येषां तपो ब्रह्मचर्यं येषु सत्यं प्रतिष्ठितम् ॥ 15 ॥

Tadye Ha Vai Tatprajaapativratam Charanti Te Mithunamut-paadayante; Teshaamevaisha Brahmaloko Yeshaam Tapo Brahmacharyam Yeshu Satyam Pratishthitam. (15)

Those abiding by the laws of the Lord of creatures control their passion and have few children; they observe austerity, celibacy and truthfulness, and attain the lunar world.

तेषामसौ विरजो ब्रह्मलोको न येषु जिह्ममनृतं न माया चेति ॥ 16 ॥

Teshaamasau Virajo Brahmaloko Na Yeshu Jihmamamanritam Na Maayaa Cheti. (16)

The blemishless world of Brahman belongs to those only in whom there is no crookedness, falsehood or duplicity.

SECOND QUESTION

अथ हैनं भार्गवो वैदर्भि: पप्रच्छ। भगवन्कत्येव देवा: प्रजां विधारयन्ते कतर
एतत्प्रकाशयन्ते क: पुनरेषां वरिष्ठ इति ॥ 1 ॥

Atha Hainam Bhaargavo Vaidarbhih Paprachchha;
Bhagavankatyeva Devaah Prajaam Vidhaarayante? Katara
Etatprakaashayante? Kah Punareshaam Varishtha Iti. (1)

Then Bhargava came to Pippalada and asked him: O Holy
One, which are those deities who have the care of living
beings? Who amongst them is the Enlightener, and who is
the Chief?

तस्मै स होवाचाकाशो ह वा एष देवो वायुरग्निराप: पृथिवी वाङ्मनश्चक्षु:
श्रोत्रं च। ते प्रकाश्याभिवदन्ति वयमेतद्बाणमवष्टभ्य विधारयाम:॥ 2 ॥

Tasmai Sa Hovaachaakaasho Ha Vaa Esha Devo
Vaayuragniraapah Prithivee Vaanmanashchakshuh Shrotram Cha;
Te Prakaashya Abhivadanti Vayavmetadbaanamavashtabhya
Vidhaarayaamah. (2)

And Pippalada answered in the following manner: These
deities are ether, air, fire, water, earth, speech, mind, eyes
and ears. Seeing their own splendour, they boasted: We are
the rulers of the body because we are its supporters.

तान्वरिष्ठ: प्राण उवाच। मा मोहमापद्यथाहमेवैतत्पञ्चधाऽऽत्मानं प्रविभज्यैतद्-
बाणमवष्टभ्य विधारयामीति तेऽश्रद्दधाना बभूवु:॥ 3 ॥

Taanvarishthah Praana Uvaacha; Maa Mohamaapadyatha
Ahamevaitat Panchadhaatmaanam Pravibhajyaitad Baanama-
vashtabhya Vidhaarayaameeti Te Shraddadhaanaa Vabhoovuh. (3)

But prana, the chief amongst them, reproved them, saying:
Don't delude yourselves. It is I alone, dividing myself fivefold,

who supports and keeps the body intact. But the other deities were incredulous.

सोऽभिमानादूर्ध्वमुत्क्रमत इव तस्मिन्नुत्क्रामत्यथेतरे सर्व एवोत्क्रामन्ते
तस्मिं श्च प्रतिष्ठमाने सर्व एव प्रातिष्ठन्ते। तद्यथा मक्षिका
मधुकरराजानमुत्क्रामन्तं सर्वा एवोत्क्रामन्ते तस्मिं श्च प्रतिष्ठमाने सर्वा एव
प्रातिष्ठन्त एवं वाङ्मनश्चक्षुःश्रोत्रं च ते प्रीताः प्राणं स्तुन्वन्ति ॥ 4 ॥

Sobhimaanaat Oordhvam Utkramata Iva Tasminnutkraa-matyathetare Sarva Evotkraamante Tasminshcha Pratishthamaane Sarva Eva Praatishthante; Tadyathaa Makshikaa Madhu-kararaajaanam Utkraamantam Sarvaa Evotkraamante Tasminshcha Pratishthamaane Sarvaa Eva Praatishthanta Evam Vaanmanashchakshuh Shrotram Cha Te Preetaah Praanam Stunvanti. (4)

In a fit of wrath, prana withdrew himself from the body. Immediately, all the deities found themselves leaving with him, and when prana returned the deities found themselves back in their former places. Just as bees leave the hive when their queen departs and return when she returns, so did the deities behave. Satisfied with this evidence, the deities now give worship to prana.

एषोऽग्निस्तपत्येष सूर्य एष पर्जन्यो मघवानेष वायुः ।
एष पृथिवी रयिर्देवः सदसच्चामृतं च यत् ॥ 5 ॥

Eshognistapatyesha Soorya Esha Parjanyo Maghavaanesha Vaayuh; Esha Prithivee Rayirdevah Sadasachchaamritam Cha Yat. (5)

Prana, as fire burns, as the sun gives light, as the clouds pour down rain, he is Indra, the air, earth, food (moon). He is both gross and subtle, and he is immortal.

अरा इव रथनाभौ प्राणे सर्वं प्रतिष्ठितम् ।
ऋचो यजूूँषि सामानि यज्ञ: क्षत्रं ब्रह्म च ॥ 6 ॥

Araa Iva Rathanaabhau Praane Sarvam Pratishthitam; Reecho Yajoomshi Saamaani Yajnah Kshatram Brahma Cha. (6)

As spokes are centred in the hub of the wheel, similarly, the scriptures, sacrifices, kshatriyas and brahmanas all have their centre in prana.

प्रजापतिश्चरसि गर्भे त्वमेव प्रतिजायसे ।
तुभ्यं प्राण प्रजास्त्विमा बलिं हरन्ति य: प्राणै: प्रतितिष्ठसि ॥ 7 ॥

Prajaapatishcharasi Garbhe Tvameva Pratijaayase; Tubhyam Praana Prajaastvimaa Balim Haranti Yah Praanaih Pratitishthasi. (7)

Prana is the Lord of creation. He moves in the womb and is born in an image resembling the parents. O prana, you abide in the multiplicity of pranas and they offer you worship.

देवानामसि वह्निनतम: पितृणां प्रथमा स्वधा ।
ऋषीणां चरितं सत्यमथर्वाङ्गिरसामसि ॥ 8 ॥

Devaanaamasi Vahnitamah Pitreenaam Prathamaa Svadhaa; Risheenaam Charitam Satyam Atharvaangirasaamasi. (8)

You are first and foremost amongst the messengers to the gods and ancestors. You are the truth the rishis hold in great esteem.

इन्द्रस्त्वं प्राण तेजसा रुद्रोऽसि परिरक्षिता ।
त्वमन्तरिक्षे चरसि सूर्यस्त्वं ज्योतिषां पति: ॥ 9 ॥

Indrastvam Praana Tejasaa Rudrosi Parirakshitaa; Tvamantarikshe Charasi Sooryastvam Jyotishaam Patih. (9)

O prana, you are Indra; in your brave aspect you are Rudra and you are the protector also. You pass through the sky. You are the sun, O Lord of all light.

यदा त्वमभिवर्षस्यथेमा: प्राण ते ऽप्रजा: ।
आनन्दरूपास्तिष्ठन्ति कामायान्नं भविष्यतीति ॥ 10 ॥

Yadaa Tvamabhivarshasyathemaah Praana Te Prajaah;
Aanandaroopaastishthanti Kaamaayaannam Bhavishyateeti. (10)

O prana, when you pour down the rain showers, you make your creatures happy, thinking there will be more food for them.

व्रात्यस्त्वं प्राणैकर्षिरत्ता विश्वस्य सत्पति: ।
वयमाद्यस्य दातार: पिता त्वं मातरिश्व न: ॥ 11 ॥

Vraatyastvam Praanaikarshirattaa Vishvasya Satpatih;
Vayamaadyasya Daataarah Pitaa Tvam Maatarishva Nah. (11)

O prana, you are purity itself; you are the one seer, you are the sacrificial fire, the Lord of the world. It is we who offer you enjoyment (food), and you are our creator.

या ते तनूर्वाचि प्रतिष्ठिता या श्रोत्रे या च चक्षुषि ।
या च मनसि सन्तता शिवां तां कुरु मोत्क्रमी:॥ 12 ॥

Yaa Te Tanoorvaachi Pratishthitaa Yaa Shrotre Yaa Cha
Chakshushi; Yaa Cha Manasi Santataa Shivaam Taam Kuru
Motkrameeh. (12)

O prana, remain in the body calm and quiet; do not leave the body. You are the Lord who abides within the speech, ear, eye and mind.

प्राणस्येदं वशे सर्वं त्रिदिवे यत्प्रतिष्ठितम् ।
मातेव पुत्रान् रक्षस्व श्रीश्च प्रज्ञां च विधेहि न इति ॥ 13 ॥

Praanasyedam Vashe Sarvam Tridive Yatpratishthitam; Maateva
Putraan Rakshasva Shreeshcha Prajnaam Cha Vidhehi Na Iti. (13)

All that exists within the three worlds is ruled by you. O
prana, grant us prosperity and knowledge, and care for us
like a mother.

THIRD QUESTION

अथ हैनं कौसल्यश्चाश्वलायन: पप्रच्छ। भगवन्कुत एष प्राणो जायते
कथमायात्यस्मिञ्शरीर आत्मानं वा प्रविभज्य कथं प्रातिष्ठते केनोत्क्रमते
कथं बाह्यमभिधत्ते कथमध्यात्ममिति ॥ १ ॥

Atha Hainam Kausalyah Cha Ashvalaayanah Paprachchha;
Bhagavan Kuta Esha Praano Jaayate Kathamaayaatyasmin Shareera?
Aatmaanam Vaa Pravibhajya Katham Praatishthate? Kenotkramate?
Katham Baahyamabhidhatte? Kathamadhyaatmamiti. (1)

Then came Kausalya to Pippalada and questioned him thus:
O Honoured One, from where does prana originate? How
does he enter the body, and in what form does he remain
after dividing himself up? How does he leave the body?
How does he support that which is external to the body, and
hold together that which is internal?

तस्मै स होवाचातिप्रश्नान्पृच्छसि ब्रह्मिष्ठोऽसीति तस्मात्तेऽहं ब्रवीमि ॥ २ ॥

Tasmai Sa Hovaachaatiprashnaan Prichchhasi Brahmishthoseeti
Tasmaatteham Braveemi. (2)

And Pippalada made the following reply: This question
concerning the origin of prana, which is transcendental, is
diffcult, but since you are a firm devotee of Brahman and a
deserving aspirant, I will explain it.

आत्मन एष प्राणो जायते यथैषा पुरुषे छायैतस्मिन्नेतदा ततं मनो
कृतेनायात्यस्मिञ्शरीरे ॥ ३ ॥

Aatmana Esha Praano Jaayate. Yathaishaa Purushe Chhaayai-
tasminnetadaa Tatam Manokriten Aayaatyasminshareere. (3)

Prana springs from the Self (Atman). Prana is inseparable
from the Self, as is the shadow from he who casts the
shadow. Prana enters the body through the mind.

19

यथा सम्राडेवाधिकृतान्विनियुङ्क्ते। एतान्ग्रामानेतान्ग्रामानधितिष्ठस्वेत्येवमेवैष प्राण इतरान् प्राणान्पृथक्पृथगेव संनिधत्ते ॥ 4 ॥

Yathaa Samraadeva Adhikritaan Viniyunkte; Etaan Graamaan-
etaan Graamaan Adhitishthasvetyevamevaisha Praana Itaraan
Praanaan Prithakprithageva Samnidhatte. (4)

Just as an emperor posts his officials in different parts of his realm to govern them, similarly, the chief prana allots functions to the lower pranas.

पायूपस्थेऽपानं चक्षुःश्रोत्रे मुखनासिकाभ्यां प्राणः स्वयं प्रातिष्ठते मध्ये तु समानः। एष ह्येतद्धुतमन्नं समं नयति तस्मादेताः सप्तार्चिषो भवन्ति ॥ 5 ॥

Paayoopasthepaanam Chakshuhshrotre Mukhanaasikaabhyaam
Praanah Svayam Praatishthate Madhye Tu Samaanah; Esha
Hyetaddhutamannam Samam Nayati Tasmaadetaah Saptaarchisho
Bhavanti. (5)

Prana himself resides in the eyes, ears, mouth and nose; apana is located in the organs of reproduction and excretion; samana abides in the stomach and governs digestion. Out of these emerge the seven flames.

हृदि ह्येष आत्मा। अत्रैतदेकशतं नाडीनां तासां शतं शतमेकैकस्यां द्वासप्ततिर्द्वासप्ततिः प्रतिशाखानाडीसहस्राणि भवन्त्यासु व्यानश्चरति ॥ 6 ॥

Hridi Hyesha Aatmaa; Atraitadekashatam Naadeenaam Taasaam
Shatam Shatamekaikasyaam Dvaasaptatirdvaasaptatih Prati-
shaakhaanaadee Sahasraani Bhavantyaasu Vyaanashcharati. (6)

The Self (Atman) abides within the heart; from here emerge one hundred main nadis, each branches into one hundred nadis and these branch into seventy-two thousand minor nadis. In these nadis, vyana moves.

अथैकयोर्ध्व उदानः पुण्येन पुण्यं लोकं नयति पापेन पापमुभाभ्यामेव मनुष्यलोकम् ॥ 7 ॥

Athaikayordhva Udaanah Punyena Punyam Lokam Nayati Paapena Paapamubhaabhyaameva Manushyalokam. (7)

Udana resides in the nadi passing through the centre of the spine. If udana is in the higher part due to virtuous deeds, a virtuous world will be attained after death; if in a lower part due to sinful works, a sinful world will be reached; and if there is a combination of both elements, the human world will be returned to.

आदित्यो ह वै बाह्यः प्राण उदयत्येष ह्येनं चाक्षुषं प्राणमनुगृह्णानः । पृथिव्यां या देवता सैषा पुरुषस्यापानमवष्टभ्यान्तरा यदाकाशः स समानो वायुर्व्यानः ॥ 8 ॥

Aadityo Ha Vai Baahyah Praana Udayatyesha Hyenam Chaakshusham Praanamanugrihnaanah; Prithivyaam Yaa Devataa Saishaa Purushasya Apaanam Avashtabhya Antaraa Yadaakaashah Sa Samaano Vaayurvyaanah. (8)

The sun is the external prana. When he rises, he gives grace (vision) to the prana of the eye. The deity of earth draws apana to his downward duty. The ether is samana, and air (wind) is vyana.

तेजो ह वा उदानस्तस्मादुपशान्ततेजाः पुनर्भवमिन्द्रियैर्मनसि सम्पद्यमानैः ॥ 9 ॥

Tejo Ha Vaa Udaanah Tasmaat Upashaantatejaah Punarbhavam Indriyaih Manasi Sampadyamaanaih. (9)

Fire is known as udana, and he who extinguishes the fire or udana in the body attains or goes for rebirth with all the senses dissolved.

यच्चित्तस्तेनैष प्राणमायाति प्राणस्तेजसा युक्तः सहात्मना यथा संकल्पितं लोकं नयति ॥ 10 ॥

Yachchittah Tenaisha Praanamaayaati Praanastejasaa Yuktah Sahaatmanaa Yathaa Sankalpitam Lokam Nayati. (10)

When a man dies, the thought held in the mind enters into prana. Prana and udana accompany the soul and take it to its desired world.

य एवं विद्वान्प्राणं वेद न हास्य प्रजा हीयतेऽमृतो भवति तदेष श्लोकः ॥ 11 ॥

Ya Evam Vidvaan Praanam Veda Na Haasya Prajaa Heeyatemrito Bhavati Tadesha Shlokah. (11)

The progeny of one who is wise and a knower of prana will become immortal.

उत्पत्तिमायतिं स्थानं विभुत्वं चैव पञ्चधा ।
अध्यात्मं चैव प्राणस्य विज्ञायामृतमश्नुते
विज्ञायामृतमश्नुत   इति ॥ 12 ॥

Utpattim Aayatim Sthaanam Vibhutvam Chaiva Panchadhaa; Adhyaatmam Chaiva Praanasya Vijnaaya Amritamashnute Vijnaaya Amritamashnuta Iti. (12)

He who knows the origin, the place of entrance, the rulership of the fivefold pranas, and their interior aspect, truly attains immortality.

FOURTH QUESTION

अथ हैनं सौर्यायणी गार्ग्य: पप्रच्छ भगवन्नेतस्मिन्पुरुषे कानि स्वपन्ति कान्यस्मिञ्जाग्रति कतर एष देव: स्वप्नान्पश्यति कस्यैतत्सुखं भवति कस्मिन्नु सर्वे संप्रतिष्ठिता भवन्तीति ॥ 1 ॥

Atha Hainam Sauryaayanee Gaargyah Paprachchha; Bhagavan Etasmin Purushe Kaani Svapanti Kaanyasminjaagrati Katara Esha Devah Svapnaan Pashyati Kasyaitatsukham Bhavati Kasminnu Sarve Sampratishthitaa Bhavanteeti. (1)

Then Gargya came to Pippalada and asked him: O Adored One. Which organs cease to function in sleep, and which are active in sleep? Which deity is the enjoyer of dreams? From whom is this enjoyment derived, and in whom are all these finally absorbed?

तस्मै स होवाच यथा गार्ग्य मरीचयोऽर्कस्यास्तं गच्छत: सर्वा एतस्मिंस्तेजोमण्डल एकीभवन्ति । ता: पुन: पुनरुदयत: प्रचरन्त्येवं ह वै तत्सर्वं परे देवे मनस्येकीभवति । तेन तर्ह्येष पुरुषो न शृणोति न पश्यति न जिघ्रति न रसयते न स्पृशते नाभिवदते नादत्ते नानन्दयते न विसृजते नेयायते स्वपितीत्याचक्षते ॥ 2 ॥

Tasmai Sa Hovaacha; Yathaa Gaargya Mareechayorkasyaastam Gachchhatah Sarvaa Etasmins Tejomandala Ekeebhavanti; Taah Punah Punarudayatah Pracharantyevam Ha Vai Tatsarvam Pare Deve Manasyekeebhavati; Tena Tarhyesha Purusho Na Shrinoti, Na Pashyati, Na Jighrati, Na Rasayate, Na Sprishate, Naabhivadate, Naadatte, Naanandayate, Na Visrijate, Neyaayate, Svapiti Iti Aachakshate. (2)

And Pippalada replied: O Gargya, just as the rays of the setting sun are absorbed back into its shining disc and re-emerge when the sun rises, similarly, in sleep the senses are absorbed into the mind, the superior god. Therefore, the sleeper does not hear, speak, taste, touch, feel, move, grasp, enjoy or evacuate.

प्राणाग्नय एवैतस्मिन्पुरे जाग्रति। गार्हपत्यो ह वा एषोऽपानो व्यानोऽन्वाहार्यपचनो यद्गार्हपत्यात् प्रणीयते प्रणयनादाहवनीय: प्राण: ॥ 3 ॥

Praanaagnaya Evaitasmin Pure Jaagrati; Gaarhapatyo Ha Vaa Eshopaano Vyaanah Anvaahaaryapachano Yadgaarhapatyaat Praneeyate Pranayanaat Aahavaneeyah Praanah. (3)

Only the fires of prana remain awake in the city of the body. Apana is the Garhapatya fire, vyana is the Anvaharyapachan fire and prana is the Ahavaniya fire because it comes from the Garhapatya fire.

यदुच्छ्वासनि:श्वासावेतावाहुती समं नयतीति स समान:। मनो ह वाव यजमान:। इष्टफलमेवोदान: । स एनं यजमानमहरहर्ब्रह्म गमयति ॥ 4 ॥

Yaduchchhvaasanihshvaasau Etaavaahutee Samam Nayateeti Sa Samaanah; Mano Ha Vaava Yajamaanah; Ishtaphalamevodaanah; Sa Enam Yjamaanam Ahararbrahma Gamayati. (4)

Samana is the priest called Hota. He maintains the equilibrium between inhalation and exhalation: the two oblations. The mind is the sacrificer, and udana the fruit of the sacrifice. The priest leads the sacrificer every day to Brahman (in deep sleep).

अत्रैष देव: स्वप्ने महिमानमनुभवति। यद्दृष्टं दृष्टमनुपश्यति श्रुतं श्रुतमेवार्थमनुशृणोति। देशदिगन्तरैश्च प्रत्यनुभूतं पुन: पुन: प्रत्यनुभवति दृष्टं चादृष्टं च श्रुतं चाश्रुतं चानुभूतं चाननुभूतं च सच्चासच्च सर्वं पश्यति सर्व: पश्यति ॥ 5 ॥

Atraisha Devah Svapne Mahimaanam Anubhavati; Yaddrishtam Drishtam Anupashyati Shrutam Shrutamevaartham Anushrinoti; Deshadigantaraishcha Pratyanubhootam Punah Punah Pratya-nubhavati Drishtam Chaadrishtam Cha Shrutam Chaashrutam

Chaanubhootam Chaananubhootam Cha Sachchaasachcha Sarvam Pashyati Sarvah Pashyati. (5)

The deity (mind) enjoys greatness in dreams. He sees again what he has seen, hears again what he has heard, enjoys again what he has enjoyed in different countries and quarters of the world. Whatever is seen and unseen, heard and unheard, experienced and unexperienced, real and unreal, he being all, experiences it.

स यदा तेजसाभिभूसो भवत्यत्रैष देव: स्वप्नान्न पश्यत्यथ तदैतस्मिञ्शरीर एतत्सुखं भवति ॥ 6 ॥

Sa Yadaa Tejasaabhibhooto Bhavati Atraisha Devah Svapnaanna Pashyatyatha Tadaitasminshareera Etatsukham Bhavati. (6)

And when the deity (mind) is overpowered by light, he ceases to dream, and all the body is full of bliss.

स यथा सोम्य वयांसि वासोवृक्षं संप्रतिष्ठन्ते एवं ह वै तत्सर्वं पर आत्मनि संप्रतिष्ठते ॥ 7 ॥

Sa Yathaa Somya Vayaamsi Vaaso Vriksham Sampratishante. Evam Ha Vai Tatsarvam Para Aatmani Sampratishthate. (7)

O Loved One, as birds fly to the trees for shelter, so also do the (senses) proceed to the Self (Atman).

पृथिवी च पृथिवीमात्रा चापश्चापोमात्रा च तेजश्च तेजोमात्रा च वायुश्च वायुमात्रा चाकाशश्चाकाशमात्रा च चक्षुश्च द्रष्टव्यं च श्रोत्रं च श्रोतव्यं च घ्राणं च घ्रातव्यं च रसश्च रसयितव्यं च त्वक्च स्पर्शयितव्यं च वाक्च वक्तव्यं च हस्तौ चादातव्यं चोपस्थश्चानन्दयितव्यं च पायुश्च विसर्जयितव्यं च पादौ च गन्तव्यं च मनश्च मन्तव्यं च बुद्धिश्च बोद्धव्यं चाहङ्कारश्चाहङ्कर्तव्यं च चित्तं च चेतयितव्यं च तेजश्च विद्योतयितव्यं च प्राणश्च विधारयितव्यं च ॥ 8 ॥

Prithivee Cha Prithiveemaatraa Chaapashchaapomaatraa Cha Tejashcha Tejomaatraa Cha Vaayushcha Vaayumaatraa Chaakaashashchaakaashamaatraa Cha Chakshushcha Drashtavyam Cha Shrotram Cha Shrotavyam Cha Ghraanam Cha Ghraatavyam Cha Rasashcha Rasayitavyam Cha Tvakcha Sparshayitavyam Cha Vaakcha Vaktavyam Cha Hastau Chaadaatavyam Chopasthashcha Aanandayitavyam Cha Paayushcha Visarjayitavyam Cha Paadau Cha Gantavyam Cha Manashcha Mantavyam Cha Buddhishcha Boddhavyam Chaanhankaarashchaahankartavyam Cha Chittam Cha Chetayitavyam Cha Tejashcha Vidyotayitavyam Cha Praanashcha Vidhaarayitavyam Cha. (8)

Earth and its essential elements, water and its essential elements, fire and its essential elements, air and its essential elements, space and its essential elements, the eye and what it perceives, the ear and what it hears, the nose and what it smells, the tongue and what it tastes, the skin and what it feels, the organ of excretion and its waste, the speech and what is said, the hands and what is grasped, the feet and what is walked upon, passion and its enjoyment, the mind and its thoughts, the intellect and what is known, the ego and what it appropriates, the chitta and what it is conscious of, light and what it illuminates, prana and its supporters, all are absorbed in the supreme Self in deep sleep.

एष हि द्रष्टा स्प्रष्टा श्रोता घ्राता रसयिता मान्ता बोद्धा कर्ता विज्ञानात्मा पुरुष: स परेऽक्षरे आत्मनि संप्रतिष्ठते ॥ 9 ॥

Esha Hi Drashtaa Sprashtaa Shrotaa Ghraataa Rasayitaa Mantaa Boddhaa Kartaa Vijnaanaatmaa Purushah Sa Parekshara Aatmani Sampratishthate. (9)

For He is the seer, the feeler, the hearer, the smeller, the taster, the thinker, the knower, the doer – the consciousness, the immortal, the Purusha.

परमेवाक्षरं प्रतिपद्यते स यो ह वै तदच्छायमशरीरमलोहितं शुभ्रमक्षरं वेदयते
यस्तु सोम्य। स सर्वज्ञ: सर्वो भवति। तदेष श्लोक:॥ 10॥

*Paramevaaksharam Pratipadyate Sa Yo Ha Vai Tadachchhaa-
yamashareeramalohitam Shubhramaksharam Vedayate Yastu
Somya; Sa Sarvajnah Sarvo Bhavati; Tadesha Shlokah.* (10)

He who realizes the Everlasting One who is without shadow,
without body, without colour, pure and immortal, definitely
attains the supreme Self, O Beloved, and becomes omniscient
and omnipresent.

विज्ञानात्मा सह देवैश्च सर्वै:
        प्राणा भूतानि संप्रतिष्ठन्ति यत्र ।
तदक्षरं वेदयते यस्तु सोम्य
        स सर्वज्ञ: सर्वमेवाविवेशेति ॥ 11॥

*Vijnaanaatmaa Saha Devaishcha Sarvaih
Praanaa Bhootaani Sampratishthanti Yatra;
Tadaksharam Vedayate Yastu Somya
Sa Sarvajnah Sarvamevaavivesheti.* (11)

He who realizes the immortal Self in which the individual
soul with all its deities, faculties and elements becomes
merged, surely becomes omniscient and enters into all.

FIFTH QUESTION

अथ हैनं शैब्य: सत्यकाम: पप्रच्छ। स यो ह वै तद्भगवन्मनुष्येषु प्रायणान्तमोङ्कारमभिध्यायीत। कतमं वाव स तेन लोकं जयतीति ॥ 1 ॥

Atha Hainam Shaibyah Satyakaamah Paprachchha; Sa Yo Ha Vai Tadbhagavan Manushyeshu Praayanaantamonkaarama-bhidhyaayeeta; Katamam Vaava Sa Tena Lokam Jayateeti. (1)

Then Satyakama asked: What world will a man attain who meditates on Om throughout his life?

तस्मै स होवाच एतद्वै सत्यकाम परं चापरं च ब्रह्म यदोङ्कार:। तस्माद्विद्वानेतेनैवायतनेनैकतरमन्वेति ॥ 2 ॥

Tasmai Sa Hovaacha Etadvai Satyakaama Param Chaaparam Cha Brahma Yadonkaarah; Tasmaad Vidvaanetenaivaayatane-naikataramanveti. (2)

Pippalada replied: O Satyakama, Om is both the higher and lower Brahman. He who meditates on Om will surely attain one of them.

स यद्येकमात्रमभिध्यायीत स तेनैव संवेदितस्तूर्णमेव जगत्यामभिसम्पद्यते। तमृचो मनुष्यलोकमुपनयन्ते स तत्र तपसा ब्रह्मचर्येण श्रद्धया सम्पन्नो महिमानमनुभवति ॥ 3 ॥

Sa Yadyekamaatramabhidhyaayeeta Sa Tenaiva Samveditastoorna-meva Jagatyaamabhisampadyate; Tamricho Manushyalokam-upanayante Sa Tatra Tapasaa Brahmacharyena Shraddhayaa Sampanno Mahimaanamanubhavati. (3)

He who meditates on Om with but little understanding gains some enlightenment, and the Rik verses will bear him back quickly to be reborn on this earth. If he then observes austerity, celibacy and faith, he will certainly achieve spiritual greatness.

अथ यदि द्विमात्रेण मनसि सम्पद्यते सोऽन्तरिक्षं यजुर्भिरुन्नीयते सोमलोकं स
सोमलोके विभूतिमनुभूय पुनरावर्तते ॥ 4 ॥

*Atha Yadi Dvimaatrena Manasi Sampadyate Sontariksham
Yajurbhirunneeyate Somalokam Sa Somaloke Vibhootimanubhooya
Punaraavartate.* (4)

And he who meditates on Om with greater understanding
gains greater illumination, and after death is transported to
the sky by the Yajus verses. He enjoys the magnificence of
the lunar world, before returning to this earth.

य: पुनरेतं त्रिमात्रेणोमित्येतेनैवाक्षरेण परं पुरुषमभिध्यायीत स तेजसि सूर्ये
संपन्न:। तथा पादोदरस्त्वचा विनिर्मुच्यत एवं ह वै स पाप्मना विनिर्मुक्त: स
सामभिरुन्नीयते ब्रह्मलोकं स एतस्माज्जीवघनात्परात्परं पुरिशयं पुरुषमीक्षते
तदेतौ श्लोकौ भवत: ॥ 5 ॥

*Yah Punaretam Trimaatrenomityetenaivaaksharena Param
Purushamabhidhyaayeeta Sa Tejasi Soorye Sampannah; Yathaa
Paadodarastvachaa Vinirmuchyata Evam Ha Vai Sa Paapmanaa
Vinirmuktah Sa Saamabhirunneeyate Brahmalokam Sa
Etasmaajjeevaghanaat Paraatparam Purishayam Purusha-
meekshate Tadetau Shlokau Bhavatah.* (5)

But he who meditates on the supreme Purusha with the
help of Om is united with the life-giving sun. Just as a snake
sheds its skin, so also will his sins fall from him, and the
Sama hymns will transport him to the world of Brahma, and
he will know Purusha abiding in all hearts. About that there
are the following two verses.

तिस्रो मात्रा मृत्युमत्य: प्रयुक्ता
अन्योन्यसक्ता अनविप्रयुक्ता: ।
क्रियासु बाह्याभ्यन्तरमध्यमासु
सम्यक्प्रयुक्तासु न कम्पते ज्ञ: ॥ 6 ॥

Tisro Maatraa Mrityumatyah Prayuktaa Anyonyasaktaa Anavi-prayuktaah; Kriyaasu Baahya Abhyantaramadhyamaasu Samyak Prayuktaasu Na Kampate Jnah. (6)

He who understands Om in part, whose three sounds are the waking, dreaming and deep sleep states, remains in the thrall of the rebirth cycle. He who realizes Om in its wholeness rises above these.

ऋग्भिरेतं   यजुर्भिरन्तरिक्षं
   सामभिर्यत्तत्कवयो   वेदयन्ते ।
तमोङ्कारेणैवायतनेनान्वेति विद्वान्
   यत्तच्छान्तमजरममृतमभयं परं चेति ॥ 7 ॥

Rigbhiretam Yajurbhirantariksham Saamabhiryat Tat Kavayo Vedayante; Tamonkaarenaivaayatanenaanveti Vidvaan Yattach-chhaantam Ajaram Amritam Abhayam Param Cheti. (7)

He who is enlightened knows that this world is attained by the Rik verses, the lunar world by the Yajus verses and the world of Brahman by the Sama verses. The wise attain this threefold world through Om alone. Through Om alone can one achieve the Supreme, the imperishable, deathless and immortal state, and thus one becomes fearless.

SIXTH QUESTION

अथ हैनं सुकेशा भारद्वाज: पप्रच्छ। भगवन्हिरण्यनाभ: कौसल्यो राजपुत्रो
मामुपेत्यैतं प्रश्नमपृच्छत। षोडशकलं भारद्वाज पुरुषं वेत्थ तमहं कुमारमब्रुवं
नाहमिमं वेद यद्यहमिममवेदिषं कथं ते नावक्ष्यमिति समूलो वा एष परिशुष्यति
योऽनृतमभिवदति तस्मान्नार्हाम्यनृतं वक्तुं स तूष्णीं रथमारुह्य प्रवव्राज। तं
त्वा पृच्छामि क्वासौ पुरुष इति ॥ 1 ॥

*Atha Hainam Sukeshaa Bhaaradvaajah Paprachchha; Bhagavan
Hiranyanaabhah Kausalyo Raajaputro Maamupetyaitam Prashnam
Aprichchhata; Shodashakalam Bhaaradvaaja Purusham Vettha
Tamaham Kumaaram Abruvam Naahamimam Veda.
Yadyahamimam Avedisham Katham Te Naavakshyamiti Samoolo
Vaa Esha Parishushyati Yoanritamabhivadati Tasmaannraarhaam-
yanritam Vaktum Sa Tooshneem Rathamaaruhya Pravavraaja;
Tam Tvaa Prichchhaami Kvaasau Purusha Iti. (1)*

Lastly Sukesha came to Pippalada and said: O Worshipful
One, one day Hiranyanabha, prince of Kausalya, asked me
whether I knew Purusha and his sixteen parts. I replied that
I did not, and if I had known, I would certainly have told
him. I did not dare tell an untruth since he who lies perishes
root and all. Thereupon the prince mounted his chariot
and silently rode away. Can you explain that Purusha to
me?

तस्मै स होवाच। इहैवान्त:शरीरे सोम्य स पुरुषो यस्मिन्नेता: षोडश कला:
प्रभवन्तीति ॥ 2 ॥

*Tasmai Sa Hovaacha; Ihaivaantah Shareere Somya Sa Purusho
Yasminnetaah Shodasha Kalaah Prabhavanteeti. (2)*

And Pippalada replied: O humble young man, Purusha
abides within the body itself, possessing sixteen parts.

31

स ईक्षांचक्रे। कस्मिन्नहमुत्क्रान्त उत्क्रान्तो भविष्यामि कस्मिन्वा प्रतिष्ठिते प्रतिष्ठास्यामीति ॥ ३ ॥

Sa Eekshaam Chakre; Kasminnahamutkraanta Utkraanto Bhavishyaami Kasminvaa Pratishthite Pratishthaasyaameeti. (3)

Purusha pondered: What is that which when it vanishes, I vanish also, and when it remains, I remain?

स प्राणमसृजत प्राणाच्छ्रद्धां खं वायुर्ज्योतिराप: पृथिवीन्द्रियं मनोऽ न्नमन्नाद्वीर्यं तपो मन्त्रा: कर्म लोका लोकेषु च नाम च ॥ ४ ॥

Sa Praanamasrijata Praanaachchhraddhaam Kham Vaayurjyoti-raapah Prithiveendriyam Manah Annam Annaadveeryam Tapo Mantraah Karma Lokaa Lokeshu Cha Naama Cha. (4)

Then Purusha created prana; from prana he created desire; from desire – ether, air, fire, water, earth, the senses, mind and food; and from food, strength, penance, the scriptures, rites, and the worlds, and the names in the worlds.

स यथेमा नद्य: स्यन्दमाना: समुद्रायणा: समुद्रं प्राप्यास्तं गच्छन्ति भिद्येते तासां नामरूपे समुद्र इत्येवं प्रोच्यते। एवमेवास्य परिद्रष्टुरिमा: षोडश कला: पुरुषायणा: पुरुषं प्राप्यास्तं गच्छन्ति भिद्येते चासां नामरूपे पुरुष इत्येवं प्रोच्यते स एषोऽकलोऽमृतो भवति तदेष श्लोक: ॥ ५ ॥

Sa Yathemaa Nadyah Syandamaanaah Samudraayanaah Samudram Praapyaastam Gachchhanti Bhidyete Taasaam Naamaroope Samudra Ityevam Prochyate; Evamevaasya Pari-drashturimaah Shodasha Kalaah Purushaayanaah Purusham Praapyaastam Gachchhanti Bhidyete Chaasaam Naamaroope Purusha Ityevam Prochyate Sa Eshokalomrito Bhavati Tadesha Shlokah. (5)

As the rivers upon reaching the ocean flow into and become one with it, abandoning their name and form, similarly, the sixteen parts of the wise, who realize Purusha, merge in Him and lose their separateness. He then becomes free from the kalaas and immortal. There is the following verse about it.

अरा इव रथनाभौ कला यस्मिन्प्रतिष्ठिताः। तं वेद्यं पुरुषं वेद यथा मा वो मृत्युःपरिव्यथा इति ॥ 6 ॥

Araa Iva Rathanaabhau Kalaa Yasminpratishthitaah; Tam Vedyam Purusham Veda Yathaa Maa Vo Mrityuh Parivyathaa Iti. (6)

May you know that Purusha, the end of all knowledge, in whom the parts (kalaas) radiate like spokes from a wheel-hub, and thereby achieve release from death.

तान्होवाचैतावदेवाहमेतत्परं ब्रह्म वेद। नातः परमस्तीति ॥ 7 ॥

Taan Hovaachaitaavadevaahametatparam Brahma Veda; Naatah Paramasteeti. (7)

Then Pippalada addressed them all, saying: May you realize the supreme Brahman, for there is none higher than Him.

ते तमर्चयन्तस्त्वं हि नःपिता योऽस्माकमविद्यायाः परंपारं तारयसीति नमः परमऋषिभ्यो नमः परमऋषिभ्यः ॥ 8 ॥

Te Tamarchayantastvam Hi Nah Pitaa Yoasmaakam Avidyaayaah Param Paaram Taarayaseeti. Namah Paramareeshibhyo Namah Paramareeshibhyah. (8)

The six disciples worshipped Pippalada and said: Indeed you are a father to us. You have helped us in our crossing of the sea of ignorance.

Salutations to the great Rishis! Salutations!

SHANTI PATH

ॐ भद्रं कर्णेभिः शृणुयाम देवा भद्रं पश्येमाक्षभिर्यजत्राः।
स्थिरैरंगैस्तुष्टुवाँसस्तनूभिर्व्यशेम देवहितं यदायुः ॥ स्वस्ति न इन्द्रो
वृद्धश्रवाः स्वस्ति नः पूषा विश्ववेदाः। स्वस्ति नस्ताक्ष्यों अरिष्टनेमिः
स्वस्ति नो बृहस्पतिर्दधातु ॥

ॐ शान्तिः शान्तिः शान्तिः

*Om Bhadram Karnebhih Shrinuyaama Devaah Bhadram
Pashyemaakshabhiryajatraah; Sthirai Rangaih Tushtuvaam
Sastanoobhirvyashema Devahitam Yadaayuh. Svasti Na Indro
Vriddhashravaa Svasti Na Pooshaa Vishvavedaah; Svasti
Nastaarkshyo Arishtanemih Svasti No Brihaspatirdadhaatu.*

Om Shaantih Shaantih Shaantih.

Om. O ye Gods. May we hear auspicious words and see
auspicious sights while worshipping you. May we be blessed
in life with perfect health and vigour while singing your
praise. May the Lord Indra, the Loved One of old, be well-
inclined towards us. May He, in his kindness, be watchful of
our prosperity. May He, the nourisher and possessor of all
wealth, give us what is good for us. May the Lord, the
destroyer of evil and the protector of the great ones, protect
us too.

Om peace, peace, peace.

Kenopanishad

The Kenopanishad is in four parts. It tells of the nature of Brahman and the knowledge of the Self in dialogue form between teacher and disciple.

The nature of Brahman and the ways He can be realized are stated in the first two parts. Being the Supreme One, He is the mind of the mind, the eye of the eye, the ear of the ear, the speech of the speech and the life of the life. The mind, prana and senses cannot function without His presence. He is different from the known and is beyond the unknown.

In the third part a dialogue takes place between the Devas (gods) and the Yakshas (spirits), and the pride and false notions of the powerful Devas – Agni (fire), Vayu (air) and Indra (the supreme god) – are dispelled altogether by means of a hay stalk. From this lesson it has become well known that whatever is glorious, prosperous and powerful comes from a spark of Brahman's splendour. From Him everything is manifested: glory, brilliance, splendour, beauty, power and so many other divine attributes. Brahman expresses Himself through all these mediums. In the fourth part the methods of meditation on Brahman and its fruits are described.

When a spiritual aspirant has a strong and burning desire to know the supreme Brahman, He reveals Himself as quick as a lightning flash or in the twinkling of an eye.

This is only possible when, by abandoning the fruits of action, one possesses a pure and calm mind which is freed from worldly desire. Knowledge of Brahman definitely destroys the ignorance which causes the cycle of rebirth. One can acquire this knowledge by studying the Vedas (scriptures). It is essential to possess austerity, self-restraint and truthfulness in order to know Him. He who knows this truth and has become free of all sin will not return to this world, but will attain immortality.

SHANTI PATH

ॐ आप्यायन्तु ममाङ्गानि वाक् प्राणश्चक्षुः श्रोत्रमथो बलमिन्द्रियाणि च
सर्वाणि। सर्वं ब्रह्मोपनिषदं माहं ब्रह्म निराकुर्यां मा मा ब्रह्म निराकरोत्,
अनिराकरणमस्त्वनिराकरणं मेऽस्तु। तदात्मनि निरते य उपनिषत्सु धर्मास्ते
मयि सन्तु, ते मयि सन्तु ॥

ॐ शान्तिः शान्तिः शान्तिः

*Om Aapyaayantu Mamaangaani Vaak Praanashchakshuh
Shrotramatho Balamindriyaani Cha Sarvaani; Sarvam
Brahmopanishadam Maaham Brahma Niraakuryaam Maa Maa
Brahma Niraakarot Aniraakaranamastvaniraakaranam Meastu;
Tadaatmani Nirate Ya Upanishatsu Dharmaaste Mayi Santu Te
Mayi Santu.*

Om Shaantih Shaantih Shaantih.

Om! May all my limbs, speech, eyes, strength and all other
organs and faculties become vigilant, keenly active and well
developed. Everything is Brahman described in the
Upanishads. May I surely not be neglectful of Brahman nor
Brahman of me. Let there be no rejection of me by Brahman
and of Brahman by me. May all the virtues revealed in the
Upanishads be evident in me giving great joy to Atman. May
they be evident in me.

Om peace, peace, peace.

PART I

ॐ केनेषितं पतति प्रेषितं मन: केन प्राण: प्रथम: प्रैति युक्त: ।
केनेषितां वाचमिमां वदन्ति चक्षु: श्रोत्रं क उ देवो युनक्ति ॥ 1 ॥

Om Keneshitam Patati Preshitam Manah Kena Praanah Prathamah
Praiti Yuktah; Keneshitaam Vaachamimaam Vadanti Chakshuh
Shrotram Ka U Devo Yunakti. (1)

By whose will is the mind directed towards its goal? By
whose order does prana proceed to perform its duty? By
whose command does a person utter speech? Who directs
the eyes and ears to their respective sensory objects?

श्रोत्रस्य श्रोत्रं मनसो मनो यद्वाचो ह वाचँ स उ प्राणस्य प्राण: ।
चक्षुषश्चक्षुरतिमुच्य धीरा: प्रेत्यास्माल्लोकादमृता भवन्ति ॥ 2 ॥

Shrotrasya Shrotram Manaso Mano Yadvaacho Ha Vaacham Sa
U Praanasya Praanah; Chakshushash Chakshuratimuchya
Dheeraah Pretyaasmaallokaadamritaa Bhavanti. (2)

It is the ear of the ear, the eye of the eye, the speech of the
speech, the mind of the mind, and the life of the life. When
the wise abandon 'I-ness' and rise above the life of the
senses, they achieve immortality.

न तत्र चक्षुर्गच्छति न वाग्गच्छति नो मनो न विद्मो न विजानीमो
यथैतदनुशिष्यादन्यदेव तद्विदितादथो अविदितादधि। इति शुश्रुम पूर्वेषां ये
नस्तद्व्याचचक्षिरे ॥ 3 ॥

Na Tatra Chakshurgachchhati Na Vaaggachchhati No Mano Na
Vidmo Na Vijaaneemo Yathaitadanushishyaadanyadeva Tad-
viditaadatho Aviditaadadhi; Iti Shushruma Poorveshaam Ye
Nastadvyaachachakshire. (3)

The eye does not go there, not the speech, nor the mind. We cannot say Brahman is this or that, hence we are unable to instruct one another about Him or the process of the same. That (Brahman) is surely different from the known and is beyond the unknown. This we have heard from the ancient teachers who explained it to us.

यद्वाचानभ्युदितं येन वागभ्युद्यते ।
तदेव ब्रह्म त्वं विद्धि नेदं यदिदमुपासते ॥ 4 ॥

Yadvaahaanabhyuditam Yena Vaagabhyudyate; Tadeva Brahma Tvam Viddhi Nedam Yadidamupaasate. (4)

That which is not uttered by speech, but which enlightens the speech, that alone is Brahman, and not that which people worship.

यन्मनसा न मनुते येनाहुर्मनो मतम् ।
तदेव ब्रह्म त्वं विद्धि नेदं यदिदमुपासते ॥ 5 ॥

Yanmanasaa Na Manute Yenaahurmano Matam; Tadeva Brahma Tvam Viddhi Nedam Yadidamupaasate. (5)

That which one cannot think with the mind, but by which, they say, the mind is made to think is Brahman, and not that which people worship.

यच्चक्षुषा न पश्यति येन चक्षूꣽषि पश्यति ।
तदेव ब्रह्म त्वं विद्धि नेदं यदिदमुपासते ॥ 6 ॥

Yachchakshushaa Na Pashyati Yena Chakshoomshi Pashyati; Tadeva Brahma Tvam Viddhi Nedam Yadidamupaasate. (6)

That which one cannot see with the eyes, but by which the eyes are enabled to see, know That alone to be Brahman, and not that which people worship.

यच्छ्रोत्रेण न शृणोति येन श्रोत्रमिदꣳश्रुतम् ।
तदेव ब्रह्म त्वं विद्धि नेदं यदिदमुपासते ॥ 7 ॥

Yachchhrotrena Na Shrinoti Yena Shrotramidam Shrutam;
Tadeva Brahma Tvam Viddhi Nedam Yadidamupaasate. (7)

That which one cannot hear with the ears, but by which the
ears are made to hear, know That alone to be Brahman, and
not that which people worship.

यत् प्राणेन न प्राणिति येन प्राणः प्रणीयते ।
तदेव ब्रह्म त्वं विद्धि नेदं यदिदमुपासते ॥ 8 ॥

Yat Praanena Na Praaniti Yena Praanah Praneeyate; Tadeva
Brahma Tvam Viddhi Nedam Yadidamupaasate. (8)

That which one cannot smell with the nose, but which
directs the nose to the object of smell, know That alone to be
Brahman, and not that which people worship.

PART II

यदि मन्यसे सुवेदेति दभ्रमेवापि नूनं त्वं वेत्थ ब्रह्मणो रूपम् ।
यदस्य त्वं यदस्य च देवेष्वथ नु मीमाँ स्यमेव मे मन्ये विदितम् ॥ 1 ॥

Yadi Manyase Suvedeti Dabhramevaapi Noonam Tvam Vettha Brahmano Roopam; Yadasya Tvam Yadasya Cha Deveshvatha Nu Meemaamsyameva Te Manye Viditam. (1)

Teacher: If you think you know Brahman very well, then you only know the partial manifestation which is the human body and the forms of the gods. So you should go deeper in your enquiry of Brahman.

नाहं मन्ये सुवेदेति नो न वेदेति च ।
यो नस्तद्वेद तद्वेद नो न वेदेति वेद च ॥ 2 ॥

Naaham Manye Suvedeti No Na Vedeti Cha; Yo Nastadveda Tadveda No Na Vedeti Veda Cha. (2)

Disciple: I do not think I do not know Brahman well, but that is not that I do not know Him. I know and also I do not know. Brahman within us knows Him and He also knows that he knows Him not.

यस्यामतं तस्य मतं मतं यस्य न वेद सः ।
अविज्ञातं विजानतां विज्ञातमविजानताम् ॥ 3 ॥

Yasyaamatam Tasya Matam Matam Yasya Na Veda Sah; Avijnaatam Vijaanataam Vijnaatamavijaanataam. (3)

It is known to him who does not know and unknown to him who knows.

प्रतिबोधविदितं मतममृत्वं हि विन्दते ।
आत्मना विन्दते वीर्यं विद्यया विन्दतेऽमृतम् ॥ 4 ॥

Pratibodhaviditam Matamamritvam Hi Vindate; Aatmanaa Vindate Veeryam Vidyayaa Vindateamritam. (4)

Brahman is known really well when he is known in every state of consciousness, since by that knowledge one receives immortality. Through the Self one gains strength and through knowledge immortality.

इह चेदवेदीदथ सत्यमस्ति न चेदिहावेदीन्महती विनष्टि: ।
भूतेषु भूतेषु विचित्य धीरा: प्रेत्यास्माल्लोकादमृता भवन्ति ॥ 5 ॥

Iha Chedavedeedatha Satyamasti Na Chedihaavedeenmahatee Vinashtih; Bhooteshu Bhooteshu Vichitya Dheeraah Pretyaas- maallokaadamritaa Bhavanti. (5)

He who knows Brahman whilst on earth has achieved the sole object of life; they who do not, suffer great misfortune. The wise, perceiving the oneness of all beings in Atman, rise above sensory phenomena and are immortal.

PART III

ब्रह्म ह देवेभ्यो विजिग्ये तस्य ह ब्रह्मणो विजये देवा अमहीयन्त त
ऐक्षन्तास्माकमेवायं विजयोऽस्माकमेवायं महिमेति ॥ 1 ॥

*Brahma Ha Devebhyo Vijigye Tasya Ha Brahmano Vijaye Devaa
Amaheeyanta Ta Aikshantaasmaakamevaayam Vijayoasmaakame-
vaayam Mahimeti.* (1)

It was Brahman Himself who gave the Devas (gods) victory,
from which they derive their glory. But they believed that
the victory and glory were their achievement.

तद्धैषां विजज्ञौ तेभ्यो ह प्रादुर्बभूव तन्न व्यजानत किमिदं यक्षमिति ॥ 2 ॥

*Taddhaishaam Vijajnau Tebhyo Ha Praadurbabhoova Tanna
Vyajaanata Kimidam Yakshamiti.* (2)

Brahman knew their attitude of pride and conceit, and He
appeared before them disguised as a Yaksha (spirit) to
destroy their self-deception. The Devas did not recognize
Him and were unaware of His plan.

तेऽग्निमब्रुवञ्जातवेद एतद् विजानीहि किमिदं यक्षमिति तथेति ॥ 3 ॥

*Teagnimabruvanjaataveda Etad Vijaaneehi Kimidam Yakshamiti
Tatheti.* (3)

And turning to Fire they said: O Jataveda, go and discover
the identity of this Yaksha.

तदभ्यद्रवत् तमभ्यवदत् कोऽसीत्यग्निर्वा अहमस्मीत्यब्रवीज्जातवेदा वा
अहमस्मीति ॥ 4 ॥

*Tadabhyadravat Tamabhyavadat Koaseetyagnirvaa Ahamasmeetya-
braveejjaatavedaa Vaa Ahamasmeeti.* (4)

43

Fire went to the Yaksha. Brahman, thus disguised, asked him who he was. And Fire replied: I am Fire, otherwise known as Jataveda.

तस्मिँ स्त्वयि किं वीर्यमिति। अपीदँ सर्वं दहेयं, यदिदं पृथिव्यामिति ॥ 5 ॥

Tasminstvayi Kim Veeryamiti; Apeedam Sarvam Daheyam, Yadidam Prithivyaamiti. (5)

Then Brahman inquired: What power do you possess such as you are? Fire replied: I can burn all things on earth.

तस्मै तृणं निदधावेतद्दहेति। तदुपप्रेयाय सर्वजवेन तन्न शशाक दग्धुं स तत एव निववृते, नैतदशकं विज्ञातुं यदेतद् यक्षमिति ॥ 6 ॥

Tasmai Trinam Nidadhaavetaddaheti; Tadupapreyaaya Sarva-javena Tanna Shashaaka Dagdhum Sa Tata Eva Nivavrite, Naitadashakam Vijnaatum Yadetad Yakshamiti. (6)

Thereupon Brahman placed a hay stalk before Fire saying: Burn this. And Fire rushed at the hay stalk with all his might, but the hay stalk remained unburnt. Immediately, Fire returned to the Devas and told them he was unable to discover the identity of the Yaksha.

अथ वायुमब्रुवन् वायवेतद् विजानीहि किमेतद् यक्षमिति तथेति ॥ 7 ॥

Atha Vaayamubruvan Vaayavetad Vijaaneehi Kimetad Yakshamiti Tatheti. (7)

The Devas now turned to Air and said: You, Air, find out for us what this Yaksha is.

तदभ्यद्रवत् तमभ्यवदत् कोऽसीति। वायुर्वा अहमस्मीत्यब्रवीन्मातरिश्वा वा अहमस्मीति ॥ 8 ॥

Tadabhyadravat Tamabhyavadat Koaseeti; Vaayurvaa Ahamasmeeti Abraveen Maatarishvaa Vaa Ahamasmeeti. (8)

So this time Air went to the Yaksha. Brahman asked Air who he was and Air told Him he was Vayu or Air, otherwise known as Matarishva.

तस्मिँ स्वयि किं वीर्यमिति? अपीदँ सर्वमाददीयम् यदिदं पृथिव्यामिति ॥ 9 ॥

Tasminstvayi Kim Veeryamiti? Apeedam Sarvamaadadeeyam Yadidam Prithivyaamiti. (9)

Then Brahman enquired what powers he possessed, and Air replied that he could blow away anything on earth.

तस्मै तृणं निदधावेतदादत्स्वेति। तदुपप्रेयाय सर्वजवेन तन्न शशाकादातुं स तत एव निववृते, नैतदशकं विज्ञातुं यदेतद् यक्षमिति ॥ 10 ॥

Tasmai Trinam Nidadhaavetadaadatsveti; Tadupapreyaaya Sarvajavena Tanna Shashaakaadaatum Sa Tata Eva Nivavrite, Naitadashakam Vijnaatum Yadetad Yakshamiti. (10)

Thereupon Brahman placed the hay stalk before Air and asked him to blow it away. Air rushed at it with all his might, but the hay stalk remained perfectly still. Air straightaway returned to the Devas and informed them of his lack of success in discovering the identity of the Yaksha.

अथेन्द्रमब्रुवन् मघवन्नेतद् विजानीहि किमेतद् यक्षमिति। तथेति। तदभ्यद्रवत् । तस्मात् तिरोदधे ॥ 11 ॥

45

*Athendram Abruvan Maghavannetad Vijaaneehi Kimetad
Yakshamiti; Tatheti; Tadabhyadravat; Tasmaat Tirodadhe.* (11)

Finally, the Devas and addressed Indra: O Maghavan, they
said. Can you find out who this Yaksha is? But when Indra
started in the direction of the Yaksha, He vanished from
sight.

स तस्मिन्नेवाकाशे स्त्रियमाजगाम बहुशोभमानामुमाँ हैमवतीं ताँ होवाच
किमेतद् यक्षमिति ॥ 12 ॥

*Sa Tasminnevaakaashe Striyamaajagaama Bahushobhamaanaamu-
man Haimavateem Taam Hovaacha Kimetad Yakshamiti.* (12)

And in His place he saw Uma, a beautiful and golden
complexioned woman, Himavat's daughter. Indra enquired
of her the identity of the Yaksha.

PART IV

सा ब्रह्मेति होवाच। ब्रह्मणो वा एतद्विजये महीयध्वमिति, ततो हैव विदाञ्चकार
ब्रह्मेति ॥ 1 ॥

*Saa Brahmeti Hovaacha; Brahmano Vaa Etadvijaye Maheeyadhva-
miti, Tato Haiva Vidaanchakaara Brahmeti.* (1)

And Uma explained to him that it had been Brahman
Himself and that the victory and glory of the Devas had
been due to Brahman alone. This truth could only be made
known from Uma's lips.

तस्माद्वा एते देवा अतितरामिवान्यान् देवान् यदग्निर्वायुरिन्द्रस्ते ह्येनन्नेदिष्ठं
पस्पृशुस्ते ह्येनत् प्रथमो विदाञ्चकार ब्रह्मेति ॥ 2 ॥

*Tasmaadvaa Ete Devaa Atitaraamivaanyaan Devaanyadagnirvaa-
yurindraste Hyenannedishtham Pasprishuste Hyenat Prathamo
Vidaanchakaara Brahmeti.* (2)

Thus indeed Fire, Air and Indra exceed the other gods in
greatness, since they came into such close contact with
Brahman and were the first to know Him.

तस्माद् वा इन्द्रोऽतितरामिवान्यान् देवान् स ह्येनन्नेदिष्ठं पस्पर्श, स ह्येनत्
प्रथमो विदाञ्चकार ब्रह्मेति ॥ 3 ॥

*Tasmaad Vaa Indroatitaraamivaanyaan Devaan Sa Hyenanne-
dishtham Pasparsha Sa Hyenat Prathamo Vidaanchakaara
Brahmeti.* (3)

And Indra is foremost among the gods because he was the
first to know that the Yaksha was Brahman.

तस्यैष आदेशो यदेतद् विद्युती व्यद्युतदा इतीन्न्यमीमिषदा इत्यधिदैवतम्
॥ 4 ॥

*Tasyaisha Aadesho Yadetad Vidyuto Vyadyutadaa Iteennyamee-
mishadaa Ityadhidaivatam.* (4)

This story explains the identity of Brahman. He appears
and disappears as quick as a lightning flash or in the twinkling
of an eye.

अथाध्यात्मं यदेतद्गच्छतीव च मनोऽनेन चैतदुपस्मरत्यभीक्ष्णं सङ्कल्पः
॥ 5 ॥

*Athaadhyaatmam Yadetadgachchhateeva Cha Manoanena Chaita-
dupasmaratyabheekshnam Sankalpah.* (5)

Now the relation of Brahman with Atman is stated: mind
remembers Brahman and Brahman makes mind remember
as quick as a lightning flash or in the twinkling of an eye.

तद्ध तद्वनं नाम तद्वनमित्युपासितव्यं स य एतदेवं वेदाभि हैनं सर्वाणि
भूतानि संवाञ्छन्ति ॥ 6 ॥

*Taddha Tadvanam Naama Tadvanamityupaasitavyam Sa Ya
Etadevam Vedaabhi Hainam Sarvaani Bhootaani Samvaanchhanti.*
(6)

It is well known that Brahman is adored by all; similarly,
those who know him are loved universally.

उपनिषदं भो ब्रूहीत्युक्ता त उपनिषद् ब्राह्मीं वाव त उपनिषदमब्रूमेति ॥ 7 ॥

*Upanishadam Bho Brooheetyuktaa Ta Upanishad Braahmeem
Vaava Ta Upanishadamabroometi.* (7)

Then did the disciple ask for more of this Upanishad to be
told. Whereupon the teacher replied: I have completed this

Upanishad about Brahman, and nothing more remains to be told.

तस्यै तपो दम: कर्मेति प्रतिष्ठा वेदा: सर्वाङ्गानि सत्यमायतनम् ॥ 8 ॥

Tasyai Tapo Damah Karmeti Pratishthaa Vedaah Sarvaangaani Satyamaayatanam. (8)

Austerity, self-restraint and performance of duty without attachment are the means to purify the heart; the Vedas and scriptures are the foundations of this knowledge, and truth is its essence.

यो वा एतामेवं वेदापहत्य पाप्मानमनन्ते स्वर्गे लोके ज्येये प्रतितिष्ठति प्रतितिष्ठति ॥ 9 ॥

Yo Vaa Etaamevam Vedaapahatya Paapmaanamanante Svarge Loke Jyeye Pratitishthati Pratitishthati. (9)

He who knows this, and being free of all sin remains steadfastly in the boundless and highest Brahman, is forever established in Him. He will be released from the cycle of rebirth and will not return to this world.

SHANTI PATH

ॐ आप्यायन्तु ममाङ्गानि वाक् प्राणश्चक्षुः श्रोत्रमथो बलमिन्द्रियाणि च सर्वाणि । सर्वं ब्रह्मोपनिषदं माहं ब्रह्म निराकुर्यां मा मा ब्रह्म निराकरोत् , अनिराकरणमस्त्वनिराकरणं मेऽस्तु। तदात्मनि निरते य उपनिषत्सु धर्मास्ते मयि सन्तु, ते मयि सन्तु ॥

ॐ शान्तिः शान्तिः शान्तिः

Om Aapyaayantu Mamaangaani Vaak Praanashchakshuh Shrotramatho Balamindriyaani Cha Sarvaani; Sarvam Brahmopanishadam Maaham Brahma Niraakuryaam Maa Maa Brahma Niraakarot Aniraakaranamastvaniraakaranam Meastu; Tadaatmani Nirate Ya Upanishatsu Dharmaaste Mayi Santu Te Mayi Santu.

Om Shaantih Shaantih Shaantih.

Om! May all my limbs, speech, eyes, strength and all other organs and faculties become vigilant, keenly active and well developed. Everything is Brahman described in the Upanishads. May I surely not be neglectful of Brahman nor Brahman of me. Let there be no rejection of me by Brahman and of Brahman by me. May all the virtues revealed in the Upanishads be evident in me giving great joy to Atman. May they be evident in me.

Om peace, peace, peace.

Mandukyopanishad

The subject matter of this Upanishad is the Ultimate Reality, which is discussed in a clear and direct way. The Ultimate is hard to grasp being beyond time, space and cause, and for which a symbol has to be used. Om, the word of all words, is the symbol of this Upanishad. Om is composed of the sounds – A, U, M. These three sounds symbolize the gross, subtle and causal aspects of Brahman. Om is the means to know Brahman, and is inseparable from Him. If you realize Om, you know Brahman. Therefore, it is essential to have a direct understanding of Om, by which the immortal Self, the supreme Brahman, the ultimate goal, is realized.

Atman is associated with the waking, the dreaming and the deep sleep states. Finally these states are merged in Turiya, the Ultimate Reality. Atman becomes identical with Brahman – the indivisible, the transcendent, the incomprehensible, the cessation of all phenomena, the blissful – when Atman, the Om, merges his Self in the Self and attains Self-realization, which is the Ultimate Reality.

SHANTI PATH

ॐ भद्रं कर्णेभिः शृणुयाम देवा भद्रं पश्येमाक्षभिर्यजत्राः । स्थिरैरंगै-
स्तुष्टुवासस्तनूभिर्व्यशेम देवहितं यदायुः ॥ स्वस्ति न इन्द्रो वृद्धश्रवाः
स्वस्ति नः पूषा विश्ववेदाः । स्वस्ति नस्ताक्ष्र्यो अरिष्टनेमिः स्वस्ति नो
बृहस्पतिर्दधातु ॥

ॐ शान्तिः शान्तिः शान्तिः

Om Bhadram Karnebhih Shrinuyaama Devaah Bhadram
Pashyemaakshabhiryajatraah; Sthirai Rangaih Tushtuvaam
Sastanoobhirvyashema Devahitam Yadaayuh. Svasti Na Indro
Vriddhashravaa Svasti Na Pooshaa Vishvavedaah; Svasti
Nastaarkshyo Arishtanemih Svasti No Brihaspatirdadhaatu.

Om Shaantih Shaantih Shaantih.

Om. O Ye Gods. May we hear auspicious words and see
auspicious sights while worshipping you. May we be blessed
in life with perfect health and vigour while singing your
praise. May the Lord Indra, the Loved One of old, be well-
inclined towards us. May He, in his kindness, be watchful of
our prosperity. May He, the nourisher and the possessor of
all wealth, give us what is good for us. May the Lord, the
destroyer of evil and the protector of the great ones, protect
us too.

Om peace, peace, peace.

ओमित्येतदक्षरमिदꣳ सर्वं तस्योपव्याख्यानं भूतं भवद्भविष्यदिति सर्वमोङ्कार
एव। यच्चान्यत् त्रिकालातीतं तदप्योङ्कार एव ॥ 1 ॥

*Omityetadaksharamidam Sarvam Tasyopavyaakhyaanam Bhootam
Bhavadbhavishyaditi Sarvamonkaara Eva; Yachchaanyat
Trikaalaateetam Tadapyonkaara Eva. (1)*

The word Om is the universe. Everything that exists in the
past, present, and future is Om. And that which exists
beyond the threefold division of time is Om.

सर्वꣳ ह्येतद् ब्रह्मायमात्मा ब्रह्म सोऽयमात्मा चतुष्पात् ॥ 2 ॥

*Sarvam Hyetad Brahmaayamaatmaa Brahma Soayamaatmaa
Chatushpaat. (2)*

And everything that is, is Brahman. The Self (Atman) is
Brahman. The following are His four aspects.

जागरितस्थानो बहिष्प्रज्ञः सप्ताङ्ग एकोनविंशतिमुखः स्थूलभुग्वैश्वानरः प्रथमः
पादः ॥ 3 ॥

*Jaagaritasthaano Bahishprajnah Saptaanga Ekonavinshatimukhah
Sthoolabhugvaishvaanarah Prathamah Paadah. (3)*

The first aspect is the waking state, the awareness of external
things, the terrain of Vaishvanara. Seven limbs and nineteen
mouths are possessed by him, and his enjoyment lies in the
visible objects of the world.

स्वप्नस्थानोऽन्तः प्रज्ञः सप्ताङ्गएकोनविंशतिमुखः प्रविविक्तभुक्तैजसो द्वितीयः
पादः ॥ 4 ॥

*Svapnasthaanoantah Prajnah Saptaanga Ekonavinshatimukhah
Praviviktabhuktaijaso Dviteeyah Paadah. (4)*

The dreaming state is the second aspect, over which Tejas rules. Seven limbs and nineteen mouths belong to him, and the objects he enjoys are invisible.

यत्र सुप्तो न कञ्चन कामं कामयते न कञ्चन स्वप्नं पश्यति तत्सुषुप्तम् ।
सुषुप्तस्थान एकीभूतः प्रज्ञानघन एवानन्दमयो ह्यानन्दभुक्चेतोमुखः
प्रज्ञस्तृतीयः पादः ॥ 5 ॥

Yatra Supto Na Kanchana Kaamam Kaamayate Na Kanchana Svapnam Pashyati Tatsushuptam; Sushuptasthaana Ekeebhootah Prajnaanaghana Evaanandamayo Hyaanandabhuk Chetomukhah Praajnastriteeyah Paadah. (5)

The third aspect is deep dreamless sleep, lying beyond desire. Prajna is the Lord of this territory; he abides in deep sleep in which all things have vanished, and he enjoys bliss. Prajna lies at the gateway to the dreaming and waking states.

एष सर्वेश्वर एष सर्वज्ञ एषोऽन्तर्याम्येष योनिः सर्वस्य प्रभवाप्ययौ हि
भूतानाम् ॥ 6 ॥

Esha Sarvehvara Esha Sarvajna Eshoantaryaamyesha Yonih Sarvasya Prabhavaapyayau Hi Bhootaanaam. (6)

Prajna is the Lord supreme, the knower supreme, the authority supreme, the source supreme, the creator and destroyer of all beings.

नान्तःप्रज्ञं न बहिष्प्रज्ञं नोभयतःप्रज्ञं न प्रज्ञानघनं न प्रज्ञं नाप्रज्ञम् ।
अदृष्टमव्यवहार्यमग्राह्यमलक्षणमचिन्त्यमव्यपदेश्यमेकात्मप्रत्ययसारं
प्रपञ्चोपशमं शान्तं शिवमद्वैतं चतुर्थं मन्यन्ते स आत्मा स विज्ञेयः ॥ 7 ॥

Naantahprajnam Na Bahishprajnam Nobhayatah Prajnam Na Prajnaanaghanam Na Prajnam Naaprajnam; Adrishtam Avyavahaaryam Agraahyam Alakshanam Achintyam Avyapadeshyam

Ekaatmapratyayasaaram Prapanchopashamam Shaantam Shiva-madvaitam Chaturtham Manyante Sa Aatmaa Sa Vijneyah. (7)

Turiya, Lord of the fourth aspect, according to the wise, remains unaware of the external, intermediate, and internal worlds. He lies beyond both consciousness and unconsciousness; it is indescribable, bearing no relation to anything, where sight cannot penetrate, nor thought. Turiya enjoys pure awareness and experiences peace, bliss, and non-duality. He is none other than Atman. Realize Him.

सोऽयमात्माध्यक्षरमोङ्कारोऽधिमात्रं पादा मात्रा मात्राश्च पादा अकार उकारो मकार इति ॥ 8 ॥

Soayamaatmaa Adhyakysharam Omkaaroadhimaatram Paadaa Maatraa Maatraashcha Paadaa Akaara Ukaaro Makaara Iti. (8)

Om is the sacred word of Atman. The sounds of Om are A, U, M, and symbolize the different aspects of Atman.

जागरितस्थानो वैश्वानरोऽकार: प्रथमा मात्राऽऽप्तेरादिमत्त्वाद्वाऽऽप्नोति ह वै सर्वान्कामानादिश्च भवति य एवं वेद ॥ 9 ॥

Jaagaritasthaano Vaishvaanaroakaarah Prathamaa Maatraa Aapteraadimattvaad Vaa Aapnoti Ha Vai Sarvaan Kaamaa-naadishcha Bhavati Ya Evam Veda. (9)

'A', the first sound, is the sound of the waking state, ruled by Vaishvanara. He who knows this truth has all desires fulfilled and is the first among men.

स्वप्नस्थानस्तैजस उकारो द्वितीया मात्रोत्कर्षादुभयत्वाद्वोत्कर्षति ह वै ज्ञानसन्ततिं समानश्च भवति नास्याब्रह्मवित्कुले भवति य एवं वेद ॥ 10 ॥

Svapnasthaanastaijasa Ukaaro Dviteeyaa Maatraa Utkar-shaadubhayatvaad Vaa Utkarshati Ha Vai Jnaanasantatim

55

Samaanashcha Bhavati Naasyaabrahmavit Kule Bhavati Ya Evam Veda. (10)

'U', the second sound, represents the state of dreaming, of which Tejas is the ruler. The knower of this truth becomes exceedingly wise, and is held in reverence by all. None to whom Brahman is unknown will be born into his family.

सुषुप्तस्थानः प्राज्ञो मकारस्तृतीया मात्रा मितेरपीतेर्वा मिनोति ह वा इदं सर्वमपीतिश्च भवति य एवं वेद ॥ 11 ॥

Sushuptasthaanah Praajno Makaarastriteeyaa Maatraa Miterapeetervaa Minoti Ha Vaa Idam Sarvamapeetishcha Bhavati Ya Evam Veda. (11)

'M', the third sound, symbolizes deep sleep, the enjoyer of which is Prajna. 'M' is both the measure and the end; therefore, he who knows this truth measures everything by his knowledge and becomes realized in Atman, the cause behind the universe.

अमात्रश्चतुर्थोऽव्यहार्यः प्रपञ्चोपशमः शिवोऽद्वैत एवमोङ्कार आत्मैव संविशत्यात्मनाऽऽत्मानं य एवं वेद – य एवं वेद ॥ 12 ॥

Amaatrashchaturthah Avyahaaryah Prapanchopashamah Shivoadvaita Evamonkaara Aatmaiva Samvishatyaatmanaa Aatmaanam Ya Evam Veda – Ya Evam Veda. (12)

The fourth aspect is 'Om' itself, the sacred, the indivisible word. Om is Atman, the transcendent, the beyond understanding, the cessation of all phenomena, the blissful, the non-dual. The knower of this highest Truth is merged in Atman and attains the final goal, which is Brahman.

SHANTI PATH

ॐ भद्रं कर्णेभि: शृणुयाम देवा भद्रं पश्येमाक्षभिर्यजत्रा: । स्थिरैरंगै-
स्तुष्टुवाससतनूभिर्व्यशेम देवहितं यदायु: ॥ स्वस्ति न इन्द्रो वृद्धश्रवा:
स्वस्ति न: पूषा विश्ववेदा: । स्वस्ति नस्ताक्ष्र्यो अरिष्टनेमि: स्वस्ति नो
बृहस्पतिर्दधातु ॥

ॐ शान्ति: शान्ति: शान्ति:

*Om Bhadram Karnebhih Shrinuyaama Devaah Bhadram
Pashyemaakshabhiryajatraah; Sthirai Rangaih Tushtuvaam
Sastanoobhirvyashema Devahitam Yadaayuh. Svasti Na Indro
Vriddhashravaa Svasti Na Pooshaa Vishvavedaah; Svasti
Nastaarkshyo Arishtanemih Svasti No Brihaspatirdadhaatu.*

Om Shaantih Shaantih Shaantih.

Om. O Ye Gods. May we hear auspicious words and see
auspicious sights while worshipping you. May we be blessed
in life with perfect health and vigour while singing your
praise. May the Lord Indra, the Loved One of old, be well-
inclined towards us. May He, in his kindness, be watchful of
our prosperity. May He, the nourisher and the possessor of
all wealth, give us what is good for us. May the Lord, the
destroyer of evil and the protector of the great ones, protect
us too.

Om peace, peace, peace.

Mundakopanishad

There are two probable meanings of the word 'mundaka': (i) *Mundaka* means a shaven-headed person, i.e. a sannyasin or monk. Sannyasa or renunciation is essential for attaining knowledge of the Self. A sannyasin is qualified for divine knowledge since he can devote himself entirely to spiritual studies and meditation. (ii) The second meaning is the following: in this Upanishad the clear-cut division between higher knowledge, or Para Vidya, and the lower knowledge, or Apara Vidya, is explained. Para Vidya, or knowledge of the Self, removes the superimposed ignorance and doubt from the mind like hair being shaved off with a razor, hence the name.

There are three sections in this Upanishad, and each is divided into two parts. The first part of the first section explains how knowledge of Brahman was passed down through the ages. Also the nature and source of the science of Brahman is described and defined, and the two kinds of knowledge – Para (higher) and Apara (lower). Knowledge of Brahman can be attained by the grace of the guru after renunciation of all worldly desires and egoism.

In the second part, all the sacrificial works for purification of the heart and the fruits of the sacrifices which are perishable and temporary are discussed, and also the requirement of cultivating austerity, faith, concentration and love of solitude while surrendering to a wise and intelligent teacher in a proper manner to attain knowledge of Brahman.

In the first part of the second section a description of the cosmology is given. Here is described vividly how the Self, prana, mind, all the organs, the five elements, all religions, rites, oceans, rivers, mountains and herbs came into being. Purusha, the supreme, is All – the entire universe, karmas, tapas and immortality. If one realizes Him within the heart, ignorance will fall away.

The second part shows the way to knowledge of Brahman: by meditation with the symbolic sound, Om. It discusses the link between the supreme Self, or immortal soul, and the world and the individual soul – this being the immortal soul residing in the human heart, shining there in all its brightness.

The third section gives an allegory of two birds seated on the self-same tree. It describes the spiritual practices and ethical virtues required by the spiritual aspirant; and there is a beautiful description of how, when knowledge of the supreme Self is attained, the meaning of all existence is understood.

If the deep significance of this Upanishad is meditated upon, the aspirant will find inspiration to cultivate the dispassion, discrimination, devotion and purity necessary to realize the supreme Purusha.

SHANTI PATH

ॐ भद्रं कर्णेभि: शृणुयाम देवा भद्रं पश्येमाक्षभिर्यजत्रा: । स्थिरैरंगै-
स्तुष्टुवा[ँ]सस्तनूभिर्व्यशेम देवहितं यदायु: ॥ स्वस्ति न इन्द्रो वृद्धश्रवा:
स्वस्ति न: पूषा विश्ववेदा: । स्वस्ति नस्ताक्ष्र्यो अरिष्टनेमि: स्वस्ति नो
बृहस्पतिर्दधातु ॥

ॐ शान्ति: शान्ति: शान्ति:

Om Bhadram Karnebhih Shrinuyaama Devaah Bhadram
Pashyemaakshabhiryajatraah; Sthirai Rangaih Tushtuvaam
Sastanoobhirvyashema Devahitam Yadaayuh. Svasti Na Indro
Vriddhashravaa Svasti Na Pooshaa Vishvavedaah; Svasti
Nastaarkshyo Arishtanemih Svasti No Brihaspatirdadhaatu.

Om Shaantih Shaantih Shaantih.

Om. O Ye Gods. May we hear auspicious words and see
auspicious sights while worshipping you. May we be blessed
in life with perfect health and vigour while singing your
praise. May the Lord Indra, the Loved One of old, be well-
inclined towards us. May He, in his kindness, be watchful of
our prosperity. May He, the nourisher and the possessor of
all wealth, give us what is good for us. May the Lord, the
destroyer of evil and the protector of the great ones, protect
us too.

Om peace, peace, peace.

SECTION 1: PART I

ॐ ब्रह्मा देवानां प्रथम: सम्बभूव
विश्वस्य कर्ता भुवनस्य गोप्ता ।
स ब्रह्मविद्यां सर्वविद्याप्रतिष्ठा-
मथर्वाय ज्येष्ठपुत्राय प्राह ॥ 1 ॥

*Om Brahma Devaanam Prathamah Sambabhoova Vishvasya Kartaa
Bhuvanasya Goptaa; Sa Brahmavidyaam Sarvavidyaapratishthaam
Atharvaaya Jyeshthaputraaya Praaha. (1)*

Brahma, the creator and preserver of the universe and the first
of the gods, rose up. And He gave the knowledge of Brahman,
the root of all knowledge, to Atharvan, his eldest son.

अथर्वणे यां प्रवदेत ब्रह्मा-
थर्वा तां पुरोवाचाङ्गिरे ब्रह्मविद्याम् ।
स भारद्वाजाय सत्यवहाय
प्राह भारद्वाजोऽङ्गिरसे परावराम् ॥ 2 ॥

*Atharvane Yaam Pravadeta Brahmaa Athaarvaa Taam Puro-
vaachaangire Brahmavidyaam; Sa Bhaaradvaajaaya Satyavahaaya
Praaha Bhaaradvaajoangirase Paraavaraam. (2)*

Atharvan gave this knowledge of Brahman he had received
from Brahma to Angira; Angira gave it to Satyavaha of the
Bharadvaja family, and Satyavaha passed on the knowledge
to Angiras in the traditional manner – from elder to the
inheritor of the next generation.

शौनको ह वै महाशालोऽङ्गिरसं विधिवदुपसन्न: पप्रच्छ ।
कस्मिन्नु भगवो विज्ञाते सर्वमिदं विज्ञातं भवतीति ॥ 3 ॥

*Shaunako Ha Vai Mahaashaaloangirasam Vidhivadupasannah
Paprachchha; Kasminnu Bhagavo Vijnaate Sarvamidam Vijnaatam
Bhavateeti. (3)*

In the manner customary in the scriptures, Saunaka, the renowned householder, came to Angiras and said: O Venerable One, tell me what that is, that being known, all other things become known?

तस्मै स होवाच । द्वे विद्ये वेदितव्ये इति ह स्म यद्ब्रह्मविदो वदन्ति परा चैवापरा च ॥ 4 ॥

Tasmai Sa Hovaacha; Dve Vidye Veditavye Iti Ha Sma Yadbrahmavido Vadanti Paraa Chaivaaparaa Cha. (4)

And Angiras replied: According to those learned in the Vedas there are two kinds of knowledge, Para (higher) and Apara (lower)

तत्रापरा ऋग्वेदो यजुर्वेद: सामवेदोऽथर्ववेद: शिक्षा कल्पो व्याकरणं निरुक्तं छन्दो ज्योतिषमिति। अथ परा यया तदक्षरमधिगम्यते ॥ 5 ॥

Tatraaparaa Rigvedo Yajurvedah Saamavedah Atharvavedah Shikshaa Kalpo Vyaakaranam Niruktam Chhando Jyotishamiti; Atha Paraa Yayaa Tadaksharam Adhigamyate. (5)

The lower knowledge includes the study of Rigveda, Samaveda, Yajurveda and Atharvaveda, Shiksha, Kalpa, the code of rituals, grammar, Nirukta, Chhanda and astrology. The higher knowledge leads one to direct realization of the immortal Brahman.

यत्तदद्रेश्यमग्राह्यमगोत्रमवर्णमचक्षु:श्रोत्रं तदपाणिपादम् । नित्यं विभुं सर्वगतं सुसूक्ष्मं तदव्ययं यद्भूतयोनिं परिपश्यन्ति धीरा: ॥ 6 ॥

Yattadadreshyam Agraahyam Agotram Avarnam Achakshuh Shrotram Tadapaanidpaadam; Nityam Vibhum Sarvagatam Susookshmam Tadavyayam Yadbhootayonim Paripashyanti Dheeraah. (6)

In this higher knowledge the wise experience in all animate forms the invisible and intangible, the causeless and indefinable, that which is without ears, eyes or feet, that which is everlasting, multi-formed, all-pervasive, subtler than the subtlest, indestructible and the source of all.

यथोर्णनाभि: सृजते गृह्णते च
यथा पृथिव्यामोषधय: सम्भवन्ति ।
यथा सत: पुरुषात्केशलोमानि
तथाक्षरात्सम्भवतीह विश्वम् ॥ 7 ॥

Yathornanaabhih Srijate Grihnate Cha Yathaa Prithivyaamo-shadhaya Sambhavanti; Yathaa Satah Purushaat Keshalomaani Tathaaksharaat Sambhavateeha Vishvam. (7)

As threads come from the spider and are withdrawn, as herbs from the earth and hair from the human body, likewise the entire universe springs from immortal Brahman.

तपसा चीयते ब्रह्म ततोऽन्नमभिजायते ।
अन्नात्प्राणो मन: सत्यं लोका: कर्मसु चामृतम् ॥ 8 ॥

Tapasaa Cheeyate Brahma Tatoannamabhijaayate; Annaatpraano Manah Satyam Lokaah Karmasu Chaamritam. (8)

God willed that He should express Himself in joy in creation; He brought forth sustenance, from sustenance mind, from mind the five elements, from the five elements the worlds, and from the worlds karma and its fruits.

यः सर्वज्ञः सर्वविद्यस्य ज्ञानमयं तपः ।
तस्मादेतब्रह्म नाम रूपमन्नं च जायते ॥ 9 ॥

Yah Sarvajnah Savavidyasya Jnaanamanyam Tapah; Tasmaa-
detabrahma Naama Roopamannam Cha Jaayate. (9)

From Brahman, the intimate knower of all, whose will is
knowledge itself, issued Brahma, name, form and sustenance.

SECTION 1: PART II

तदेतत्सत्यं मन्त्रेषु कर्माणि कवयो यान्यपश्यंस्तानि त्रेतायां बहुधा संततानि ।
तान्याचरथ नियतं सत्यकामा एष व: पन्था: सुकृतस्य लोके ॥ 1 ॥

*Tadetat Satyam Mantreshu Karmaani Kavayo Yaanyapashyanstaani
Tretaayaam Bahudhaa Santataani; Taanyaacharatha Niyatam
Satyakaamaa Esha Vah Panthaah Sukritasya Loke.* (1)

The right performance of sacrificial works, which the wise
have read in the mantras of the Vedas, was true of the Treta
age. Perform these regularly, desiring good results, O seekers
after Truth; in this way you will attain their fruits.

यदा लेलायते ह्यर्चि: समिद्धे हव्यवाहने ।
तदाज्यभागावन्तरेणाहुती: प्रतिपादयेत् ॥ 2 ॥

*Yadaa Lelaayate Hyarchih Samiddhe Havyavaahane;
Tadaajyabhaagaavantarenaahuteeh Pratipaadayet.* (2)

When the fire is lit and the flames rise up, offer oblations in
the centre of the fire with deep faith.

यस्याग्निहोत्रमदर्शमपौर्णमास-
मचातुर्मास्यमनाग्रयणमतिथिवर्जितं च ।
अहुतमवैश्वदेवमविधिना हुत-
मासप्तमांस्तस्य लोकान् हिनस्ति ॥ 3 ॥

*Yasyaagnihotram Adarsham Apaurnamaasam Achaaturmaasya-
manaagrayanam Atithivarjitam Cha; Ahutamavaishvadevam
Avidhinaahutam Asaptamaanstasya Lokaan Hinasti.* (3)

If the Agnihotra sacrifice is not performed during the new
moon, or full moon, or during the four months of the
autumn season, if guests are not present, if the hour is
incorrect, or the oblations to the Vaishvadevas omitted; that

is, if the sacrifice is not performed according to the scriptures, misfortune will follow one in the seven worlds.

काली कराली च मनोजवा च
सुलोहिता या च सुधूम्रवर्णा ।
स्फुलिङ्गिनी विश्वरुची च देवी
लेलायमाना इति सप्त जिह्वाः ॥ 4 ॥

Kaalee Karaalee Cha Manojavaa Cha Sulohitaa Yaa Cha Sudhoomravarnaa; Sphulinginee Vishvaruchee Cha Devee Lelaayamaanaa Iti Sapta Jivhaah. (4)

There are seven tongues of flame – the black, the terrible, the swift as mind, the deep red, the smoky and the brilliant.

एतेषु यश्चरते भ्राजमानेषु
यथाकालं चाहुतयो ह्याददायन् ।
तं नयन्त्येताः सूर्यस्य रश्मयो
यत्र देवानां पतिरेकोऽधिवासः ॥ 5 ॥

Eteshu Yashcharate Bhraajamaaneshu Yathaakaalam Chaahutayo Hyaadadaayan; Tam Nayantyetaah Sooryasya Rashmayo Yatra Devaanaam Patirekoadhivaasah. (5)

If one performs Agnihotra in the brilliant flame at the proper hour, the oblations will become the sun's rays and will bear the sacrificer up to the abode of Indra, the greatest of the gods.

एह्येहीति तमाहुतयः सुवर्चसः
सूर्यस्य रश्मिभिर्यजमानं वहन्ति ।
प्रियां वाचमभिवदन्त्योऽर्चयन्त्य
एष वः पुण्यः सुकृतो ब्रह्मलोकः ॥ 6 ॥

Ehyeheeti Tamaahutayah Suvarchasah Sooryasya Rashmi-bhiryajamaanam Vahanti; Priyaam Vaachanabhivadantyo-archayantya Esha Vah Punyah Sukrito Brahmalokah. (6)

These oblations transformed into sun's rays greet the sacrificer with the welcoming words: Come hither, come hither – while raising him up to the heaven of Brahman. And they say: Your attainment to the world of Brahman is the reward of your good works.

प्लवा ह्येते अदृढा यज्ञरूपा
अष्टादशोक्तमवरं येषु कर्म ।
एतच्छ्रेयो येऽभिनन्दन्ति मूढा
जरामृत्युं ते पुनरेवापि यन्ति ॥ 7 ॥

Plavaa Hyete Adridhaa Yajnaroopaa Ashtaadashoktamavaram Yeshu Karma; Etachchhreyo Yeabhinandanti Moodhaa Jaraa-mrityum Te Punarevaapi Yanti. (7)

The fruits of eighteen types of sacrifices alone are finite and perishable. Those ignorant ones who perform them believing they will attain bliss, only become the victims of old age and death.

अविद्यायामन्तरे वर्तमानाः स्वयंधीराः पण्डितं मन्यमानाः ।
जङ्घन्यमानाः परियन्ति मूढा अन्धेनैव नीयमाना यथान्धाः ॥ 8 ॥

Avidyaayaamantare Vartamaanaah Svayam Dheeraah Panditam Manyamaanaah; Janghanyamaanaah Pariyanti Moodhaa Andhenaiva Neeyamaanaa Yathaandhaah. (8)

The ignorant, spending their lives in ignorance, but thinking themselves to be wise and intelligent, experience great suffering and misery, and resemble the blind led by the blind.

अविद्यायां बहुधा वर्तमाना
वयं कृतार्था इत्यभिमन्यन्ति बाला: ।
यत्कर्मिणो न प्रवेदयन्ति रागात्
तेनातुरा:   क्षीणलोकाश्च्यवन्ते ॥ 9 ॥

Avidyaayaam Bahudhaa Vartamaanaa Vayam Kritaarthaa
Ityabhimanyanti Baalaah; Yatkarmino Na Pravedayanti Raagaat
Tenaaturaah Ksheenaloka Ashchyavante. (9)

The ignorant, the truth being unknown to them, and all the
time engrossed in their ignorance, fancy they have achieved
their goal in life, and bound by attachment and passion they
are reduced to misery and sorrow. They sink lower and
lower, and when in the afterworld their good deeds are
spent, they are again reborn on this earth.

इष्टापूर्तं मन्यमाना वरिष्ठं नान्यच्छ्रेयो वेदयन्ते प्रमूढा ।
नाकस्य पृष्ठे ते सुकृतेऽनुभूत्वेमं लोकं हीनतरं वा विशन्ति ॥ 10 ॥

Ishtaapoortam Manyamaanaa Varishtham Naanyachchhreyo
Vedayante Pramoodhaah; Naakasya Prishthe Te Sukrite-
anubhootvemam Lokam Heenataram Vaa Vishanti. (10)

These ignorant persons lack real knowledge of the Self, and
in their conceit think their sacrifices and other charitable
works to be the highest good. After deriving enjoyment
from their pious works in heaven, they return to human life
or to a lower worldly form.

तप:श्रद्धे ये ह्या, पवसन्त्यरण्ये
शान्ता विद्वांसो भैक्ष्यचर्यां चरन्त: ।
सूर्यद्वारेण ते विरजा: प्रयान्ति
यत्रामृत: स पुरुषो ह्यव्ययात्मा ॥ 11 ॥

Tapahshraddhe Ye Hyupavasantyaranye Shaantaa Vidvaanso Bhaikshyacharyaam Charantah; Sooryadvaarena Te Virajaah Prayaanti Yatraamritah Sa Purusho Hyavyayaatmaa. (11)

But those who dedicate their lives to the practice of austerity and devotion in the forest and live on alms are released from virtue and vice and go via the sun to reside in Purusha, the immortal One.

परीक्ष्य लोकान् कर्मचितान् ब्राह्मणो
निर्वेदमायान्नास्त्यकृतः   कृतेन ।
तद्विज्ञानार्थं स गुरुमेवाभिगच्छेत्
समित्पाणिः श्रोत्रियं ब्रह्मनिष्ठम् ॥ 12 ॥

Pareekshya Lokaan Karmachitaan Braahmano Nirvidam Aayaanaastyakritah Kritena; Tadvijaanaartham Sa Gurumevaabhigachchhet Samitpaanih Shrotriyam Brahmanishtham. (12)

The aspirant, who has by intensely studying the karmic worlds concluded that the eternal cannot be gained by karma, who is free of desires, for the sake of this knowledge, let him only approach, with sacrificial fuel in hand, a teacher learned in the scriptures and established in Brahman.

तस्मै स विद्वानुपसन्नाय सम्यक्
प्रशान्तचित्ताय   शमान्विताय ।
येनाक्षरं पुरुषं वेद सत्यं
प्रोवाच तां तत्त्वतो ब्रह्मविद्याम् ॥ 13 ॥

Tasmai Sa Vidvaanupasannaaya Samyak Prashaantachittaaya Shamaanvitaaya; Yenaaksharam Purusham Veda Satyam Provaacha Taam Tattvato Brahmavidyaam. (13)

The teacher should clearly explain this supreme knowledge to that disciple who possesses controlled senses and equanimity of mind.

SECTION 2: PART I

तदेतत्सत्यं यथा सुदीप्तात्पावकाद् विस्फुलिङ्गा:
सहस्रश: प्रभवन्ते सरूपा: ।
तथाक्षराद् विविधा: सोम्य भावा:
प्रजायन्ते तत्र चैवापियन्ति ॥ 1 ॥

*Tadetat Satyam Yathaa Sudeeptaat Paavakaad Visphulingaah
Sahasrashah Prabhavante Saroopaah; Tathaaksharaad Vividhaah
Somya Bhaavaah Prajaayante Tatra Cha Eva Apiyanti. (1)*

That is the truth. As a flaming fire sends forth a thousand
sparks, similarly, O gentle youth, from immortal Brahman
spring various jivas (souls) who return to Him once more.

दिव्यो ह्यमूर्त: पुरुष: सबाह्याभ्यन्तरो ह्यज: ।
अप्राणो ह्यमना: शुभ्रो ह्यक्षरात् परत: पर: ॥ 2 ॥

*Divyo Hyamoortah Purushah Sabaahyaabhyantaro Hyajah;
Apraano Hyamanaah Shubhro Hyaksharaat Paratah Parah. (2)*

Ever radiant He is and formless, existing both within and
without, unborn, beyond prana and mind, pure and supreme
– the Imperishable One.

एतस्माज्जायते प्राणो मन: सर्वेन्द्रियाणि च ।
खं वायुर्ज्योतिराप: पृथिवी विश्वस्य धारिणी ॥ 3 ॥

*Estasmaajjaayate Praano Manah Sarvendriyaani Cha; Kham
Vaayurjyotiaraapah Prithivee Vishvasya Dhaarinee. (3)*

From Him issue prana, mind, the senses, space, air, fire,
water and the earth, the supporter of the world.

अग्निर्मूर्धा चक्षुषी चन्द्रसूर्यौ
दिश: श्रोत्रे वाग् विवृताश्च वेदा: ।
वायु: प्राणो हृदयं विश्वमस्य
पद्भ्यां पृथिवी ह्येष सर्वभूतान्तरात्मा ॥ 4 ॥

Agnirmoordhaa Chakshushee Chandrasooryau Dishah Shrotre Vaag
Vivritaashcha Vedaah; Vaayuh Praano Hridayam Vishvamasya
Padbhyaam Prithivee Hyesha Sarvabhootaantaraatmaa. (4)

Fire is His head, the sun and moon are His eyes, the
directions are His ears, exposition of Vedas is His speech,
the wind is His breath, the universe is His heart and the
whole earth is His feet; He is truly the Inner Self of all.

तस्मादग्नि: समिधो यस्य सूर्य:
सोमात्पर्जन्य ओषधय: पृथिव्याम् ।
पुमान् रेत: सिञ्चति योषितायां
बह्वी: प्रजा: पुरुषात् सम्प्रसूता: ॥ 5 ॥

Tasmaadagnih Samidho Yasya Sooryah Somaatparjanya
Oshadhayah Prithivyaam; Pumaan Retah Sinchati Yoshitaayaam
Bahveeh Prajaah Purushaat Samprasootaah. (5)

From Him issues the (first) fire, the sun, the light of the
heavens; (and the second fire), the clouds carrying rain; (and
the third fire), the herbs and cereals of the earth succoured
by the clouds; (and the fourth fire), man who is nourished by
these; (and the fifth fire), the casting of man's seed in woman.
In this way all animate things originate in Him.

तस्मादृच: साम यजूंषि दीक्षा
यज्ञाश्च सर्वे क्रतवो दक्षिणाश्च ।
संवत्सरश्च यजमानश्च लोका:
सोमो यत्र पवते यत्र सूर्य: ॥ 6 ॥

71

*Tasmaadrichah Saama Yajoonshi Deekshaa Yajnaashcha Sarve
Kratavo Dakshinaashcha; Samvatsarashcha Yajamaanashcha
Lokaah Somo Yatra Pavate Yatra Sooryah.* (6)

The Rig, Sama, Yajur, initiation rites, all sacrificial offerings,
the sacrificer, times for sacrifices and fees to priests, also the
worlds which are purified by the moon and illumined by the
sun, all have issued from Him.

तस्माच्च देवा बहुधा सम्प्रसूता:
साध्या मनुष्या: पशवो वयांसि ।
प्राणापानौ व्रीहियवौ तपश्च
श्रद्धा सत्यं ब्रह्मचर्यं विधिश्च ॥ 7 ॥

*Tasmaachcha Devaa Bahudhaa Samprasootaah Saadhyaa
Manushyaah Pashavo Vayaansi; Praanaapaanau Vreehiyavau
Tapashcha Shraddhaa Satyam Brahmacharyam Vidhishcha.* (7)

From Him also have issued the gods of the various orders,
mankind, birds and beasts, all animate things, rice and
barley, truth, devotion, austerity, celibacy and spiritual
injunctions.

सप्त प्राणा: प्रभवन्ति तस्मात्
सप्तार्चिष: समिध: सप्त होमा: ।
सप्त इमे लोका येषु चरन्ति प्राणा
गुहाशया निहिता: सप्त सप्त ॥ 8 ॥

*Sapta Praanah Prabhavanti Tasmaat Saptaarichishah Samidhah
Sapta Homaah; Sapta Ime Lokaa Yeshu Charanti Praanaa
Guhaashayaa Nihitaah Sapta Sapta.* (8)

The seven pranas, the seven flames, the seven kinds of fuel,
the seven oblations, and the seven worlds the senses pass
through to reside in groups of seven in the heart cave, from
Him are manifested.

अत: समुद्रा गिरयश्च सर्वेऽस्मात्स्यन्दन्ते सिन्धव: सर्वरूपा: ।
अतश्च सर्वा ओषधयो रसश्च येनैष भूतैस्तिष्ठते ह्यन्तरात्मा ॥ 9 ॥

Atah Samudraa Girayashcha Sarve-Asmaatsyandante Sindhavah
Sarvaroopaah; Atashcha Sarvaa Oshadhayo Rasashcha Yenaisha
Bhootaistishthate Hyantaraatmaa. (9)

From Him spring all oceans and mountains, the various
rivers, the varieties of herbs and cereals, and the sustenance
by which the inner Self exists in the gross physical sheath.

पुरुष एवेदं विश्वं कर्म तपो ब्रह्म परामृतम् ।
एतद्यो वेद निहितं गुहायां सोऽविद्याग्रन्थिं विकिरतीह सोम्य ॥ 10 ॥

Purusha Evedam Vishvam Karma Tapo Brahma Paraamritam;
Etadyo Veda Nihitam Guhaayaam So Avidyaagranthim Vikirateeha
Somya. (10)

O Loved One, the entire universe is Purusha alone. All
sacrificial works, austerity, Brahman, and the greatest
immortals, issue from Him. He who knows Purusha, residing
in the heart cave, must break the knot of ignorance whilst
still in this life.

आवि: संनिहितं गुहाचरं नाम महत्पदमत्रैतत्समर्पितम् । एजत्प्राणन्निमिषच्च
यदेतज्जानथ सदसद्वरेण्यं परं विज्ञानाद्यद्वरिष्ठं प्रजानाम् ॥ 1 ॥

Aavih Sannihitam Guhaacharam Naama Mahatpadamatraitat
Samarpitam; Ejatpraanannimishachcha Yadetajjaanatha Sada-
sadvarenyam Param Vijnaanaadyadvarishtham Prajaanaam. (1)

He is ever radiant who moves in the heart caves of all. The
highest goal is Him, who has form and no form, adored by
all. All sentient things that move and breathe in Him exist.
Know this highest Truth, beyond the reach of both the
intellect and the senses.

यदर्चिमद्यदणुभ्योऽणु च यस्मिँल्लोका निहिता लोकिनश्च । तदेतदक्षरं ब्रह्म
स प्राणस्तदु वाङ्मन: । तदेतत्सत्यं तदमृतं तद्वेद्धव्यं सोम्य विद्धि ॥ 2 ॥

Yadarchimadyadanubhyoanu Cha Yasminllokaa Nihitaa Lokinash-
cha; Tadetadaksharam Brahma Sa Praanastadu Vaangmanah;
Tadetat Satyam Tadamritam Tad Veddhavyam Somya Viddhi. (2)

The radiant, the smallest of the small, the foundation of the
entire universe and this abode of the universe and its inhabit-
ants: all are Him. So also are life, speech and mind, Truth and
immortality. This is the target. O Loved One, strike here.

धनुर्गृ हीत्वौपनिषदं महास्त्रं शरं ह्युपासानिशितं संधयीत ।
आयम्य तद् भावगतेन चेतसा लक्ष्यं तदेवाक्षरं सोम्य विद्धि ॥ 3 ॥

Dhanurgriheetvaupanishadam Mahaastram Sharam Hyupaasaani-
shitam Sandhayeeta; Aayamya Tad Bhaavagatena Chetasaa
Lakshyam Tadevaaksharam Somya Viddhi. (3)

Take the great weapon of the Upanishads, the bow. Fix in
the arrow sharpened by meditation. With the mind draw it

and aim at Brahman, the immortal. O Beloved Youth, hit this target.

प्रणवो धनुः शरो ह्यात्मा ब्रह्म तल्लक्ष्यमुच्यते ।
अप्रमत्तेन वेद्धव्यं शरवत्तन्मयो भवेत् ॥ ४ ॥

Pranavo Dhanuh Sharo Hyaatmaa Brahma Tallokshyamuchyate;
Apramattena Veddhavyam Sharavat Tanmayo Bhavet. (4)

Om is the bow, the soul (Atman) is the arrow and the target is Brahman. He succeeds who possesses a one-pointed mind; the arrow becomes fixed in its mark; he is merged in Brahman.

यस्मिन् द्यौः पृथिवी चान्तरिक्षमोतं मनः सह प्राणैश्च सर्वैः ।
तमेवैकं जानथ आत्मानमन्या वाचो विमुञ्चथामृतस्यैष सेतुः ॥ ५ ॥

Yasmin Dyauh Prithivee Chaantarikshamotam Manah Saha
Praanaishcha Sarvaih; Tamevaikam Jaanatha Aatmaanamanyaa
Vaacho Vimunchathaamritasyaisha Setuh. (5)

Know Him, the Unique One, the sustainer of space, earth, mind and the forces of life. Abandon all other beliefs. The bridge crossing the ocean of life and reaching to immortality lies here.

अरा इव रथनाभौ संहता यत्र नाड्यः स एषोऽन्तश्चरते बहुधा जायमानः ।
ओमित्येवं ध्यायथ आत्मानं स्वस्ति वः पाराय तमसः परस्तात् ॥ ६ ॥

Araa Iva Rathanaabhau Samhataa Yatra Naadyah Sa Eshoantash-
charate Bahudhaa Jaayamaanah; Omityevam Dhyaayatha
Aatmaanam Svasti Vah Paaraaya Tamasah Parastaat. (6)

He moves in the heart, at the place where the nadis meet like spokes at a wheel-hub, in different forms. With the help of Om meditate on the Self, that you may cross from the darkness to the beyond without difficulties.

य: सर्वज्ञ: सर्वविद् यस्यैष महिमा भुवि ।
दिव्ये ब्रह्मपुरे ह्येष व्योम्न्यात्मा प्रतिष्ठित: ॥
मनोमय: प्राणशरीरनेता प्रतिष्ठितोऽन्ने हृदयं संनिधाय ।
तद्विज्ञानेन परिपश्यन्ति धीरा आनन्दरूपममृतं यद् विभाति ॥ 7 ॥

Yah Sarvajnah Sarvavid Yasyaisha Mahimaa Bhuvi; Divye Brahmapure Hyesha Byomnyaatmaa Pratishthitah. Manomayah Praanashareeranetaa Pratishthitoanne Hridayam Sannidhaaya; Tad Vijnaanena Paripashyanti Dheeraa Aanandaroopamamritam Yad Vibhaati. (7)

The all-knowing Self, knowing all intimately, whose greatness is experienced in the world, resides in the shining sky of the heart, the city of Brahman ever growing in radiance. Life, mind and body are ruled by Him. Within the whole body is His presence. The food of the body is His sustenance and the heart is His residence. Have perfect knowledge of Him and attain bliss and immortality like the wise.

भिद्यते हृदयग्रन्थिश्छिद्यन्ते सर्वसंशया: ।
क्षीयन्ते चास्य कर्माणि तस्मिन्दृष्टे परावरे ॥ 8 ॥

Bhidyate Hiridayagranthishchhidyante Sarvasanshayaah; Ksheeyante Chaasya Karmaani Tasmin Drishte Paraavare. (8)

The knot of the heart is released of he who is a realizer of the Self, the higher and lower Brahman; all doubts disappeared, all karmas vanished.

हिरण्मये परे कोशे विरजं ब्रह्म निष्कलम् ।
तच्छुभ्रंज्योतिषां ज्योतिस्तद्यदात्मविदो विदुः ॥ ९ ॥

Hiranmaye Pare Koshe Virajam Brahma Nishkalam;
Tachchhubhram Jyotishaam Jyotistadyadaatmavido Viduh. (9)

Within the innermost sheath He resides, indivisible and
without blemish, the pure One and light of all that shines.
So know the knowers of Brahman.

न तत्र सूर्यो भाति न चन्द्रतारकं
      नेमा विद्युतो भान्ति कुतोऽयमग्निः ।
तमेव   भान्तमनुभाति   सर्वं
      तस्य   भासा   सर्वमिदं विभाति   ॥ १० ॥

Na Tatra Sooryo Bhaati Na Chandrataarakam Nemaa Vidyuto
Bhaanti Kutoayamagnih; Tameva Bhaantamanubhaati Sarvam
Tasya Bhaasaa Sarvamidam Vibhaati. (10)

There the light of the sun does not penetrate, nor of the
moon, of the stars, of lightning, and even less of fires
kindled on earth. When He shines the whole universe is
radiant with His reflected light.

ब्रह्मैवेदममृतं पुरस्तात्ब्रह्म पश्चात्ब्रह्म दक्षिणतश्चोत्तरेण ।
अधश्चोर्ध्वं   च   प्रसृतं   ब्रह्मैवेदं विश्वमिदं वरिष्ठम् ॥ ११ ॥

Brahmaivedamamritam Purastaat Brahma Pashchaat Brahma
Dakshinataashchottarena; Adhashchordhvam Cha Prasritam
Brahmaivedam Vishvamidam Varishtham. (11)

All, certainly, is immortal Brahman. Above, below, before,
behind and on every side: the entire universe is Brahman
alone. It is the greatest.

द्वा सुपर्णा सयुजा सखाया समानं वृक्षं परिषस्वजाते ।
तयोरन्य: पिप्पलं स्वाद्वत्त्यनश्नन्नन्यो अभिचाकशीति ॥ 1 ॥

Dvaa Suparnaa Sayujaa Sakhaayaa Samaanam Vriksham Parishasvajaate; Tayoranyah Pippalam Svaadvattyah Anashnannanyo Abhichaakasheeti. (1)

Two birds, both fast friends, were perched on the self-same tree. One was eating the delicious fruits of the tree, but the other did not eat.

समाने वृक्षे पुरुषो निमग्नोऽनीशया शोचति मुह्यमान: ।
जुष्टं यदा पश्यत्यन्यमीशमस्य महिमानमिति वीतशोक: ॥ 2 ॥

Samaane Vrikshe Purusho Nimagno Aneeshayaa Shochati Muhyamaanah; Jushtam Yadaa Pashyatyanyam Eeshamasya Mahimaanamiti Veetashokah. (2)

Although resting on the self-same tree, the one who is jiva (individual soul), existing in ignorance and delusion, laments his powerlessness. But his depression is dispelled completely when he sees the glory of the other, the Lord, whom all worship.

यदा पश्य: पश्यते रुक्मवर्णं
कर्तारमीशं पुरुषं ब्रह्मयोनिम् ।
तदा विद्वान् पुण्यपापे विधूय
निरञ्जन: परमं साम्यमुपैति ॥ 3 ॥

Yadaa Pashyah Pashyate Rukmavarnam Kartaarameesham Purusham Brahmayonim; Tadaa Vidvaan Punyapaape Vidhooya Niranjanah Paramam Saamyamupaiti. (3)

When the golden-coloured Brahman, the ruler, the source of all creation, the Lord, is realized by the seer, then, released from actions of merit and demerit and blemishless, he achieves unity in Him.

प्राणो ह्येष यः सर्वभूतैर्विभाति
विजानन् विद्वान् भवते नातिवादी ।
आत्मक्रीड आत्मरतिः क्रियावा-
नेष ब्रह्मविदां वरिष्ठः ॥ 4 ॥

Praano Hyesha Yah Sarvabhootaih Vibhaati Vijaanan Vidvaan Bhavate Naativaadee; Aatmakreeda Aatmaratih Kriyaavaanesha Brahmavidaam Varishthah. (4)

The vital energy (prana) radiant in all animate things is the Lord. The truly wise experience pure joy in Him. He whose delight is in the Self, whose joy is in the Self and whose life is spiritual becomes foremost among His followers.

सत्येन लभ्यस्तपसा ह्येष आत्मा
सम्यग्ज्ञानेन ब्रह्मचर्येण नित्यम् ।
अन्तःशरीरे ज्योतिर्मयो हि शुभ्रो
ये पश्यन्ति यतयः क्षीणदोषाः ॥ 5 ॥

Satyena Labhyastapasaa Hyesha Aatmaa Samyagjnaanena Brahmacharyena Nityam; Antahshareere Jyotirmayo Hi Shubhro Yam Pashyanti Yatayah Ksheenadoshaah. (5)

Truthfulness, austerity, wisdom and celibacy reveal the Self. By practising these unceasingly, perfect knowledge is achieved, and when all impurities are thus dissolved the self-controlled sadhaka, pure and radiant of body, attains Brahman.

सत्यमेव जयति नानृतं
सत्येन पन्था विततो देवयान: ।
येनाक्रमन्त्यृषयो ह्याप्तकामा
यत्र तत् सत्यस्य परमं निधानम् ॥ 6 ॥

Satyameva Jayati Naanritam Satyena Panthaa Vitato Devayaanah;
Yenaakramantyrishayo Hyaaptakaamaa Yatra Tat Satyasya
Paramam Nidhaanam. (6)

The truthful alone, and not the untruthful, are victorious.
Truth widens the divine path along which the sages,
desireless, advance to that supreme abode of Truth.

बृहच्च तद् दिव्यमचिन्त्यरूपं
सूक्ष्माच्च तत् सूक्ष्मतरं विभाति ।
दूरात् सुदूरे तदिहान्तिके च
पश्यत्स्विहैव निहितं गुहायाम् ॥ 7 ॥

Brihachcha Tad Divyamachintyaroopam Sookshmaachcha Tat
Sookshmataram Vibhaati; Doorat Sudoore Tadihaantike Cha
Pashyatsvihaiva Nihitam Guhaayaam. (7)

He is beyond thought, all radiant, vast, divine and of extreme
subtlety. He lies beyond the beyond, yet abides within the
body, and He is discovered by sages in the heart.

न चक्षुषा गृह्यते नापि वाचा
नान्यैर्देवैस्तपसा कर्मण वा ।
ज्ञानप्रसादेन विशुद्धसत्त्व-
स्ततस्तु तं पश्यते निष्कलं ध्यायमान: ॥ 8 ॥

Na Chakshushaa Grihyate Naapi Vaachaa Naanyairdevaistapasaa
Karmanaa Vaa; Jnaanaprasaadena Vishuddhasattvastatastu Tam
Pashyate Nishkalam Dhyaayamaanah. (8)

The eyes cannot see Him, speech cannot describe Him, the senses cannot grasp Him, rituals and austerity cannot reveal Him. Only when the mind is calm and pure through knowledge can He be realized in meditation.

एषोऽणुरात्मा चेतसा वेदितव्यो
यस्मिन् प्राण: पञ्चधा संविवेश ।
प्राणैश्चितं सर्वमोतं प्रजानां
यस्मिन् विशुद्धे विभवत्येष आत्मा ॥ 9 ॥

Eshoanuraatmaa Chetasaa Veditavyo Yasmin Praanah Panchadhaa Sanvivesh; Praanaishchitam Sarvamotam Prajaanaam Yasmin Vishuddhe Vibhavatyesha Aatmaa. (9)

The mind existing in the human frame becomes the knower of the subtle truth of the Self. It is full of prana which has the five sensory outlets and is absorbed in worldly objects. But when the mind is purified, the Self spontaneously shines through.

यं यं लोकं मनसा संविभाति
विशुद्धसत्त्व: कामयते यांश्च कामान् ।
तं तं लोकं जायते तांश्च कामां-
स्तस्मादात्मज्ञं ह्यर्चयेद् भूतिकाम: ॥ 10 ॥

Yam Yam Lokam Manasaa Sanvibhaati Vishuddhasattvah Kaamayate Yaanshcha Kaaman; Tam Tam Lokam Jaayate Taanshcha Kaamaamstasmaadaatmajnam Hyarchayed Bhootikaamah. (10)

He who wants to enjoy prosperity should worship the Self-realized man, the possessor of a purified mind, for all his desires are granted in this and other worlds.

स वेदैतत् परमं ब्रह्म धाम
यत्र विश्वं निहितं भाति शुभ्रम् ।
उपासते पुरुषं ये ह्यकामा-
स्ते शुक्रमेतदतिवर्तन्ति धीराः ॥ 1 ॥

Sa Vedaitat Paramam Brahma Dhaama Yatra Vishvam Nihitam Bhaati Shubhram; Upaasate Purusham Ye Hayakaamaaste Shukrametadativartanti Dheeraah. (1)

The wise, free from worldly desires, should worship such a man, a knower of Brahman, the supporter of the whole universe and the all-radiant, for then they will transcend the cycle of rebirth.

कामान् यः कामयते मन्यमानः
स कामभिर्जायते तत्र तत्र ।
पर्याप्तकामस्य कृतात्मनस्त्व-
हैव सर्वे प्रविलीयन्ति कामाः ॥ 2 ॥

Kaamaan Yah Kaamayate Manyamaanah Sa Kaamabhirjaayate Tatra Tatra; Paryaapta Kaamasya Kritaatmanastu Ihaiva Sarve Pravileeyanti Kaamaah. (2)

Those who are full of desires and dwell on them continually are born here and there so that these desires might be satisfied. Those realized ones, however, abandon all desires even in this life only.

नायमात्मा प्रवचनेन लभ्यो
न मेधया न बहुना श्रुतेन ।
यमेवैष वृणुते तेन लभ्य-
स्तस्यैष आत्मा विवृणुते तनूँ स्वाम् ॥ 3 ॥

Naayamaatmaa Pravachanena Labhyo Na Medhayaa Na Bahunaa Shrutena; Yamevaisha Vrinute Tena Labhyastasyaisha Aatmaa Vivrinute Tanoom Svaam. (3)

Discourse or intelligence or much knowledge do not lead to the Self; only a burning desire for Brahman brings revelation.

नायमात्मा बलहीनेन लभ्यो
न च प्रमादात्तपसो वाप्यलिङ्गात् ।
एतैरुपायैर्यतते यस्तु विद्वां-
स्तस्यैष आत्मा विशते ब्रह्मधाम ॥ 4 ॥

Naayamaatmaa Balaheenena Labhyo Na Cha Pramaadaat Tapaso Vaapyalingaat; Etairupaayairyatate Yastu Vidvaans Tasyaisha Aatmaa Vishate Brahmadhaama. (4)

The Self is not known by those who possess weak personalities, who lack eagerness and who practise incorrect austerity, but only by the wise who with sincerity practise the means.

सम्प्राप्यैनमृषयो ज्ञानतृप्ताः
कृतात्मानो वीतरागाः प्रशान्ताः ।
ते सर्वगं सर्वतः प्राप्य धीरा
युक्तात्मानः सर्वमेवाविशन्ति ॥ 5 ॥

Sampraapyainamrishayo Jnaanatriptaah Kritaatmaano Veetaraagaah Prashaantaah; Te Sarvagam Sarvatah Praapya Dheeraa Yuktaatmaanah Sarvamevaavishanti. (5)

The sages, the realized beings, are satiated and find fulfilment in this knowledge. They become desireless and experience peace. Knowing the omnipresence of all-pervading Atman, the pure and wise enter into Him.

वेदान्तविज्ञानसुनिश्चितार्था:
संन्यासयोगाद् यतय: शुद्धसत्त्वा: ।
ते ब्रह्मलोकेषु परान्तकाले
परामृता: परिमुच्यन्ति सर्वे ॥ 6 ॥

Vedaantavijnaanasunishchitaarthaah Sannyaasayogaad Yatayah Shuddhasattvaah; Te Brahmalokeshu Paraantakaale Paraamritaah Parimuchyanti Sarve. (6)

The heaven of Brahman is attained by those aspirants who are purified through renunciation and study of the scriptures, and thereby well established in the Self. When leaving the world, they are fully liberated.

गता: कला: पञ्चदश प्रतिष्ठा
देवाश्च सर्वे प्रतिदेवतासु ।
कर्माणि विज्ञानमयश्च आत्मा
परेऽव्यये सर्व एकीभवन्ति ॥ 7 ॥

Gataah Kalaah Panchadasha Pratishtaa Devaashcha Sarve Pratidevataasu; Karmaani Vijnaanamayashcha Aatmaa Pareavyaye Sarva Ekeebhavanti. (7)

The fifteen parts (kalaas) of these realized beings return to their sources, their senses return to their respective deities, whilst their karma and individual souls merge with the ultimate and infinite Brahman.

यथा नद्य: स्यन्दमाना: समुद्रे-
ऽस्तं गच्छन्ति नामरूपे विहाय ।
तथा विद्वान् नामरूपाद् विमुक्त:
परात्परं पुरुषमुपैति दिव्यम् ॥ 8 ॥

Yathaa Nadyah Syandamaanaah Samudreastam Gachchhanti Naamaroope Vihaaya; Tathaa Vidvaan Naamaroopaad Vimuktah Paraatparam Purushamupaiti Divyam. (8)

As the rivers flow into and become one with the ocean, abandoning name and form, so also the wise, freed from name and form, merge with the highest Reality, the supreme Divinity.

स यो ह वै तत्परमं ब्रह्म वेद ब्रह्मैव भवति नास्याब्रह्मवित्कुले भवति।
तरति शोकं तरति पाप्मानं गुहग्रन्थिभ्यो विमुक्तोऽमृतो भवति ॥ 9 ॥

Sa Yo Ha Vai Tat Paramam Brahma Veda Brahmaiva Bhavati Naasyaaabrahmavit Kule Bhavati; Tarati Shokam Tarati Paapmaanam Guhaagranthibhyo Vimuktoamrito Bhavati. (9)

The knower of Brahman in Him is united; the knot of ignorance in the heart is released; he rises above sun and suffering, and is immortal. Into his family none ignorant of Brahman is born.

तदेतदृचाभ्युक्तम्-
क्रियावन्तः श्रोत्रिया ब्रह्मनिष्ठाः
    स्वयं जुह्वत एकर्षि श्रद्धयन्तः ।
तेषामेवैतां ब्रह्मविद्यां वदेत
    शिरोव्रतं विधिवद्यैस्तु चीर्णम् ॥ 10 ॥

Tadetadrichaabhyuktam:
Kriyaavantah Shrotriyaa Brahmanishthaah Svayam Juhvata Ekarshim Shraddhayantah. Teshaavmevaitaam Brahmavidyaam Vadeta Shirovratam Vidhivad Yaistu Cheernam. (10)

The following Vedic verse concerns the imparting of the highest knowledge. The knowledge of Brahman should be given to those only who perform the rites, are learned in the Vedas, have deep faith, offer oblations in the Ekarshi fire and observe Shirovrata as directed in the scriptures.

तदेतत् सत्यमृषिरङ्गिरा: पुरोवाच नैतदचीर्णव्रतोऽधीते ।
नम: परमऋषिभ्यो   नम: परमऋषिभ्य: ॥ 11 ॥

Tadetat Satyamrishirangiraah Purovaacha Naitadacheerna-
vratoadheete; Namah Paramarishibyo Namah Paramarishibhyah. (11)

This true science of Brahman was expounded by Angiras
Rishi (to his disciple Saunaka) in ancient times. He who is
spiritually unprepared should not study this science.

Salutations, great Rishis. Salutations.

SHANTI PATH

ॐ भद्रं कर्णेभिः शृणुयाम देवा भद्रं पश्येमाक्षभिर्यजत्राः । स्थिरैरंगै-
स्तुष्टुवाꣳसस्तनूभिर्व्यशेम देवहितं यदायुः ॥ स्वस्ति न इन्द्रो वृद्धश्रवाः
स्वस्ति नः पूषा विश्ववेदाः । स्वस्ति नस्ताक्ष्र्यो अरिष्टनेमिः स्वस्ति नो
बृहस्पतिर्दधातु ॥

ॐ शान्तिः शान्तिः शान्तिः

*Om Bhadram Karnebhih Shrinuyaama Devaah Bhadram
Pashyemaakshabhiryajatraah; Sthirai Rangaih Tushtuvaam
Sastanoobhirvyashema Devahitam Yadaayuh. Svasti Na Indro
Vriddhashravaa Svasti Na Pooshaa Vishvavedaah; Svasti
Nastaarkshyo Arishtanemih Svasti No Brihaspatirdadhaatu.*

Om Shaantih Shaantih Shaantih.

Om. O Ye Gods. May we hear auspicious words and see
auspicious sights while worshipping you. May we be blessed
in life with perfect health and vigour while singing your
praise. May the Lord Indra, the Loved One of old, be well-
inclined towards us. May He, in his kindness, be watchful of
our prosperity. May He, the nourisher and the possessor of
all wealth, give us what is good for us. May the Lord, the
destroyer of evil and the protector of the great ones, protect
us too.

Om peace, peace, peace.

Ishavasya Upanishad

The Vedas are four in number. The first one is known as Rigveda, the second as Yajurveda, the third as Samaveda and the fourth and last one, in chronological order, Atharvaveda. Ishavasya Upanishad is the last chapter of Yajurveda. The whole text of Yajurveda is divided into forty chapters. The first thirty-nine chapters of this Veda talk about the mantras in connection with rituals, ceremonies, worship, poems, incantations, hymns, etc., and the last chapter of Yajurveda talks of nothing but the Supreme Knowledge. Therefore, this Upanishad is considered to be the seed of the entire Indian philosophy in general and of Vedantic philosophy in particular. Many scholars of East and West consider that in India, the Vedantic philosophy of Parabrahma, the Supreme Being, is the science and philosophy of Brahma Vidya, and the cosmic truth developed from this little Upanishad. Hence, this Upanishad is also known as Vedanta Upanishad, but Ishavasya is its most popular name.

The first two lines of Ishavasya Upanishad are the shanti mantra, or the mystic syllables of peace. It is a tradition that an Upanishad begins and ends with a mantra called shanti mantra. The meaning of this mantra with which the Ishavasya Upanishad begins is wonderful.

SHANTI PATH

ॐ पूर्णमद: पूर्णमिदं पूर्णात् पूर्णमुदच्यते । पूर्णस्य पूर्णमादाय
पूर्णमेवावशिष्यते ॥

ॐ शान्ति: शान्ति: शान्ति:

Om Poornamadah Poornamidam Poornaat Poornamudachyate;
Poornasya Poornamaadaaya Poornameva Avashishyate.

Om Shaantih Shaantih Shaantih.

That is full, this is full. From full, the full is taken, the full
has come. If you remove the full from the full, the full alone
remains.

Om peace, peace, peace.

ॐ ईशा वास्यमिद: सर्वं यत्किञ्च जगत्यां जगत् ।
तेन त्यक्तेन भुञ्जीथा मा गृध: कस्यस्विद् धनम् ॥ 1 ॥

Om Eeshaa Vaasyamidam Sarvam Yatkincha Jagatyaam Jagat;
Tena Tyaktena Bhunjeethaa Maa Gridhah Kasyasvid Dhanam. (1)

All this, whatsoever moves in this universe, is indwelled by
Isha; therefore, through renunciation do thou enjoy, and
do not covet anybody's wealth.

कुर्वन्नेवेह   कर्माणि   जिजीविषेच्छत: समा: ।
एवं त्वयि नान्यथेतोऽस्ति न कर्म लिप्यते नरे ॥ 2 ॥

Kurvanneveha Karmaani Jijeevishechchhatam Samaah; Evam
Tvayi Naanyathetoasti Na Karma Lipyate Nare. (2)

Let every man wish to live for a hundred years while
performing karmas in this world. Thus, other than this,
there is no way out for you; karmas do not bind the man.

असुर्या नाम ते लोका अन्धेन तमसाऽऽवृता: ।
ता:स्ते प्रेत्याभिगच्छन्ति ये के चात्महनो जना: ॥ 3 ॥

Asuryaa Naama Te Lokaa Andhena Tamasaavritaah; Taanste
Pretyaabhigachchhanti Ye Ke Chaatmahano Janaah. (3)

There are worlds covered with blinding darkness. They are
known as sunless worlds. The killers of the self depart to
these worlds.

अनेजदेकं मनसो जवीयो नैनद्देवा आप्नुवन् पूर्वमर्षत् ।
तद्धावतोऽन्यानत्येति तिष्ठत्तस्मिन्नपो मातरिश्वा दधाति ॥ 4 ॥

Anejadekam   Manaso   Javeeyo   Nainaddevaa   Aapnuvan
Poorvamarshat; Taddhaavatoanyaanatyeti Tishthat Tasminnapo
Maatarishvaa Dadhaati. (4)

Atma is motionless, but is swifter than the mind. The senses can never overtake it. It runs ahead of them. While sitting, it goes faster than those who run after it. In this Atma, the air (prana) places the karmas.

तदेजति तन्नैजति तद् दूरे तद्वन्तिके ।
तदन्तरस्य सर्वस्य तदु सर्वस्यास्य बाह्यतः ॥ 5 ॥

Tadejati Tannaijati Tad Doore Tadvantike; Tadantarasya Sarvasya Tadu Sarvasyaasya Baahyatah. (5)

That moves on and does not move. It is far and near. It is inside and outside of all.

यस्तु सर्वाणि भूतान्यात्मन्येवानुपश्यति ।
सर्वभूतेषु चात्मानं ततो न विजुगुप्सते ॥ 6 ॥

Yastu Sarvaani Bhootaani Aatmanyeva Anupashyati; Sarva-bhooteshu Chaatmaanam Tato Na Vijugupsate. (6)

He who constantly sees all beings in the higher Self, or in the spiritual consciousness, and the Self in all beings does not hate.

यस्मिन् सर्वाणि भूतान्यात्मैवाभूद् विजानतः ।
तत्र को मोहः कः शोक एकत्वमनुपश्यतः ॥ 7 ॥

Yasmin Sarvaani Bhootaani Aatmaivaabhood Vijaanatah; Tatra Ko Mohah Kah Skoka Ekatvam Anupashyatah. (7)

When all beings become one in one's own higher consciousness, then what delusion and what grief is there for one who is constantly seeing oneness?

स पर्यगाच्छुक्रमकायमव्रण-
मस्नाविरꣳ शुद्धमपापविद्धम् ।
कविर्मनीषी परिभूः स्वयम्भूर्याथातथ्यतो-
ऽर्थान् व्यदधाच्छाश्वतीभ्यः समाभ्यः ॥ 8 ॥

*Sa Paryagaat Shukram Akaayam Avranam Asnaaviram Shuddham
Apaapaviddham; Kavirmaneeshee Paribhooh Svayambhooh
Yaathaatathyatah Arthaan Vyadadhaat Shaashvateebhyah
Samaabhyah. (8)*

He is all-pervading, bright, bodiless and unscathed. He has
no muscles. He is pure and sinless. The wise ones say that
He is omniscient and Self-born. He has been functioning
everywhere since eternity.

अन्धं तमः प्रविशन्ति येऽविद्यामुपासते ।
ततो भूय इव ते तमो य उ विद्यायाꣳ रताः ॥ 9 ॥

*Andham Tamah Pravishanti Yeavidyaamupaasate; Tato Bhooya
Iva Te Tamo Ya U Vidyaayaam Rataah. (9)*

Those who follow the path of avidya enter into blinding
darkness. More than that, those who are engrossed in vidya
also enter into the great blinding darkness.

अन्यदेवाहुर्विद्ययान्यदाहुरविद्यया ।
इति शुश्रुम धीराणां ये नस्तद् विचचक्षिरे ॥ 10 ॥

*Anyadevaahuh Vidyayaa Anyad Aahuh Avidyayaa; Iti Shushruma
Dheeraanaam Ye Nastad Vichachakshire. (10)*

We have heard from the wise ones, who explained to us that
thus definitely from vidya it is different, and from avidya it
is different; so it is explained.

विद्यां चाविद्यां च यस्तद् वेदोभयꣳ सह ।
अविद्यया मृत्युं तीर्त्वा विद्ययामृतमश्नुते ॥ 11 ॥

Vidyaam Chaavidyaam Cha Yastad Vedobhayam Saha; Avidyayaa Mrityum Teertvaa Vidyayaamritamashnute. (11)

He who knows both vidya and avidya together crosses death by avidya and obtains immortality by vidya.

अन्धं तमः प्रविशन्ति येऽसम्भूतिमुपासते ।
ततो भूय इव ते तमो य उ सम्भूत्याꣳ रताः ॥ 12 ॥

Andham Tamah Pravishanti Yeasambhootimupaasate; Tato Bhooya Iva Te Tamo Ya U Sambhootyaam Rataah. (12)

Those who worship the unmanifest reality enter into blinding darkness. Those who worship the manifest also enter into a denser realm of darkness.

अन्यदेवाहुः सम्भवादन्यदाहुरसम्भवात् ।
इति शुश्रुम धीराणां ये नस्तद्विचचक्षिरे ॥ 13 ॥

Anyadevaahuh Sambhavaat Anyadaahuh Asambhavaat; Iti Shushruma Dheeraanaam Ye Nastadvichachakshire. (13)

By meditating on the manifest definitely a different thing is obtained, and by meditation on the unmanifest something else is obtained – that is what they say.

सम्भूतिं च विनाशं च यस्तद् वेदोभयꣳ सह ।
विनाशेन मृत्युं तीर्त्वा सम्भूत्यामृतमश्नुते ॥ 14 ॥

Sambhootim Cha Vinaasham Cha Yastad Vedobhayam Saha; Vinaashena Mrityum Teertvaa Sambhootyaamritam Ashnute. (14)

He who knows the impersonal God and the personal God both as one overcomes death through the impersonal God and obtains immortality through the personal God.

हिरण्मयेन पात्रेण सत्यस्यापिहितं मुखम् ।
तत्त्वं पूषन्नपावृणु सत्यधर्माय दृष्टये ॥ 15 ॥

Hiranmayena Paatrena Satyasyaapihitam Mukham; Tattvam Pooshan Apaavrinu Satyadharmaaya Drishtaye. (15)

The face of truth is covered by a golden vessel. O Nourisher, open that so that I, the practitioner of truth, may behold Thee.

पूषन्नेकर्षे यम सूर्य प्राजा-
पत्य व्यूह रश्मीन् समूह ।
तेजो यत्ते रूपं कल्याणतमं तत्ते पश्यामि
योऽसावसौ पुरुषः सोऽहमस्मि ॥ 16 ॥

Pooshannekarshe Yama Soorya Praajaapatya Vyooha Rashmeen Samooha; Tejo Yatte Roopam Kalyaanatamam Tatte Pashyaami Yoasaavasau Purushah Soahamasmi. (16)

O Pushan (nourisher); O Ekarshe (seer of one); O Yama (controller); O Surya (sun); O Prajapataya (son of Prajapati); do thou disperse thy rays and concentrate thy brilliance, so that I may see thy auspicious form. Who is that purusha? He I am!

वायुरनिलममृतमथेदं भस्मान्तः शरीरम् ।
ॐ क्रतो स्मर कृतः स्मर क्रतो स्मर कृतः स्मर ॥ 17 ॥

Vaayuranilam Amritam Athedam Bhasmaantam Shareeram; Om Krato Smara Kritam Smara Krato Smara Kritam Smara. (17)

Let my prana into universal prana; let this body to ashes; Om, O universal Atma, remember, do thou remember actions; O universal Soul, remember actions!

अग्ने नय सुपथा राये अस्मान् विश्वानि देव वयुनानि विद्वान् ।
युयोध्यस्मज्जुहुराणमेनो भूयिष्ठां ते नम उक्तिं विधेम ॥ 18 ॥

Agne Naya Supathaa Raaye Asmaan Vishvaani Deva Vayunaani Vidvaan; Yuyodhya Asmat Juhuraanameno Bhooyishthaam Te Nama Uktim Vidhema. (18)

O Agni, lead us on to prosperity through a good path; O God! Thou the knower of our deeds, remove from us complicated sins. We offer Thee our best salutations.

SHANTI PATH

ॐ पूर्णमद: पूर्णमिदं पूर्णात् पूर्णमुदच्यते । पूर्णस्य पूर्णमादाय पूर्णमेवावशिष्यते ॥

ॐ शान्ति: शान्ति: शान्ति:

Om Poornamadah Poornamidam Poornaat Poornamudachyate;
Poornasya Poornamaadaaya Poornameva Avashishyate.

Om Shaantih Shaantih Shaantih.

That is full, this is full. From full, the full is taken, the full has come. If you remove the full from the full, the full alone remains.

Om peace, peace, peace.

Kathopanishad

This is the most popular of the Upanishads due to its charming presentation of the eternal truths and sublime teachings of Vedanta in a narrative form. Philosophy and poetry go hand in hand in the Upanishad, and some regard it as the greatest philosophical poem ever written. It is well known throughout the world and has been translated into practically all the major languages.

The colourful story of the Upanishad, so beautifully narrated, runs like this. Vajashravasa, desiring divine bounty, gave away all he possessed in a sacrifice. He had a son called Nachiketa who, though still a young boy, was filled with an intense and unshakeable desire to do good to his father. Therefore, when he saw that worn out cows were being presented as sacrificial gifts, he became very anxious about this niggardliness of his father, and going to him he asked: To whom will you give me? This he repeated three times, at which has father, anger aroused, replied: To death I shall give you. Nachiketa obediently went to Yama, the Lord of Death, and had to wait at his place for three days and nights without food, as Yama was absent. When Yama returned, the Brahmin boy-guest was received courteously and, apologizing for the poor treatment he had been given, Yama offered to grant him three boons, one in respect of each night without hospitality.

Nachiketa, who typifies the ideal spiritual aspirant, asked as his first boon for peace of mind and joy for his father. As his second boon, he requested the knowledge of the fire sacrificer to heaven. Yama, pleased by the intelligence, sincerity and devotion of the boy, named the fire sacrifice Nachiketa, after him. As his third boon, Nachiketa asked for a definite answer as to the truth or falsity of existence after death. Yama's answer to this young Brahmin boy's enquiry forms the principal part of this Upanishad, and is of great philosophical importance. It is concerned with transcendental truths that lie beyond logic and intellect.

Yama gradually revealed the secrets of the knowledge of Brahman during his explanation of the source of the world, the necessity of having a realized teacher, and of practising yoga. The qualified aspirant who follows the entire technique of Brahma Vidya, so vividly outlined in this Upanishad, will surely realize the Self and attain immortality as Nachiketa did.

SHANTI PATH

ॐ सह नाववतु । सह नौ भुनक्तु । सह वीर्यं करवावहै । तेजस्वि नावधीतमस्तु । मा विद्विषावहै ॥

ॐ शान्ति: शान्ति शान्ति

Om Saha Naavavatu; Saha Nau Bhunaktu; Saha Veeryam Karavaavahai; Tejasvi Naavadheetamastu; Maa Vidvishaavahai.

Om Shaantih Shaantih Shaantih.

Om. May the Lord protect both teacher and disciple, and may He cherish us both. May we work with full energy, that our study be perfect and give good results. May we never feel ill will toward the other.

Om peace, peace, peace.

SECTION 1: PART I

ॐ उशन् ह वै वाजश्रवस: सर्ववेदसं ददौ ।
तस्य ह नचिकेता नाम पुत्र आस ॥ 1 ॥

Om Ushan Ha Vai Vaajashravasah Sarvavedasam Dadau; Tasya Ha Nachiketaa Naama Putra Aasa. (1)

Desiring heavenly bounty, Vajashravasa gave all he possessed in a sacrifice. He had a son called Nachiketa.

तरूह कुमार:सन्तं दक्षिणासु नीयमानासु श्रद्धाऽऽविवेश सोऽमन्यत ॥ 2 ॥

Tam Ha Kumaaram Santam Dakshinaasu Neeyamaanaasu Shraddhaa Aavivesha Shoamanyata. (2)

When the final gifts were brought to the priests for distribution Nachiketa, who though still a boy, had deep concern about the welfare of his father, thought to himself:

पीतोदका जग्धतृणा दुग्धदोहा निरिन्द्रिया: ।
अनन्दा नाम ते लोकास्तान् स गच्छति ता ददत् ॥ 3 ॥

Peetodakaa Jagdhatrinaa Dugdhadohaa Nirindriyaah; Anandaa Naama Te Lokaastaan Sa Gachchhati Taa Dadat. (3)

That is certainly a joyless world one attains who gives such aged, worn-out cows as presents in a sacrifice, which are too weak to drink water or eat grass, have no milk and are barren.

स होवाच पितरं तत कस्मै मां दास्यसीति ।
द्वितीयं तृतीयं तरूहोवाच मृत्यवे त्वा ददामीति ॥ 4 ॥

Sa Hovaacha Pitaram Tata Kasmai Maam Daasyaseeti; Dviteeyam Triteeyam Tam Hovaacha Mrityave Tvaa Dadaameeti. (4)

Nachiketa went to his father and said: To whom will you give me? This he repeated once, twice, thrice. Then his father replied with anger: To death I shall give you.

बहूनामेमि प्रथमो बहूनामेमि मध्यम: ।
किं ःस्विद्यमस्य कर्तव्यं यन्मयाद्य करिष्यति ॥ 5 ॥

Bahoonaamemi Prathamo Bahoonaamemi Madhyamah; Kim Svidyamasya Kartavyam Yanmayaadya Karishyati. (5)

Nachiketa considered for a while: Among my fellows I am the most outstanding, or at least of middle rank. What will my father gain by giving me to Yama, the god of death?

अनुपश्य यथा पूर्वे प्रतिपश्य तथापरे ।
सस्यमिव मर्त्य: पच्यते सस्यमिवाजायते पुन: ॥ 6 ॥

Anupashya Yathaa Poorve Pratipashya Tathaapare; Sasyamiva Martyah Pachyate Sasyamivaajaayate Punah. (6)

Remember how our ancestors passed away, and this generation will also. Men perish and fall down like corn, and like corn they rise again.

वैश्वानर: प्रविशत्यतिथिर्ब्राह्मणो गृहान् ।
तस्यैताः ःशान्तिं कुर्वन्ति हर वैवस्वतोदकम् ॥ 7 ॥

Vaishvaanarah Pravishati Atithirbraahmano Grihaan; Tasyaitaam Shaantim Kurvanti Hara Vaivasvatodakam. (7)

A Brahmin guest enters the house like radiant light. Pacify him (O Yama) and fetch water for him.

आशाप्रतीक्षे संगतःसूनृतां च
इष्टापूर्ते पुत्रपशूंश्च सर्वान् ।
एतद् वृङ्क्ते पुरुषस्याल्पमेधसो
यस्यानश्नन् वसति ब्राह्मणो गृहे ॥ 8 ॥

Aashaaprateekshe Samgatam Soonritaam Cha Ishtaapoorte
Putrapashoomshcha Sarvaan; Etad Vrinkte Purushasyaal-
pamedhaso Yasyaanashnan Vasati Braahmano Grihe. (8)

Hopes, expectations, the fruits of good company, friendly
discourse, sacred and pious deeds, and all children and
animals are lost to that ignorant man in whose house a
Brahmin stays without a meal.

तिस्रो रात्रीर्यदवात्सीगृहे मे
अनश्नन् ब्रह्मन्नतिथिर्नमस्यः ।
नमस्तेऽस्तु ब्रह्मन् स्वस्ति मेऽस्तु
तस्मात् प्रति त्रीन् वरान् वृणीष्व ॥ 9 ॥

Tisro Raatreeryadavaatseergrihe Me Anashnan Brahman
Atithirnamasyah; Namsteastu Brahman Svasti Meastu Tasmaat
Prati Treen Varaan Vrineeshva. (9)

Yama said: O Brahman, you are an honourable guest, but in
my absence you stayed in my house for three nights without
a meal. Choose, therefore, three boons, one in respect of
each of these nights as compensation. O Brahman, my
salutations to you. Be good to me.

शान्तसंकल्पः सुमना यथा स्याद्वीतमन्युर्गौतमो माभि मृत्यो ।
त्वत्प्रसृष्टं माभिवदेत्प्रतीत एतत्त्रयाणां प्रथमं वरं वृणे ॥ 10 ॥

Shaantasankalpah Sumanaa Yathaa Syaad Veetamanyurgautamo
Maabhi Mrityo; Tvatprasrishtam Maabhivadet Prateeta Etattra-
yaanaam Prathamam Varam Vrine. (10)

Nachiketa said: O Death, as the first of the three boons, grant that my father may be cheerful and free from anger and anxiety concerning me, and may he recognize and welcome me when I am sent back by you.

यथा पुरस्ताद् भविता प्रतीत
औद्दालकिरारुणिर्मत्प्रसृष्ट: ।
सुखं रात्री: शयिता वीतमन्यु-
स्त्वां ददृशिवान्मृत्युमुखात्प्रमुक्तम् ॥ ११ ॥

Yathaa Purastaad Bhavitaa Prateeta Auddaalakih Arunirmat-prasrishtah; Sukham Raatreeh Shayitaa Veetamanyuh Tvaam Dadrishivaan Mrityumukhaat Pramuktam. (11)

Yama replied: By my grace, Auddalaki, the son of Aruna, will recognize and love you as before. When he sees you, freed from my jaws of death, his anger will vanish and he will sleep soundly at night.

स्वर्गे लोके न भयं किंचनास्ति
न तत्र त्वं न जरया बिभेति ।
उभे तीर्त्वाशनायापिपासे
शोकातिगो मोदते स्वर्गलोके ॥ १२ ॥

Svarge Loke Na Bhayam Kinchanaasti Na Tatra Tvam Na Jarayaa Bibheti; Ubhe Teertvaashanaayaapipaase Shokaatigo Modate Svargaloke. (12)

Nachiketa said: In heaven there is not fear, nor are you there, O Death, nor is anyone subject to old age. They have conquered hunger and thirst and they are merry and free from sorrow in heaven.

स त्वमग्निः स्वर्ग्यमध्येषि मृत्यो
प्रब्रूहि त्वः श्रद्दधानाय मह्यम् ।
स्वर्गलोका अमृतत्वं भजन्त
एतद् द्वितीयेन वृणे वरेण ॥ 13 ॥

*Sa Tvamagnim Svargyamadhyeshi Mrityo Prabroohi Tvam
Shraddadhaanaaya Mahyam; Svargalokaa Amritatvam Bhajanta
Etad Dviteeyena Vrine Varena. (13)*

O Death, you know that fire sacrifice which leads to heaven.
Tell it me, for I am full of faith. By that, the heaven seekers
attain immortality. This is my second boon.

प्र ते ब्रवीमि तदु मे निबोध
स्वर्ग्यमग्निं नचिकेतः प्रजानन् ।
अनन्तलोकाप्तिमथो प्रतिष्ठां
विद्धि त्वमेतं निहितं गुहायाम् ॥ 14 ॥

*Pra Te Braveemi Tadu Me Nibodha Svargyamagnim Nachiketah
Prajaanan; Anantalokaaptimatho Pratishthaam Viddhi Tvametam
Nihitam Guhaayaam. (14)*

Yama replied: I indeed know that fire sacrifice which leads
to heaven, and I shall tell it you, O Nachiketa. Be instructed
by me. That is the way to attain heaven, which is the support
of the world and exists in the heart cave of the enlightened.

लोकादिमग्निं तमुवाच तस्मै
या इष्टका यावतीर्वा यथा वा ।
स चापि तत्प्रत्यवदद्यथोक्त-
मथास्य मृत्युःपुनरेवाह तुष्टः ॥ 15 ॥

*Lokaadimagnim Tamuvaacha Tasmai Yaa Ishtakaa Yaavateervaa
Yatha Vaa; Sa Chaapi Tat Pratyavadad Yathoktam Athaasya
Mrityuh Punarevaaha Tushtah. (15)*

Yama explained to him that fire sacrifice, which is the source of the world, and also the kind and number of bricks required, how these are placed, and how it should be lit. Then Nachiketa repeated the instructions, and Yama was very satisfied.

तमब्रवीत् प्रीयमाणो महात्मा
वरं तवेहाद्य ददामि भूय: ।
तवैव नाम्ना भवितायमग्नि:
सृङ्कां चेमामनेकरूपां गृहाण ॥ 16 ॥

Tamabraveet Preeyamaano Mahaatmaa Varam Tavehaadya Dadaami Bhooyah; Tavaiva Naamnaa Bhavitaayamagnih Srinkaam Chemaamanekaroopaam Grihaana. (16)

Being very pleased, the generous-hearted Yama said to him: I shall grant you an extra boon – the fire sacrifice shall be known by your name, and also take this mala of precious stones.

त्रिणाचिकेतस्त्रिभिरेत्य संधिं
त्रिकर्मकृत् तरति जन्ममृत्यू ।
ब्रह्मजज्ञं देवमीड्यं विदित्वा
निचाय्येमा ाःशान्तिमत्यन्तमेति ॥ 17 ॥

Trinaachiketastribhiretya Sandhim Trikarmakrit Tarati Janma-mrityoo; Brahmajajnam Devameedyam Viditvaa Nichaayyemaam Shaantimatyantameti. (17)

One who performs the Nachiketa fire sacrifice thrice with full dedication, and performs the three duties, (of renunciation, austerity and charity), overcomes birth and death. When he has realized this radiant, omniscient and worshipful fire of the Brahman, he achieves the highest peace.

त्रिणाचिकेतस्त्रयमेतद्विदित्वा
य एवंविद्वाँश्चिनुतेनाचिकेतम् ।
स मृत्युपाशान् पुरत: प्रणोद्य
शोकातिगो मोदते स्वर्गलोके ॥ 18 ॥

Trinaachiketah Trayametad Viditvaa Ya Evam Vidvaamshchinute
Naachiketam; Sa Mrityupaashaan Puratah Pranodya Shokaatigo
Modate Svargaloke. (18)

One who has full knowledge of the three Nachiketa fires
and the tripartite instructions concerning this Agni will cut
the chain of death and pass beyond the sorrow and tears of
this world and reach the joyful heaven.

एष तेऽग्निर्नचिकेत: स्वर्ग्यो
यमवृणाथा द्वितीयेन वरेण ।
एतमग्निं तवैव प्रवक्ष्यन्ति जनास-
स्तृतीयं वरं नचिकेतो वृणीष्व ॥ 19 ॥

Esha Teagnirnachiketah Svargyo Yamavrineethaa Dviteeyena
Varena; Etamagnim Tavaiva Pravakshyanti Janaasa Striteeyam
Varam Nachiketo Vrineeshva. (19)

This is your fire, O Nachiketa, which leads to heaven, and
your second boon. People will call this fire by your name
alone. Now, O Nachiketa, ask the third boon.

येयं प्रेते विचिकित्सा मनुष्ये-
ऽस्तीत्येके नायमस्तीति चैके ।
एतद्विद्यामनुशिष्टस्त्वयाहं
वराणामेष वरस्तृतीय: ॥ 20 ॥

Yeyam Prete Vichikitsaa Manushye Asteetyeke Naayamasteeti
Chaike; Etad Vidyaam Anushishtastvayaaham Varaanaamesha
Varastriteeyah. (20)

Nachiketa said: This doubt exists. Some say when a man dies 'he exists' and some say 'he does not'. This I should like to know. Explain it to me. This is my third boon.

देवैरत्रापि विचिकित्सितं पुरा
न हि सुविज्ञेयमणुरेष धर्म: ।
अन्यं वरं नचिकेतो वृणीष्व
मा मोपरोत्सीरति मा सृजैनम् ॥ 21 ॥

Devairatraapi Vichikitsitam Puraa Na Hi Suvijneyamanuresha Dharmah; Anyam Varam Nachiketo Vrineeshva Maa Moparot-seerati Maa Srijainam. (21)

Yama replied: Even the gods in ancient times doubted this point. It is very subtle and difficult to understand. Do not press me for the boon but choose some other, O Nachiketa. Abandon that boon and release me from the obligation.

देवैरत्रापि विचिकित्सितं किल
त्वं च मृत्यो यन्न सुविज्ञेयमात्थ ।
वक्ता चास्य त्वादृगन्यो न लभ्यो
नान्यो वरस्तुल्य एतस्य कश्चित् ॥ 22 ॥

Devairatraapi Vichikitsitam Kila Tvam Cha Mrityo Yanna Suvijneyamaattha; Vaktaa Chaasya Tvaadriganyo Na Labhyo Naanyo Varastulya Etasya Kashchit. (22)

Nachiketa said: You say, O Death, that even the gods doubted this point, and that it is not easy to understand. None but you can answer it, therefore I sincerely believe no boon can be equal to this one.

शतायुषः पुत्रपौत्रान् वृणीष्व
बहून् पशून् हस्तिहिरण्यमश्वान् ।
भूमेर्महदायतनं वृणीष्व
स्वयं च जीव शरदो यावदिच्छसि ॥ 23 ॥

Shataayushah Putrapautraan Vrineeshva Bahoon Pashoon Hastihiranyamashvaan; Bhoomermahadaayatanam Vrineeshva Svayam Cha Jeeva Sharado Yaavadichchhasi. (23)

Yama replied: Ask for sons and grandsons who will live a hundred years, for elephants, horses, gold and herds of cattle, a vast territory on earth and a long span of life.

एततुल्यं यदि मन्यसे वरं
वृणीष्व वित्तं चिरजीविकां च ।
महाभूमौ नचिकेतस्त्वमेधि
कामानां त्वा कामभाजं करोमि ॥ 24 ॥

Etattulyam Yadi Manyase Varam Vrineeshva Vittam Chirajee-vikaam Cha; Mahaabhoomau Nachiketastvam Edhi Kaamaanaam Tvaa Kaamabhaajam Karomi. (24)

And if you can think of some other boon of equal worth, ask also for that: wealth or a long life. O Nachiketa, be king of the wide earth. I shall make you the enjoyer of all your desires.

ये ये कामा दुर्लभा मर्त्यलोवे
सर्वान् कामाꣳश्छन्दतः प्रार्थयस्व ।
इमा रामाः सरथाः सतूर्या
न हीदृशा लम्भनीया मनुष्यैः ।
आभिर्मत्प्रत्ताभिः परिचारयस्व
नचिकेतो मरणं मानुप्राक्षीः ॥ 25 ॥

Ye Ye Kaamaa Durlabhaa Martyaloke Sarvaan Kaamaamsh-
chhandatah Praarthayasva; Imaa Raamaah Sarathaah Satooryaa
Na Heedrishaa Lambhaneeyaa Manushyaih; Aabhirmatprattaabhih
Parichaarayasva Nachiketo Maranam Maanupraaksheeh. (25)

Ask for even those objects of desire that are difficult to find
in this world of mortals, as you choose. Fair maidens will
wait on you and you will have chariots and musical
instruments such as are not obtainable by mortals. All this I
offer you, but do not ask about death.

श्वोभावा मर्त्यस्य यदन्तकैतत्-
सर्वेन्द्रियाणां जरयन्ति तेज: ।
अपि सर्वं जीवितमल्पमेव
तवैव वाहास्तव नृत्यगीते ॥ 26 ॥

Shvobhaavaa Martyasya Yadantakaitat Sarvendriyaanaam
Jarayanti Tejah; Api Sarvam Jeevitamalpameva Tavaiva Vaahaas-
tava Nrityageete. (26)

Nachiketa said: All these things, O Death, are not everlasting
and only decay the vigour of man's faculties. The whole
span of life is indeed short, so keep your chariots, horses,
dance and music and merry-making things with you.

न वित्तेन तर्पणीयो मनुष्यो
लप्स्यामहे वित्तमद्राक्ष्म चेत् त्वा ।
जीविष्यामो यावदीशिष्यति त्वं
वरस्तु मे वरणीय: स एव ॥ 27 ॥

Na Vittena Tarpaneeyo Manushyo Lapsyaamahe Vittama-
draakshma Chet Tvaa; Jeevishyaamo Yaavadeeshishyasi Tvam
Varastu Me Varaneeyah Sa Eva. (27)

Man cannot be satisfied with wealth or enjoy long life, seeing
you. That boon alone which I chose is fit to be craved.

अजीर्यताममृतानामुपेत्य
जीर्यन् मर्त्यः क्वधःस्थः प्रजानन् ।
अभिध्यायन् वर्णरतिप्रमोदा-
नतिदीर्घे जीविते को रमेत ॥ 28 ॥

Ajeeryataam Amritaanaamupetya Jeeryan Martyah Kvadhahsthah Prajaanan; Abhidhyaayan Varnarati Pramodaa Natideerghe Jeevite Ko Rameta. (28)

Having known the undecaying and immortal, what decaying mortal remaining in the world below will take pleasure in a long span of life after scrutinizing the enjoyments obtained from dancing and singing?

यस्मिन्निदं विचिकित्सन्ति मृत्यो
यत्साम्पराये महति ब्रूहि नस्तत् ।
योऽयं वरो गूढमनुप्रविष्टो
नान्यं तस्मान्नचिकेता वृणीते ॥ 29 ॥

Yasminnidam Vichikitsanti Mrityo Yat Saamparaaye Mahati Broohi Nastat; Yoayam Varo Goodhamanupravishto Naanyam Tasmaan-nachiketaa Vrineete. (29)

O Death, tell me that which people doubt on, regarding the supreme life after death. Only that boundless boon does Nachiketa crave.

SECTION 1: PART II

अन्यच्छ्रेयोऽन्यदुतैव प्रेयस्ते
    उभे   नानार्थे   पुरुषꣳ सिनीतः ।
तयोः श्रेय आददानस्य साधु
    भवति हीयतेऽर्थाद्य उ प्रेयो वृणीते ॥ 1 ॥

Anyat Shreyah Anyat Utaiva Preyah Te Ubhe Naanaarthe
Purusham Sineetah; Tayoh Shreya Aadadaanasya Saadhu Bhavati
Heeyatearthaadya U Preyo Vrineete. (1)

Yama said: Worldly objects give either joy or pleasure, and
both these bind man. Fortune is kind to him who chooses
the joyful, but one who follows the pleasurable remains in
delusion.

श्रेयश्च प्रेयश्च मनुष्यमेतस्तौ
    सम्परीत्य   विविनक्ति धीरः ।
श्रेयो हि धीरोऽभि प्रेयसो वृणीते
    प्रेयो मन्दो योगक्षेमाद् वृणीते ॥ 2 ॥

Shreyashcha Preyashcha Manushyametah Tau Sampareetya
Vivinakti Dheerah; Shreyo Hi Dheeroabhi Preyaso Vrineete Preyo
Mando Yogakshemaad Vrineete. (2)

The joyful and pleasurable lie before man. The wise man,
after discriminating and examining them well, prefers the
joyful, but the ignorant, due to greed and attachment,
chooses the pleasurable.

स त्वं प्रियान् प्रियरूपाꣳश्च कामा-
    नभिध्यायन्नचिकेतोऽत्यस्त्राक्षीः ।
नैताꣳ सृङ्कां वित्तमयीमवाप्तो
    यस्यां मज्जन्ति बहवो मनुष्याः ॥ 3 ॥

111

Sa Tvam Priyaan Priyaroopaanshcha Kaamaan Abhidhyaayan Nachiketoatyasraaksheeh; Naitaam Srinkaam Vittamayeemavaapto Yasyaam Majjanti Bahavo Manushyaah. (3)

O Nachiketa, you have discarded all the objects of desire and things pleasurable in appearance, not judging them at their face value. You have not taken to the miry path of wealth in which many mortals sink.

दूरमेते विपरीते विषूची
अविद्या या च विद्येति ज्ञाता ।
विद्याभीप्सिनं नचिकेतसं मन्ये
न त्वा कामा बहवोऽलोलुपन्त ॥ 4 ॥

Dooramete Vipareete Vishoochee Avidyaa Yaa Cha Vidyeti Jnaataa; Vidyaabheepsinam Nachiketasam Manye Na Tvaa Kaamaa Bahavoalolupanta. (4)

Ignorance and knowledge are quite different, leading to opposite results. They are wide apart from each other. Nachiketa, you I consider a deserving aspirant for knowledge because even an abundance of enjoyable things could not tempt you.

अविद्यायामन्तरे वर्तमाना:
स्वयं धीरा: पण्डितम्मन्यमाना: ।
दन्द्रम्यमाणा: परियन्ति मूढा
अन्धेनैव नीयमाना यथान्धा: ॥ 5 ॥

Avidyaayaamantare Vartamaanaah Svayam Dheeraah Panditam Manyamaanaah; Dandramyamaanaah Pariyanti Moodhaa Andhenaiva Neeyamaanaa Yathaandhaah. (5)

The ignorant, living in the midst of ignorance, pretending to themselves they are wise and intelligent, go round and round in circles, tottering to and fro like the blind led by the blind.

न साम्पराय: प्रतिभाति बालं
प्रमाद्यन्तं वित्तमोहेन मूढम् ।
अयं लोको नास्ति पर इति मानी
पुन: पुनर्वशमापद्यते मे ॥ 6 ॥

Na Saamparaayah Pratibhaati Baalam Pramaadyantam Vittamohena Moodham; Ayam Loko Naasti Para Iti Maanee Punah Punarvasham Aapadyate Me. (6)

The ignorant, deluded by wealth, never see the path of the hereafter. 'This is the only world and there is no other' – thinking like this, such foolish men become my victims.

श्रवणायापि बहुभिर्यो न लभ्य:
शृण्वन्तोऽपि बहवो यं न विद्यु: ।
आश्चर्यो वक्ता कुशलोऽस्य लब्धा-
ऽऽश्चर्यो ज्ञाता कुशलानुशिष्ट: ॥ 7 ॥

Shravanaayaapi Bahubhiryo Na Labhyah Shrinvantoapi Bahavo Yam Na Vidyuh; Aashcharyo Vaktaa Kushaloasya Labdhaa Aashcharyo Jnaataa Kushalaanushishtah. (7)

There are many who never come to hear of That (the Self). There are many who, even if they hear of Him, do not understand. Wonderful is the teacher of the Self, and wonderful is he who, when taught by an able teacher, understands Him.

न नरेणावरेण प्रोक्त एष
सुविज्ञेयो बहुधा चिन्त्यमान: ।
अनन्यप्रोक्ते गतिरत्र नास्ति
अणीयान् ह्यतर्क्यमणुप्रमाणात् ॥ 8 ॥

Na Narenaavarena Prokta Esha Suvijneyo Bahudhaa Chintyamaanah; Ananyaprokte Gatiratra Naasti Aneeyaan Hyatarkyam Anupramaanaat. (8)

This Atman, being subtler than the subtlest and beyond arguments, can never be grasped if taught by an unrealized man, because it should be thought of in certain ways. But when it is taught by a realized teacher, there will be no doubts.

नैषा तर्केण मतिरापनेया
प्रोक्तान्येनैव सुज्ञानाय प्रेष्ठ ।
यां त्वमाप: सत्यधृतिर्बतासि
त्वादृङ् नो भूयान्नचिकेत: प्रष्टा ॥ ९ ॥

Naishaa Tarkena Matiraapaneyaa Proktaanyenaiva Sujnaanaaya Preshtha; Yaam Tvamaapah Satyadhritirbataasi Tvaadring No Bhooyaannachiketah Prashtaa. (9)

Knowledge of the Self cannot be acquired by mere reasoning, but it becomes easy, O Dearest One, when imparted by the seer. You are really firm in Truth, therefore you have obtained this. May we get more enquirers like you, Nachiketa.

जानाम्यहं शेवधिरित्यनित्यं
न ह्यध्रुवै: प्राप्यते हि ध्रुवं तत् ।
ततो मया नाचिकेतश्चितोऽग्नि-
रनित्यैर्द्रव्यै: प्राप्तवानस्मि नित्यम् ॥ १० ॥

Jaanaamyaham Shevadhih Ityanityam Na Hyadhruvaih Praapyate Hi Dhruvam Tat; Tato Mayaa Naachiketashchito Agnih Anityah Dravyaih Praaptavaanasmi Nityam. (10)

I know that treasure does not endure, for the eternal is not attained by the non-eternal, yet I attained the relatively eternal by sacrificing the perishable objects in the Nachiketa fire.

कामस्याप्तिं जगत: प्रतिष्ठां
क्रतोरनन्त्यमभयस्य   पारम् ।
स्तोममहदुरुगायं प्रतिष्ठां
दृष्ट्वा धृत्या धीरो नचिकेतोऽत्यस्राक्षी: ॥ 11 ॥

Kaamasyaaptim Jagatah Pratishthaam Kratoranantyam Abhayasya Paaram; Stomamahat Urugaayam Pratishthaam Drishtvaa Dhrityaa Dheero Nachiketah Atyasraaksheeh. (11)

Complete fulfilment of desires, the dominion of the world, the endless rewards of sacred rites, the power of fearlessness, fame, and great and wide expanses, all these you considered with a calm mind and, being intelligent, O Nachiketa, you have renounced all with firm determination.

तं दुर्दर्शं गूढमनुप्रविष्टं
गुहाहितं गह्वरेष्ठं पूराणम् ।
अध्यात्मयोगाधिगमेन देवं
मत्वा धीरो हर्षशोकौ जहाति ॥ 12 ॥

Tam Durdarsham Goodham Anupravishtam Guhaahitam Gahvareshtham Pooraanam; Adhyaatmayogaadhigamena Devam Matvaa Dheero Harshashokau Jahaati. (12)

The wise man abandons both joy and sorrow by meditation on the Self, that ancient luminous one, difficult to perceive, subtle and unfathomable, who is seated in the heart cave in the body.

एतच्छ्रुत्वा सम्परिगृह्य मर्त्य:
प्रवृह्य धर्म्यमणुमेतमाप्य ।
स मोदते मोदनीयं हि लब्ध्वा
विवृतं सद्म नचिकेतसं मन्ये ॥ 13 ॥

*Etachchhrutvaa   Samparigrihya   Martyah   Pravrihya
Dharmyamanum Etamaapya; Sa Modate Modaneeyam Hi
Labdhvaa Vivritam Sadma Nachiketasam Manye.* (13)

Having heard and well grasped the Self, the mortal, after
separating the virtuous from the impure and discovering
the subtle Self, rejoices indeed, because he has achieved the
real cause of all rejoicing. I think the house of Brahman is
wide open for you, O Nachiketa.

अन्यत्र धर्मादन्यत्राधर्मादन्यत्रास्मात्कृताकृतात् ।
अन्यत्र भूताच्च भव्याच्च यत्तत्पश्यसि तद्वद ॥ 14 ॥

*Anyatra   Dharmaadanyatra   Adharmaat   Aanyatraasmaat
Kritaakritaat; Anyatra Bhootaachcha Bhavyaachcha Yattatpashyasi
Tadvada.* (14)

Nachiketa said: Tell me about That, which you see as
different from good and evil, cause and effect, and past and
future.

सर्वे वेद यत् पदमामनन्ति
            तपाॅहि सर्वाणि च यद् वदन्ति ।
यदिच्छन्तो ब्रह्मचर्यं चरन्ति
            तत्ते पदःॅ संग्रहेण ब्रवीम्योमित्येतत् ॥ 15 ॥

*Sarve Vedaa Yat Padamaamananti Tapaamsi Sarvaani Cha Yad
Vadanti; Yadichchhanto Brahmacharyam Charanti Tat Te Padam
Sangrahena Braveemyomityetat.* (15)

Yama replied: That goal which all the scriptures praise, the
object of all penance, and the self-controlled life devoted to
austerity and knowledge, that goal, in short, is Om.

एतद्धयेवाक्षरं ब्रह्म एतद्धयेवाक्षरं परम् ।
एतद्धयेवाक्षरं ज्ञात्वा यो यदिच्छति तस्य तत् ॥ 16 ॥

Etaddhyevaaksharam Brahma Etaddhyevaaksharam Param;
Etaddhyevaaksharam Jnaatvaa Yo Yadichchhati Tasya Tat. (16)

The word Om is indeed the Brahman and this word is
Supreme. One who knows this word obtains whatever he
wants.

एतदालम्बनः श्रेष्ठमेतदालम्बनं परम् ।
एतदालम्बनं ज्ञात्वा ब्रह्मलोके महीयते ॥ 17 ॥

Etadaalambanam Shreshtham Etadaalambanam Param;
Etadaalambanam Jnaatvaa Brahmaloke Maheeyate. (17)

This path is the highest, and the foundation. One who
knows Om is worshipped in the heaven of Brahman.

न जायते म्रियते वा विपश्चि-
न्नायं कुतश्चिन्न बभूव कश्चित् ।
अजो नित्यः शाश्वतोऽयं पुराणो
न हन्यते हन्यमाने शरीरे ॥ 18 ॥

Na Jaayate Mriyate Vaa Vipashchit Naayam Kutashchinna
Babhoova Kashchit; Ajo Nityah Shaashvatoayam Puraano Na
Hanyate Hanyamaane Shareere. (18)

The intelligent soul is not born, nor does he die. He did not
arise from anything, nor has anything come into being from
him. He is unborn, eternal and undecaying. When the body
is slain with weapons, he remains unaffected.

117

हन्ता चेन्मन्यते हन्तूँहतश्चेन्मन्यते हतम् ।
उभौ तौ न विजानीतो नायूँ हन्ति न हन्यते ॥ 19 ॥

Hantaa Chenmanyate Hantum Hatashchenmanyate Hatam; Ubhau Tau Na Vijaaneeto Naayam Hanti Na Hanyate. (19)

If the killer thinks that he kills, or the killed that he is killed, both do not know. Neither does he kill, nor is he killed.

अणोरणीयान्महतो महीया-
    नात्मास्य जन्तोर्निहितो गुहायाम् ।
तमक्रतुः पश्यति वीतशोको
    धातुप्रसादान्महिमानमात्मनः   ॥ 20 ॥

Anoraneeyaan Mahato Maheeyaan Aatmaasya Jantornihito Guhaayaam; Tamakratuh Pashyati Veetashoko Dhaatuprasaadaat Mahimaanamaatmanah. (20)

The Atman, subtler than the subtlest and greater than the greatest, dwells in the heart of every living being. One who is desireless and free from anxiety realizes the glorious Atman through the purity of senses and mind and becomes free from sorrow.

आसीनो दूरं व्रजति शयानो याति सर्वतः ।
कस्तं मदामदं देवं मदन्यो ज्ञातुमर्हति ॥ 21 ॥

Aaseeno Dooram Vrajati Shayaano Yaati Sarvatah; Kastam Madaamadam Devam Madanyo Jnaatumarhati. (21)

While at rest He goes afar, while motionless He moves everywhere. Who but the purest of the pure can know that radiant God who is both joyful and joyless.

अशरीर ँशरीरेष्वनवस्थेष्ववस्थितम् ।
महान्तं विभुमात्मानं मत्वा धीरो न शोचति ॥ 22 ॥

*Ashareeram Shareereshu Anavastheshu Avasthitam; Mahaantam
Vibhumaatmaanam Matvaa Dheero Na Shochati.* (22)

The wise man does not grieve, having known the bodiless,
all-pervading and great, seated firmly in perishable bodies.

नायमात्मा प्रवचनेन लभ्यो
        न मेधया न बहुना श्रुतेन ।
यमेवैष वृणुते तेन लभ्य-
        स्तस्यैष आत्मा विवृणुते तनूँस्वाम् ॥ 23 ॥

*Naayamaatmaa Pravachanena Labhyo Na Medhayaa Na Bahunaa
Shrutena; Yamevaisha Vrinute Tena Labhya Stasyaisha Aatmaa
Vivrinute Tanoom Svaam.* (23)

The Atman cannot be known through the study of scriptures,
or by much learning or intelligence. He is attained by him
alone who chooses Him. To him alone does the Atman
reveal His own Truth.

नाविरतो दुश्चरितान्नाशान्तो नासमाहितः ।
नाशान्तमानसो वापि प्रज्ञानेनैनमाप्नुयात् ॥ 24 ॥

*Naavirato   Dushcharitaannaashaanto   Naasamaahitah;
Naashaantamaanaso Vaapi Prajnaanenainamaapnuyaat.* (24)

One who has not kept himself aloof from doing sinful acts,
nor controlled his senses, and has not a peaceful and one-
pointed mind, can never attain the Atman through
knowledge.

यस्य ब्रह्म च क्षत्रं च उभे भवत ओदन: ।
मृत्युर्यस्योपसेचनं क इत्था वेद यत्र स: ॥ 25 ॥

Yasya Brahma Cha Kshatram Cha Ubhe Bhavata Odanah;
Mrityuryasya Upasechanam Ka Itthaa Veda Yatra Sah. (25)

Who can say where that Atman is, whose food is priests and
warriors and whose condiment is death?

SECTION 1: PART III

ऋतं पिबन्तौ सुकृतस्य लोके
    गुहां प्रविष्टौ परमे परार्धे ।
छायातपौ ब्रह्मविदो वदन्ति
    पञ्चाग्नयो ये च त्रिणाचिकेताः ॥ 1 ॥

*Ritam Pibantau Sukritasya Loke Guhaam Pravishtau Parame
Paraardhe; Chhaayaatapau Brahmavido Vadanti Panchaagnayo
Ye Cha Trinaachiketaah. (1)*

There are two in this body who are the enjoyers, lodged in
the cavity of the heart, the seat of the Supreme. The knower
of Brahman and the performer of the fivefold fires and the
threefold Nachiketa fire sacrifice call them light and shade.

यः सेतुरीजानानामक्षरं ब्रह्म यत् परम् ।
अभयं तितीर्षतां पारं नाचिकेतूं शकेमहि ॥ 2 ॥

*Yah Setureejaanaanaam Aksharam Brahma Yat Param; Abhayam
Titeershataam Paaram Naachiketam Shakemahi. (2)*

We have told of both the Nachiketa fire sacrifice, which is
the bridge across the ocean of life for all sacrificers, and also
of the undecaying supreme Brahman, the fearless and the
ultimate refuge.

आत्मानूं रथिनं विद्धि शरीरूं रथमेव तु ।
बुद्धिं तु सारथिं विद्धि मनः प्रग्रहमेव च ॥ 3 ॥

*Aatmaanam Rathinam Viddhi Shareeram Rathameva Tu; Buddhim
Tu Saarathim Viddhi Manah Pragrahameva Cha. (3)*

Know that the Atman sitting within is the master of the
chariot which is the body, know the pure discriminating
intellect to be the charioteer and the mind as the reins.

इन्द्रियाणि हयानाहुर्विषयाᳵस्तेषु गोचरान् ।
आत्मेन्द्रियमनोयुक्तं भोक्तेत्याहुर्मनीषिण: ॥ 4 ॥

Indriyaani Hayaanaahurvishayaamsteshu Gocharaan; Aatmendriya-
manoyuktam Bhoktetyaahurmaneeshinah. (4)

The senses are called the horses, and their sense objects the
roads. The wise know He is the enjoyer when He is united
with the body, the senses and the mind.

यस्त्वविज्ञानवान् भवत्ययुक्तेन मनसा सदा ।
तस्येन्द्रियाण्यवश्यानि दुष्टाश्वा इव सारथे: ॥ 5 ॥

Yastvavijnaanavaan Bhavatyayuktena Manasaa Sadaa;
Tasyendriyaanyavashyaani Dushtaashvaa Iva Saaratheh. (5)

One whose mind is always unrestrained and does not have
discrimination, his senses are uncontrollable like horses of a
charioteer which are vicious.

यस्तु विज्ञानवान् भवति युक्तेन मनसा सदा ।
तस्येन्द्रियाणि वश्यानि सदश्वा इव सारथे: ॥ 6 ॥

Yastu Vijnaanavaan Bhavati Yuktena Manasaa Sadaa;
Tasyendriyaani Vashyaani Sadashvaa Iva Saaratheh. (6)

But one whose mind is always under control and has correct
understanding, his senses are controllable like the horses of
a charioteer which are disciplined.

यस्त्वविज्ञानवान् भवत्यमनस्क: सदाशुचि: ।
न स तत्पदमाप्नोति सᳵ-सारं चाधिगच्छति ॥ 7 ॥

Yastvavijnaanavaan Bhavatyamanaskah Sadaashuchih; Na Sa Tat
Padamaapnoti Samsaaram Chaadhigachchhati. (7)

And he who has no right discrimination, who is thoughtless, impure and unsteady of mind, he never reaches the goal but moves in the round of birth and death.

यस्तु विज्ञानवान् भवति समनस्क: सदा शुचि: ।
स तु तत्पदमाप्नोति यस्माद् भूयो न जायते ॥ 8 ॥

Yastu Vijnaanavaan Bhavati Samanaskah Sadaa Shuchih; Sa Tu Tat Padamaapnoti Yasmaad Bhooyo Na Jaayate. (8)

But he who has correct understanding, who is ever pure and whose mind is well controlled, reaches that goal from where none is again born.

विज्ञानसारथिर्यस्तु मन:प्रग्रहवान् नर: ।
सोऽध्वन:पारमाप्नोति तद्विष्णो: परमं पदम् ॥ 9 ॥

Vijnaanasaarathiryastu Manahpragrahavaan Narah; Soadhvanah Paaramaapnoti Tad Vishnoh Paramam Padam. (9)

That man who has keen intelligence for his charioteer, a well-balanced mind for his reins, reaches the end of the journey, which is the Supreme place.

इन्द्रियेभ्य: परा ह्यर्था अर्थेभ्यश्च परं मन: ।
मनसस्तु परा बुद्धिर्बुद्धेरात्मा महान् पर: ॥ 10 ॥

Indriyebhyah Paraa Hyarthaa Arthebhyashcha Param Manah; Manasastu Paraa Buddhirbuddheraatmaa Mahaan Parah. (10)

The sense objects are superior to the senses, the mind is superior to the sense objects and intellect is superior to the mind. Beyond the intellect is the great soul (Self).

महत: परमव्यक्तमव्यक्तात् पुरुष: पर: ।
पुरुषान्न परं किंचित्सा काष्ठा सा परा गति: ॥ 11 ॥

Mahatah Paramavyaktam Avyaktaat Purushah Parah;
Purushaanna Param Kinehit Saa Kaashthaa Saa Paraa Gatih. (11)

The Unmanifest is superior to the great Atman, and the
Purusha is superior to the Unmanifest. Nothing is superior
to the Purusha. That is the end, the highest goal.

एष सर्वेषु भूतेषु गूढोत्मा न प्रकाशते ।
दृश्यते त्वग्र्यया बुद्ध्या सूक्ष्मया सूक्ष्मदर्शिभि: ॥ 12 ॥

Esha Sarveshu Bhooteshu Goodhotmaa Na Prakaashate; Drishyate
Tvagryayaa Buddhyaa Sookshmayaa Sookshmadarshibhih. (12)

This Atman, hidden in all things, does not reveal Himself to
all, but is perceived by those subtle seers through their keen
and subtle intellect.

यच्छेद्वाङ्मनसी प्राज्ञस्तद्यच्छेज्ज्ञान आत्मनि ।
ज्ञानमात्मनि महति नियच्छेत्तद्यच्छेच्छान्त आत्मनि ॥ 13 ॥

Yachchhed Vaan Manasee Praajnastad Yachchhejjnaana Aatmani;
Jnaanamaatmani Mahati Niyachchhet Tad Yachchhechchhaanta
Aatmani. (13)

The wise man should merge speech in mind, mind in
intellect, intellect in the great Self (Atman), and the great
Self in the peaceful Self.

उत्तिष्ठत जाग्रत प्राप्य वरान्निबोधत ।
क्षुरस्य धारा निशिता दुरत्यया दुर्गं पथस्तत्कवयो वदन्ति ॥ 14 ॥

Uttishthata Jaagrata Praapya Varaan Nibodhata; Kshurasya Dhaaraa
Nishitaa Duratyayaa Durgam Pathastat Kavayo Vadanti. (14)

Awake, arise! Learn this wisdom from the great ones. As narrow as the razor's edge is that path, difficult to traverse and hard to tread, say the wise.

अशब्दमस्पर्शमरूपमव्ययं
तथारसं नित्यमगन्धवच्च यत् ।
अनाद्यनन्तं महत: परं ध्रुवं
निचाय्य तन्मृत्युमुखात् प्रमुच्यते ॥ 15 ॥

Ashabdam Asparsham Aroopam Avyayam Tathaarasam Nityam Agandhavachcha Yat; Anaadyanantam Mahatah Param Dhruvam Nichaayya Tanmrityumukhaat Pramuchyate. (15)

One who has realized That (Atman) which is soundless, intangible, formless, undiminishing, tasteless and odourless, eternal, without beginning or end, transcendental and unchanging, is released from the jaws of death.

नाचिकेतमुपाख्यानं मृत्युप्रोक्तं सनातनम् ।
उक्त्वा श्रुत्वा च मेधावी ब्रह्मलोके महीयते ॥ 16 ॥

Naachiketamupaakhyaanam Mrityuproktam Sanaatanam; Uktvaa Shrutvaa Cha Medhaavee Brahmaloke Maheeyate. (16)

That intelligent one who hears or narrates this ancient story of Nachiketa and the instruction of Yama will be glorified in the heaven of Brahman.

य इमं परमं गुह्यं श्रावयेद् ब्रह्मसंसदि ।
प्रयत: श्राद्धकाले वा तदानन्त्याय कल्पते ।
तदानन्त्याय   कल्पत   इति ॥ 17 ॥

Ya Imam Paramam Guhyam Shraavayed Brahma Sansadi; Prayatah Shraaddhakaale Vaa Tadaanantyaaya Kalpate; Tadaanantyaaya Kalpata Iti. (17)

One who with great devotion repeats this great secret before an assembly of priests or during a ceremony to the ancestors thereby attains eternal reward, immortality.

SECTION 2: PART I

परञ्चि खानि व्यतृणत् स्वयंभू-
स्तस्मात्पराङ्पश्यति नान्तरात्मन् ।
कश्चिद्धीर: प्रत्यगात्मानमैक्ष-
दावृत्तचक्षुरमृतत्वमिच्छन्   ॥ 1 ॥

*Paraanchi Khaani Vyatrinat Svayambhoo Stasmaat Paraan Pashyati
Naantaraatman; Kashchiddheerah Pratyagaatmaanamaikshad
Aavrittachakshuramritatvamichchhan.* (1)

The Self-existent Lord of all things created the sense organs
with a powerful tendency to go outwards, and thus man sees
external objects and not the internal Self. Yet there are a few
wise men who, desiring immortality, turn their entire
attention within and see the inner Atman.

पराच: कामाननुयन्ति बाला-
स्ते मृत्योर्यन्ति विततस्य पाशम् ।
अथ धीरा अमृतत्वं विदित्वा
ध्रुवमध्रुवेष्विह   न   प्रार्थयन्ते ॥ 2 ॥

*Paraachah Kaamaananuyanti Baalaaste Mrityoryanti Vitatasya
Paasham; Atha Dheeraa Amritatvam Viditvaa Dhruva-
madhruveshviha Na Praarthayante.* (2)

The ignorant and child-like run after external pleasures
and fall into the widespread traps of death, but the wise,
having known That which is immortal and eternal in the
midst of impermanent objects, do not care for the sensory
pleasures in this world.

येन रूपं रसं गन्धं शब्दान्स्पर्शाँ ‌‌श्च मैथुनान् ।
एतेनैव विजानाति किमत्र परिशिष्यते ॥ एतद्वै तत् ॥ ३ ॥

Yena Roopam Rasam Gandham Shabdaan Sparshaamshcha Maithunaan; Etenaiva Vijaanaati Kimatra Parishishyate. Etadvai Tat. (3)

To that Atman by which one perceives form, taste, smell, sound, touch and sexual pleasure, there is nothing unknown in this world. This is verily That (Atman, you ought to know).

स्वप्नान्तं जागरितान्तं चोभौ येनानुपश्यति ।
महान्तं विभुमात्मानं मत्वा धीरो न शोचति ॥ ४ ॥

Svapnaantam Jaagaritaantam Chobhau Yenaanupashyati; Mahaantam Vibhumaatmaanam Matvaa Dheero Na Shochati. (4)

The wise man does not grieve, having realized that great and all-pervading Atman through which he perceives the things of the waking state and of dreams.

य इमं मध्वदं वेद आत्मानं जीवमन्तिकात् ।
ईशानं भूतभव्यस्य न ततो विजुगुप्सते ॥ एतद्वै तत् ॥ ५ ॥

Ya Imam Madhvadam Veda Aatmaanam Jeevamantikaat; Eeshaanam Bhootabhavyasya Na Tato Vijugupsate. Etadvai Tat. (5)

One who knows this Atman, the enjoyer of nectar, very close, and the Lord of the past and the future, does not fear. This is verily That.

य: पूर्वं तपसो जातमद्भ्य: पूर्वमजायत ।
गुहां प्रविश्य तिष्ठन्तं यो भूतेभिर्व्यपश्यत् ॥ एतद्वै तत् ॥ ६ ॥

Yah Poorvam Tapaso Jaatamadbhyah Poorvamajaayata; Guhaam Pravishya Tishthantam Yo Bhootebhirvyapashyat. Etadvai Tat. (6)

128

He who was born from austerity in ancient times, was born of waters in ancient times, who stays, having entered the secret place (of the heart) and looked forth through beings. This is verily That.

या   प्राणेन   सम्भवत्यदितिर्देवतामयी ।
गुहां प्रविश्य तिष्ठन्तीं या भूतेभिर्व्यजायत ॥ एतद्वै तत् ॥ 7 ॥

Yaa Praanena Sambhavati Aditirdevataamayee; Guhaam Pravishya Tishthanteem Yaa Bhootebhirvyajaayata. Etadvai Tat. (7)

One who knows that One, who is manifested in the form of prana and the presiding deities of the sense organs, who is self-created in the elements and who resides in the heart cavity, verily knows the Brahman. This is verily That.

अरण्योर्निहितो जातवेदा गर्भ इव सुभृतो गर्भिणीभिः ।
दिवे दिव ईड्यो जागृवद्भिर्हविष्मद्भिर्मनुष्येभिरग्निः ॥ एतद्वै तत् ॥ 8 ॥

Aranyornihito Jaatavedaa Garbha Iva Subhrito Garbhineebhih; Dive Diva Eedyo Jaagrivadbhih Havishmadbhih Manushye-bhiragnih. Etadvai Tat. (8)

The sacrificial fire lodged between the two pieces of wood, like the foetus in the womb of the mother, which is worshipped daily by sages and householders, is that same One. This is verily That.

यतश्चोदेति   सूर्योऽस्तं यत्र   च   गच्छति ।
तं देवाः सर्वे अर्पितास्तदु नात्येति कश्चन ॥ एतद्वै तत् ॥ 9 ॥

Yatashchodeti Sooryoastam Yatra Cha Gachchhati; Tam Devaah Sarve Arpitaastadu Naatyeti Kashchana. Etadvai Tat. (9)

That whence the sun rises and where it merges again, in That all the gods are fixed and no one goes beyond That. This is verily That.

यदेवेह   तदमुत्र   यदमुत्र   तदन्विह ।
मृत्यो: स मृत्युमाप्नोति य इह नानेव पश्यति ॥ 10 ॥

Yadeveha Tadamutra Yadamutra Tadanviha; Mrityoh Sa Mrityumaapnoti Ya Iha Naaneva Pashyati. (10)

Whatever is here in this world is also there in the Brahman and whatever is there is likewise here. One who sees difference here undergoes various births and deaths.

मनसैवेदमाप्तव्यं   नेह   ननास्ति   किंचन ।
मृत्यो: स मृत्युं गच्छति य इह नानेव पश्यति ॥ 11 ॥

Manasaivedamaaptavyam Neha Nanaasti Kinchana; Mrityoh Sa Mrityum Gachchhati Ya Iha Naaneva Pashyati. (11)

This the mind alone can realize and then there seems no difference at all. One who sees any difference here goes from death to death.

अङ्गुष्ठमात्र: पुरुषो मध्य आत्मनि तिष्ठति ।
ईशानो भूतभव्यस्य न ततो विजुगुप्सते ॥ एतद्वै तत् ॥ 12 ॥

Angushthamaatrah Purusho Madhya Aatmani Tishthati; Eeshaano Bhootabhavyasya Na Tato Vijugupsate. Etadvai Tat. (12)

The Purusha, the size of a thumb, resides in the physical heart. He is the Lord of the past and future and after knowing Him one fears no more. This is verily That.

अङ्गुष्ठमात्र: पुरुषो   ज्योतिरिवाधूमक: ।
ईशानो भूतभव्यस्य स एवाद्य स उ श्व: ॥एतद्वै तत् ॥ 13 ॥

Angushthamaatrah Purusho Jyotirivaadhoomakah; Eeshaano Bhootabhavyasya Sa Evaadya Sa U Shvah. Etadvai Tat. (13)

The Purusha, the size of a thumb, the Lord of the past and future, is like a flame without smoke. He exists today and will be tomorrow. This is verily That.

यथोदकं दुर्गे वृष्टं पर्वतेषु विधावति ।
एवं धर्मान् पृथक् पश्यंस्तानेवानुविधावति ॥ 14 ॥

Yathodakam Durge Vrishtam Parvateshu Vidhaavati; Evam Dharmaan Prithak Pashyanstaanevaanuvidhaavati. (14)

As rainwater having fallen on the mountain top runs down with great force, scattering rocks and laying waste hillsides, so also one who sees difference in the objects verily runs after them on all sides.

यथोदकं शुद्धे शुद्धमासिक्तं तादृगेव भवति ।
एवं मुनेर्विजानत आत्मा भवति गौतम ॥ 15 ॥

Yathodakam Shuddhe Shuddhamaasiktam Taadrigeva Bhavati; Evam Munervijaanata Aatmaa Bhavati Gautama. (15)

As pure water poured into pure water becomes the same, so does the Self of the man of knowledge, O Nachiketa.

SECTION 2: PART II

पुरमेकादशद्वारमजस्यावक्रचेतसः   ।
अनुष्ठाय न शोचति विमुक्तश्च विमुच्यते ॥ एतद्वै तत् ॥ 1 ॥

Puramekaadashadvaaram Ajasyaavakrachetasah; Anushthaaya Na Shochati Vimuktashcha Vimuchyate. Etadvai Tat. (1)

The city of the unborn (Brahman), whose consciousness is constant, has eleven gates. Meditating on Him, one grieves no more and, liberated from the bonds of ignorance, one becomes free. This is verily That.

हरॅसः शुचिषद् वसुरन्तरिक्षस-
                     द्धोता   वेदिषदतिथिर्दुरोणसत् ।
नृषद् वरसदृतसद् व्योमसदब्जा
                     गोजा ऋतजा अद्रिजा ऋतं बृहत् ॥ 2 ॥

Hamsah Shuchishad Vasurantarikshasat Hotaa Vedishadatithih Duronasat; Nrishad Varasadritasad Vyomasadabjaa Gojaa Ritajaa Adrijaa Ritam Brihat. (2)

He is the sun in the heaven, the air in the sky, the fire on the earth, the guest in the sacrificial jar (house). He is living in man, in gods, in sacrifice and in the sky. He is born in water, in earth, in mountains and in sacrifice. He is the true and the great.

ऊर्ध्वं   प्राणमुन्नयत्यपानं प्रत्यगस्यति ।
मध्ये वामनमासीनं विश्वे देवा उपासते ॥ 3 ॥

Oordhvam Praanamunnayati Apaanam Pratyagasyati; Madhye Vaamanamaaseenam Vishve Devaa Upaasate. (3)

He sends prana upwards and throws apana downwards. All gods worship that adorable one seated in the centre.

अस्य विस्रंसमानस्य शरीरस्थस्य देहिन: ।
देहिद्विमुच्यमानस्य किमत्र परिशिष्यते ॥ एतद्वै तत् ॥ 4 ॥

*Asya Visramsamaanasya Shareerasthasya Dehinah; Dehaad
Vimuchyamaanasya Kimatra Parishishyate. Etadvai Tat. (4)*

When this Atman, the dweller in the body, leaves the body,
what indeed remains in the body? This is verily That.

न प्राणेन नापानेन मर्त्यो जीवति कश्चन ।
इतरेण तु जीवन्ति यस्मिन्नेतावुपाश्रितौ ॥ 5 ॥

*Na Praanena Naapaanena Martyo Jeevati Kashchana; Itarena
Tu Jeevanti Yasminnetaavupaashritau. (5)*

No mortal lives by prana and apana (inflowing and outflowing
breath), but there is some other on whom these two depend
and all live.

हन्त ते इदं प्रवक्ष्यामि गुह्यं ब्रह्म सनातनम् ।
यथा च मरणं प्राप्य आत्मा भवति गौतम ॥ 6 ॥

*Hanta Te Idam Pravakshyaami Guhyam Brahma Sanaatanam;
Yathaa Cha Maranam Praapya Aatmaa Bhavati Gautama. (6)*

I shall explain further, O Nachiketa, the mysterious, eternal
Brahman and what happens to the Self after death.

योनिमन्ये प्रपद्यन्ते शरीरत्वाय देहिन: ।
स्थाणुमन्येऽनुसंयन्ति यथाकर्म यथाश्रुतम् ॥ 7 ॥

*Yonimanye Prapadyante Shareeratvaaya Dehinah; Sthaanumanye
Anusanyanti Yathaakarma Yathaashrutam. (7)*

According to their karma and evolution, souls enter a womb
to take bodily form, or they enter into plant life.

133

य एष सुप्तेषु जागर्ति कामं कामं पुरुषो निर्मिमाण: ।
तदेव शुक्रं तद् ब्रह्म तदेवामृतमुच्यते ॥
तस्मिँल्लोका: श्रिता: सर्वे तदु नात्येति कश्चन ।
एतद् वै तत् ॥ 8 ॥

Ya Esha Supteshu Jaagarti Kaamam Kaamam Purusho Nirmimaanah; Tadeva Shukram Tad Brahma Tadevaamrita-muchyate. Tasminllokaah Shritaah Sarve Tadu Naatyeti Kashchana; Etad Vai Tat. (8)

The Purusha, who remains awake while all sleep, creates all kinds of desires. He is verily called the Pure, the Brahman, the Immortal. He is the support of all the worlds, and no one goes beyond That. This is verily That.

अग्निर्यथैको भुवनं प्रविष्टो
रूपं रूपं प्रतिरूपो बभूव ।
एकस्तथा सर्वभूतान्तरात्मा
रूपं रूपं प्रतिरूपो बहिश्च ॥ 9 ॥

Agniryathaiko Bhuvanam Pravishto Roopam Roopam Pratiroopo Babhoova; Ekastathaa Sarvabhootaantaraatmaa Roopam Roopam Pratiroopo Bahishcha. (9)

Just as fire, though one, having entered the world, adopts the shapes of the different objects it burns, similarly, the one Atman of all living things, though one, assumes the forms of the various objects He enters (as breath), and He exists also beyond.

वायुर्यथैको भुवनं प्रविष्टो रूपं रूपं प्रतिरूपो बभूव ।
एकस्तथा सर्वभूतान्तरात्मा रूपं रूपं प्रतिरूपो बहिश्च ॥ 10 ॥

Vaayuryathaiko Bhuvanam Pravishto Roopam Roopam Pratiroopo Babhoova; Ekastathaa Sarvabhootaantaraatmaa Roopam Roopam Pratiroopo Bahishcha. (10)

Just as the air, though one, having entered the world, adopts the shapes of the different objects it enters, similarly, the one Atman of all living things, though one, assumes the forms of the various objects He enters, and He also exists beyond.

सूर्यो यथा सर्वलोकस्य चक्षुर्न लिप्यते चाक्षुषैर्बाह्यदोषैः ।
एकस्तथा सर्वभूतान्तरात्मा न लिप्यते लोकदुःखेन बाह्यः ॥ 11 ॥

Sooryo Yathaa Sarvalokasya Chakshuh Na Lipyate Chaakshu-shairbaahyadoshaih; Ekastathaa Sarvabhootaantaraatmaa Na Lipyate Lokaduhkhena Baahyah. (11)

Just as the sun, the eye of the universe, is not at all affected by the defects of the eye or the external impurities of the objects, similarly, the one Atman abiding in all living things is not the least affected by the miseries of the world.

एको वशी सर्वभूतान्तरात्मा एकं रूपं बहुधा यः करोति ।
तमात्मस्थं येऽनुपश्यन्ति धीरास्तेषां सुखं शाश्वतं नेतरेषाम् ॥ 12 ॥

Eko Vashee Sarvabhootaantaraatmaa Ekam Roopam Bahudhaa Yah Karoti; Tamaatmastham Yeanupashyanti Dheeraasteshaam Sukham Shaashvatam Netareshaam. (12)

The supreme ruler and soul of all living things is One, and out of His Oneness He makes the various forms. Those wise men who realize Him within their Self enjoy infinite bliss, and none else.

नित्यो नित्यानां चेतनश्चेतनाना-
मेको बहूनां यो विदधाति कामान् ।
तमात्मस्थं येऽनुपश्यन्ति धीरा-
स्तेषां शान्तिः शाश्वती नेतरेषाम् ॥ 13 ॥

Nityo Nityaanaam Chetanashchetanaanaam Eko Bahoonaam Yo Vidadhaati Kaamaan; Tamaatmastham Yeanupshyanti Dheeraah Teshaam Shaantih Shaashvatee Netareshaam. (13)

The wise, who realize the Self as the everlasting among those who seem to be constant, the consciousness of the conscious which, though one, accomplishes the desires of the many, and as living within their Self, enjoy eternal peace, and none else.

तदेतदिति मन्यन्तेऽनिर्देश्यं परमं सुखम् ।
कथं नु तद्विजानीयां किमु भाति विभाति वा ॥ 14 ॥

Tadetaditi Manyante Anirdeshyam Paramam Sukham; Katham Nu Tadvijaaneeyaam Kimu Bhaati Vibhaati Vaa. (14)

The sages realize that indescribable supreme joy in This is That. How shall I know That? Is its splendour its own, or does it reflect the glory of another?

न तत्र सूर्यो भाति न चन्द्रतारकं
    नेमा विद्युतो भान्ति कुतोऽयमग्नि: ।
तमेव भान्तमनुभाति सर्वं
    तस्य भासा सर्वमिदं विभाति ॥ 15 ॥

Na Tatra Sooryo Bhaati Na Chandrataarakam Nemaa Vidyuto Bhaanti Kutoayamagnih; Tameva Bhaantamanubhaati Sarvam Tasya Bhaasaa Sarvamidam Vibhaati. (15)

The light of the sun does not go there, nor of the moon, stars or lightning, and least of all of fire. When He shines, everything shines. By His light all this is lit.

SECTION 2: PART III

ऊर्ध्वमूलोऽवाक्शाख   एषोऽश्वत्थ: सनातन: ।
तदेव   शुक्रं   तद्   ब्रह्म   तदेवामृतमुच्यते ।
तस्मिँल्लोका: श्रिता: सर्वे तदु नात्येति कश्चन । एतद्वै तत् ॥ 1 ॥

Oordhvamooloavaakshaakha Eshoashvatthah Sanaatanah; Tadeva
Shukram Tad Brahma Tadevaamritamuchyate; Tasminllokaah
Shritaah Sarve Tadu Naatyeti Kashchana. Etad Vai Tat. (1)

This is that ancient ashvattha tree whose roots are above
and branches below. That is verily the Pure, the Brahman,
the Immortal. All the worlds derive from That, and none go
beyond That. This is verily That.

यदिदं किं च जगत्सर्वं प्राण एजति नि:सृतम् ।
महद्भयं वज्रमुद्यतं य एतद्विदुरमृतास्ते भवन्ति ॥ 2 ॥

Yadidam Kim Cha Jagat Sarvam Praana Ejati Nihsritam;
Mahadbhayam Vajramudyatam Ya Etad Viduramritaaste Bhavanti.
(2)

This entire universe emerged from the Brahman and moves
in prana, which is the supreme Brahman. He is terrible like
the raised thunderbolt. Those who know this become
immortal.

भयादस्याग्निस्तपति   भयात्   तपति   सूर्य: ।
भयादिन्द्रश्च   वायुश्च   मृत्युर्धावति पञ्चम: ॥ 3 ॥

Bhayaat Asyaagnistapati Bhayaat Tapati Sooryah;
Bhayaadindrashcha Vaayushcha Mrityurdhaavati Panchamah. (3)

From fear of the Brahman fire burns, the sun gives light,
and from fear Indra, Vayu and Death, the fifth, fulfil their
tasks.

इह चेदशकद् बोद्धुं प्राक् शरीरस्य विस्रसः ।
ततः सर्गेसु लोकेषु शरीरत्वाय कल्पते ॥ 4 ॥

Iha Chedashakad Boddhum Praak Shareerasya Visrasah; Tatah Sargeshu Lokeshu Shareeratvaaya Kalpate. (4)

If one realizes Him before the fall of the body, he becomes free from the bondage of the world; otherwise he again takes bodily form in the worlds of creation.

यथाऽऽदर्शे तथाऽऽत्मनि यथा स्वप्ने तथा पितृलोके ।
यथाप्सु परीव ददृशे तथा गन्धर्वलोके छायातपयोरिव ब्रह्मलोके ॥ 5 ॥

Yathaa Aadarshe Tathaa Aatmani Yatha Svapne Tathaa Pitriloke; Yathaapsu Pareeva Dadrishe Tathaa Gandharvaloke Chhaayaatapayoriva Brahmaloke. (5)

Brahman is seen in the Self as in a mirror, in the world of the ancestors as in a dream, in the world of the gandharvas (celestial beings) as in water, and in the world of Brahman as light from shade.

इन्द्रियाणां पृथग्भावमुदयास्तमयौ च यत् ।
पृथगुत्पद्यमानानां मत्वा धीरो न शोचति ॥ 6 ॥

Indriyaanaam Prithagbhaavam Udayaastamayau Cha Yat; Prithagutpadyamaanaanaam Matvaa Dheero Na Shochati. (6)

A wise man, having known the distinct and separate nature of the senses and their active and dormant states, grieves no more.

इन्द्रियेभ्यः परं मनो मनसः सत्त्वमुत्तमम् ।
सत्त्वादधि महानात्मा महतोऽव्यक्तमुत्तमम् ॥ 7 ॥

Indriyebhyah Param Mano Manasah Sattvamuttamam; Sattvaadadhi Mahaanaatmaa Mahatoavyaktamuttamam. (7)

Beyond the senses is the mind, beyond the mind is the intellect and beyond the intellect is the great Atman. Superior to the great Atman is the Unmanifest.

अव्यक्तातु पर: पुरुषो व्यापकोऽलिङ्ग एव च ।
यं ज्ञात्वा मुच्यते जन्तुरमृतत्वं च गच्छति ॥ 8 ॥

Avyaktaat Tu Parah Purusho Vyaapakoalinga Eva Cha; Yam Jnaatvaa Muchyate Janturamritatvam Cha Bachchhati. (8)

And, verily, beyond the Unmanifest is the Supreme Purusha, all-pervading and aloof from attributes. One who knows Him becomes free and attains immortality.

न संदृशे तिष्ठति रूपमस्य
न चक्षुषा पश्यति कश्चनैनम् ।
हृदा मनीषा मनसाभिक्लृप्तो
य एतद् विदुरमृतास्ते भवन्ति ॥ 9 ॥

Na Sandrishe Tishthati Roopamasya Na Chakshushaa Pashyati Kashchanainam; Hridaa Maneeshaa Manasaabhiklripto Ya Etad Viduramritaaste Bhavanti. (9)

His form is beyond the power of vision. No one can see Him with the eyes. He is revealed by the pure intellect and the controlled mind, residing in the heart. Those who know Him become immortal.

यदा पञ्चावतिष्ठन्ते ज्ञानानि मनसा सह ।
बुद्धिश्च न विचेष्टति तामाहु:परमां गतिम् ॥ 10 ॥

Yadaa Panchaavatishthante Jnaanaani Manasaa Saha; Buddhishcha Na Vicheshtati Taamaahuh Paramaam Gatim. (10)

When the five senses of perception along with the mind are at rest, and even the intellect has ceased functioning, That, sages say, is the Supreme state.

तां योगमिति मन्यन्ते स्थिरामिन्द्रियधारणाम् ।
अप्रमत्तस्तदा भवति योगो हि प्रभवाप्ययौ ॥ 11 ॥

Taam Yogamiti Manyante Sthiraamindriyadhaaranaam;
Apramattastadaa Bhavati Yogo Hi Prabhavaapyayau. (11)

Firm control of the senses is called yoga. One must be ever
watchful, for yoga is hard to acquire and easy to lose.

नैव वाचा न मनसा प्राप्तुं शक्यो न चक्षुषा ।
अस्तीति ब्रुवतोऽन्यत्र कथं तदुपलभ्यते ॥ 12 ॥

Naiva Vaachaa Na Manasaa Praaptum Shakyo Na Chakshushaa;
Asteeti Bruvatoanyatra Katham Tadupalabhyate. (12)

That Atman cannot be reached by speech, nor by the eyes,
nor even by the mind. How can That be realized but by
those who say He exists?

अस्तीत्येवोपलब्धव्यस्तत्त्वभावेन चोभयो: ।
अस्तीत्येवोपलब्धस्यय तत्त्वभाव: प्रसीदति ॥ 13 ॥

Asteetyevopalabdhavyah Tattvabhaavena Chobhayoh; Asteetyevo-
patabdhasya Tattvabhaavah Praseedaati. (13)

The Self should be known as existing by faith, and as He
really is. To one who approaches Him through faith, His
true nature becomes revealed.

यदा सर्वे प्रमुच्यन्ते कामा येऽस्य हृदि श्रिता: ।
अथ मर्त्योऽमृतो भवत्यत्र ब्रह्म समश्नुते ॥ 14 ॥

Yadaa Sarve Pramuchyante Kaamaa Yeasya Hridi Shritaah; Atha
Martyoamrito Bhavatyatra Brahma Samashnute. (14)

When all desires that adhere to the heart are released here
on earth, then the mortal becomes immortal and attains
Brahman even here.

यदा सर्वे प्रभिद्यन्ते हृदयस्येह ग्रन्थयः ।
अथ मर्त्योऽमृतो भवत्येतावद्ध्यनुशासनम् ॥ 15 ॥

Yadaa Sarve Prabhidyante Hridayasyeha Granthayah; Atha Martyoamrito Bhavatyetaavaddhyanushaasanam. (15)

When all the knots of the heart are released here on earth, then the mortal becomes immortal. This is the teaching (of Vedanta).

शतं चैका च हृदयस्य नाड्य-
स्तासां मूर्धानमभिनिःसृतैका ।
तयोर्ध्वमायन्नमृतत्वमेति
विष्वङ्ङन्या उत्क्रमणे भवन्ति ॥ 16 ॥

Shatam Chaikaa Cha Hridayasya Naadyastaasaam Moordhaanam Abhinih Sritaikaa; Tayordhvamaayannamritatvameti Vishvan-nanyaa Utkramane Bhavanti. (16)

A hundred and one nerves emerge from the heart. Of them, one goes towards the crown of the head. When a man goes upwards by it, he attains immortality, but the other nerves lead different ways.

अङ्गुष्ठमात्रः पुरुषोऽन्तरात्मा
सदा जनानां हृदये सन्निविष्टः ।
तं स्वाच्छरीरात्प्रवृहेन्मुञ्जादिवेषीकां धैर्येण
तं विद्याच्छुक्रममृतं विद्याच्छुक्रममृतमिति ॥ 17 ॥

Angushthamaatrah Purushoantaraatmaa Sadaa Janaanam Hridaye Sannivishtah Tam Svaachchhareeraat Pravrihen-munjaadivesheekaam Dhairyena Tam Vidyaachchhukramamritam Vidyaachchhukramamritamiti. (17)

The Purusha, the size of a thumb, the inner Self, abides ever in the heart of all living things. One should separate Him from the body patiently, as pith from the reed. One should know Him as pure and immortal.

मृत्युप्रोक्तां नचिकेतोऽथ लब्ध्वा
विद्यामेतां योगविधिं च कृत्स्नम् ।
ब्रह्मप्राप्तो विरजोऽभूद्विमृत्यु-
रन्योऽप्येवं यो विदध्यात्ममेव ॥ 18 ॥

Mrityuproktaam Nachiketoatha Labdhvaa Vidyaametaam Yoga-vidhim Cha Kritsnam; Brahmapraapto Virajoabhood Vimrityuh Anyoapyevam Yo Vidadhyaatmameva. (18)

Nachiketa, having received this thorough instruction from Yama, and also the teaching of yoga, became free of all impurity and death and attained Brahman. Anyone who thus knows the inner Self can likewise attain Brahman.

SHANTI PATH

ॐ सह नाववतु । सह नौ भुनक्तु । सह वीर्यं करवावहै । तेजास्व
नावधीतमस्तु । मा विद्विषावहै ॥

ॐ शान्ति: शान्ति शान्ति

Om Saha Naavavatu; Saha Nau Bhunaktu; Saha Veeryam Karavaavahai; Tejasvi Naavadheetamastu; Maa Vidvishaavahai.

Om Shaantih Shaantih Shaantih.

Om. May the Lord protect both teacher and disciple, and may He cherish us both. May we work with full energy, that our study be perfect and give good results. May we never feel ill will toward the other.

Om peace, peace, peace.

Aitareya Upanishad

This short Upanishad is the part of the fourth, fifth and sixth chapters of the second Aranyaka of Aitareya Brahmana. The earlier portions of the same deal with karma along with meditation. The latter portion, mentioned in this Upanishad, directly deals with the true knowledge of Brahman, the Supreme Self, one without a second, and His identity with the individual Self.

As stated in the Vedas, in the beginning there is no creation except Atman, and that creation is willed by Him only. This whole universe is nothing but the projection of His will, based on pure consciousness; therefore, consciousness is Brahman. He has made it, right from Indra, the ruler of the gods, and Prajapati, the protector, to the smallest gross creation. He is everywhere, but devoid of all characteristics of the world, such as names, forms, activities, waking, dreaming and deep sleep states. He is fearless, decayless and deathless. To attain the Absolute, which is the chief aim of life, is not possible by any means other than true knowledge of the secondless Self. One possessing a deep, direct realization of this Atman obtains immortality.

This Upanishad, in short, is a guide to all seekers of Brahma Vidya who want to be freed from vice, passion and all sorts of impurities, and enjoy immortal bliss through knowledge of the Self.

SHANTI PATH

ॐ वाङ् मे मनसि प्रतिष्ठिता मनो मे वाचि प्रतिष्ठितमाविरावीर्म एधि ।
वेदस्य म आणीस्थः श्रुतं मे मा प्रहासीः । अनेनाधीतेनाहोरात्रान्सं-दधाम्यृतं
वदिष्यामि । सत्यं वदिष्यामि तन्मामवतु । तद्वक्तारमवतु । अवतु मामवतु
वक्तारमवतु वक्तारम् ॥

ॐ शान्तिः शान्ति : शान्तिः

Om Vaan Me Manasi Pratishthitaa Mano Me Vaachi Pratishthitam
Aaviraaveerma Edhi; Vedasya Ma Aaneesthah Shrutam Me Maa
Prahaaseeh; Anenaadheetena Ahoraatraan Sandadhaamyritam
Vadishyaami; Satyam Vadishyaami Tanmaamavatu; Tadvak-
taaramavatu; Avatumaamavatu Vaktaaram Avatu Vaktaaram.

Om Shaantih Shaantih Shaantih.

Om. May my speech be fixed upon my mind and may my
mind be fixed upon my speech. O Self-luminous Brahman,
be Thou revealed to me. May both mind and speech make
me able to understand the truth of the Vedas. May the
Vedic truth be ever present in me. Day and night I shall
dedicate to this endeavour. I shall think the truth and I shall
speak the truth. May That (Brahman) protect me. May He
protect the teacher. May He protect me. May He protect the
teacher.

Om peace, peace, peace.

SECTION 1: PART I

ॐ आत्मा वा इदमेक एवाग्र आसीत् । नान्यत्किंचन मिषत् । स ईक्षत
लोकान्नु सृजा इति ॥ 1 ॥

*Om Aatmaa Vaa Idameka Evaagra Aaseet; Naanyat Kinchana
Mishat; Sa Eekshata Lokaannu Srijaa Iti. (1)*

Verily, in the beginning this was all Atman alone, One
without a second. Atman thought to Himself: Let me create
the world.

स इमाँल्लोकानसृजत । अम्भो मरीचीर्मरमापोऽदोऽम्भः परेण दिवं द्यौः
प्रतिष्ठान्तरिक्षं मरीचयः पृथिवी मरो या अधस्तात्ता आपः ॥ 2 ॥

*Sa Imaanllokaanasrijata; Ambho Mareecheermaramaapoadoam-
bhah Parena Divam Dyauh Pratishthaaaantariksham Mareechayah
Prithivee Maro Yaa Adhastaattaa Aapah. (2)*

He created the worlds: Ambhas, the highest heaven; Marichi
(rays of light); Maram (death), the water. This water is above
the heaven. The heaven is its support, light rays are in the
space between (the earth and heaven). Earth is death. That
which is below is the water.

स ईक्षतेमे नु लोका लोकपालान्नु सृजा इति सोऽद्भ्य एव पुरुषं
समुद्धृत्यामूर्छयत् ॥ 3 ॥

*Sa Eekshateme Nu Lokaa Lokapaalaannu Srijaa Iti Soadbhya
Eva Purusham Samuddhritya Amoorchhayat. (3)*

And Atman thought: Here indeed are the created worlds.
Let me now create caretakers for them. He then made from
the waters (the five elements) the model of a human, giving
it the proper shape.

तमभ्यतपत्तस्याभितप्तस्य मुखं निरभिद्यत यथाण्डं मुखाद्वाग् वाचोऽग्निर्नासिके निरभिद्येतां नासिकाभ्यां प्राण: प्राणाद्वायुरक्षिणी निरभिद्येतामक्षिभ्यां चक्षुश्चक्षुष आदित्य: कर्णौ निरभिद्येतां कर्णाभ्यां श्रोत्रं श्रोत्रादिशस्त्वङ् निरभिद्यत त्वचो लोमानि लोमभ्य ओषधिवनस्पतयो हृदयं निरभिद्यत हृदयान्मनो मनसश्चन्द्रमा नाभिर्निरभिद्यत नाभ्या अपानोऽपानान्मृत्यु: शिश्नं निरभिद्यत शिश्नाद्रेतो रेतस आप: ॥ 4 ॥

Tamabhyatapat Tasyaabhitaptasya Mukham Nirabhidyata
Yathaandam Mukhaadvaag Vaachoagnirnaasike Nirabhidyetaam
Naasikaabhyaam Praanah Praanaadvaayurakshinee
Nirabhidyetaamakshibhyaam Chakshushchakshusha Aadityah
Karnau Nirabhidyetaam Karnaabhyaam Shrotram
Shrotraaddishastvan Nirabhidyata Tvacho Lomaani Lomabhya
Oshadhivanaspatayo Hridayam Nirabhidyata Hridayaanmano
Manasashchandramaa Naabhirnirabhidyata Naabhyaa Apaano-
apaanaan Mrityuh Shishnam Nirabhidyata Shishnaadreto Retasa
Aapah. (4)

And Atman brooded over this creation like an egg, and the mouth issued from it. From the mouth came speech and from speech, fire. The two nostrils formed. From the nostrils came the faculty of smell and from the faculty of smell, prana, and from prana came air. The eyes separated off. From the eyes came the power of vision and from vision, the sun. The ears departed. From the ears came the faculty of hearing, and from hearing, the four directions. The skin formed. From skin came the sense of touch and hair, and from hair, herbs and trees. The heart came away and from the heart came mind and from mind, the moon. The navel emerged; from the navel came apana (expiration) and from apana, death. The generative organ formed and from that organ came seed, and from seed, water.

147

SECTION 1: PART II

ता एता देवता: सृष्टा अस्मिन् महत्यर्णवे प्रापतंस्तम-
शनायापिपासाभ्यामन्ववार्जत् ता एनमब्रुवन्नायतनं न: प्रजानीहि यस्मिन्
प्रतिष्ठिता अन्नमदामेति ॥ 1 ॥

*Taa Etaa Devataah Srishtaa Asmin Mahatyarnave Praapatans Tam
Tam Ashanaayaapipaasaabhyaam Anvavaarjat; Taa
Enamabruvannaayatanam Nah Prajaaneehi Yasmin Pratishthitaa
Annamadaameti. (1)*

Thus created, these Gods, the caretakers of this universe,
fell into this great endless ocean. The Lord subjected the
whole body (virat) to hunger and thirst, and the Gods
prayed to the Lord that they might be provided with a place
where they could live and eat.

ताभ्यो गामानयत्ता अब्रुवन्न वै नोऽयमलमिति ताभ्योऽश्वमानयत्ता अब्रुवन्न
वै नोऽयमलमिति ॥ 2 ॥

*Taabhyo Gaamaanayattaa Abruvanna Vai Noayamalamiti
Taabhyoashvamaanayattaa Abruvanna Vai Noayamalamiti. (2)*

He showed them the form of a cow and they said: This is
not sufficient for us. Then He showed them the form of a
horse and they said: This also is not sufficient for us.

ताभ्य: पुरुषमानयत्ता अब्रुवन् सुकृतं बतेति । पुरुषो वाव सुकृतम् । ता
अब्रवीद्यथायतनं प्रविशतेति ॥ 3 ॥

*Taabhyah Purushamaanayattaa Abruvan Sukritam Bateti; Purusho
Vaava Sukritam; Taa Abraveedyathaayatanam Pravishateti. (3)*

Then He showed them the form of a man and they were
glad and said: This is indeed a good form. Man is really the
image of God Himself. And He told them: Enter and occupy
your respective places.

148

अग्निर्वाग्भूत्वा मुखं प्राविशद्वायु: प्राणो भूत्वा नासिके प्राविशदादि-
त्यश्चक्षुर्भूत्वाक्षिणी प्राविशद्दिश: श्रोत्रं भूत्वा कर्णौ प्राविशन्नोषधिवनस्पतयो
लोमानि भूत्वा त्वचं प्राविशंश्चन्द्रमा मनो भूत्वा हृदयं प्राविशन्मृत्युरपानो
भूत्वा नाभिं प्रविशदापो रेतो भूत्वा शिश्नं प्राविशन् ॥ ४ ॥

*Agnirvaagbhootvaa Mukham Praavishadvaayuh Praano Bhootvaa
Naasike Praavishat Aadityashchakshurbhootvaa Akshinee
Praavishaddishah Shrotram Bhootvaa Karnau Praavishann
Oshadhivanaspatayo Lomaani Bhootvaa Tvacham Praavishansh-
chandramaa Mano Bhootvaa Hridayam Praavishanmrityurapaano
Bhootvaa Naabhim Pravishadaapo Reto Bhootvaa Shishnam
Praavishan. (4)*

Then fire entered the mouth as speech; air entered the
nostrils as prana; the sun entered the eyes as vision; the
deities of the four directions entered the ears as hearing; the
deities of plants and trees entered the skin as hair; the moon
entered the heart as mind; death entered the navel as apana
(expiration); water entered the generative organ as seed.

तमशनायापिपासे अब्रुतामावाभ्यामभिप्रजानीहीति। ते अब्रवीदेतास्वेव वां
देवतास्वाभजाम्येतासु भागिन्यौ करोमीति। तस्माद्यस्यै कस्यै च देवतायै
हविर्गृह्यते भागिन्यावेवास्यामशनायापिपासे भवत: ॥ ५ ॥

*Tamashanaayaapipaase Abrutaamaavaabhyaam Abhiprajaaneeheeti.
Te Abraveedetaasveva Vaam Devataasvaabhajaamyetaasu
Bhaaginyau Karomeeti. Tasmaadyasyai Kasyai Cha Devataayai
Havirgrihyate Bhaaginyaaveva Asyaamashanaayaapipaase
Bhavatah. (5)*

Then hunger and thirst said to Him: Grant a place for us.
And He replied: I grant you to these Gods and make you
sharers in them. This is why, whenever oblation is offered to
any of these Gods, hunger and thirst verily become
shareholders in it.

SECTION 1: PART III

स ईक्षतेमे नु लोकाश्च लोकपालाश्चान्नमेभ्य: सृजा इति ॥ 1 ॥

Sa Eekshateme Nu Lokaashcha Lokapaalaashcha Annamebhyah Srijaa Iti. (1)

Then the Creator thought: Here are the worlds and their respective caretaker deities. Let me create food for them.

सोऽपोऽभ्यतपत्ताभ्योऽभितप्ताभ्यो मूर्तिरजायत। या वै सा मूर्तिरजायतान्नं वै तत् ॥ 2 ॥

Soapo Abhyatapat Taabhyah Abhitaptaabhyo Moortirajaayata; Yaa Vai Saa Moortirajaayataannam Vai Tat. (2)

And He brooded over the waters (the elements) and from the water so brooded over issued form, which is verily the food.

तदेनत् सृष्टं पराङत्यजिघांसत्तद्वाचाजिघृक्षत्तन्नाशक्नोद्वाचाग्रहीतुम् यद्धैनद्वाचाग्रहैष्यदभिव्याहृत्य हैवान्नमत्रप्स्यत् ॥ 3 ॥

Tadenat Srishtam Paraan Atyajighaansattadvaachaa Ajighrikshat Tannaashaknodvaachaa Graheetum Yaddhainadvaachaa Agrahaishyat Abhivyaakritya Haivaannam Atrapsyat. (3)

This created food tried to flee from fear. He tried to catch hold of it with speech, but with no success. Had He been successful in catching hold of it with speech, then, merely by talking about food, everyone would become satisfied.

तत्प्राणेनाजिघृक्षत्तन्नाशक्नोत्प्राणेन ग्रहीतुं स यद्धैनत्प्राणेनाग्रहैष्यदभिप्राण्य हैवान्नमत्रमत्रप्स्यत् ॥ 4 ॥

Tatpraanenaajighrikshat Tannaashaknotpraanena Graheetum Sa Yaddhainatpraanena Agrahaishyat Abhipraanya Haivaannam Atrapsyat. (4)

Then he sought to seize the food with the breath, but He could not seize it with the breath. Had He succeeded in seizing it with the breath, then everyone would become satisfied by merely smelling food.

तच्चक्षुषाजिघृक्षत्तन्नाशक्नोच्चक्षुषा ग्रहीतुं स यद्धैनच्चक्षुषाग्रहैष्यद् दृष्ट्वा हैवान्नमत्रप्स्यत् ॥ 5 ॥

Tachchakshushaa Ajighrikshat Tannaashaknot Chakshushaa Graheetum Sa Yaddhainat Chakshushaa Agrahaishyat Drishtvaa Haivaannam Atrapsyat. (5)

Then He wanted to take the food up with the eyes, but He could not do so. Had He taken it up with the eyes, then everyone would become satisfied merely by the sight of food.

तच्छ्रोत्रेणाजिघृक्षत्तन्नाशक्नोच्छ्रोत्रेण ग्रहीतुं स यद्धैनच्छ्रोत्रेणा ग्रहैष्यच्छ्रुत्वा हैवान्नमत्रप्स्यत् ॥ 6 ॥

Tachchhrotrena Ajighrikshat Tannaashaknot Shrotrena Graheetum Sa Yaddhainat Shrotrena Agrahaishyat Shrutvaa Haivaannam Atrapsyat. (6)

Then He tried to take in the food with the ears, but He could not do so. Had He taken the food in with the ears, then everyone would become satisfied by merely hearing about food.

तत्त्वचाजिघृक्षत्तन्नाशक्नोत्त्वचा ग्रहीतुं स यद्धैनत्त्वचाग्रहैष्यत्स्पृष्ट्वा हैवान्नमत्रप्स्यत् ॥ 7 ॥

Tattvachaajighrikshat Tannaashaknottvachaa Graheetum Sa Yaddhainattvachaagrahaishyat Sprishtvaa Haivaannam Atrapsyat. (7)

Then He tried to catch the food with the skin, but he could not do so. Had He caught it with the skin, then everyone would become satisfied by merely touching food.

तन्मनसाजिघृक्षत्तन्नाशक्नोन्मनसा ग्रहीतुं स यद्धैनन्मनसाग्रहैष्यद्ध्यात्वा हैवान्नमत्रप्स्यत् ॥ 8 ॥

Tanmanasaa Ajighrikshat Tannaashaknonmanasaa Graheetum Sa Yaddhainanmanasaa Agrahaishyat Dhyaatvaa Haivaannam Atrapsyat. (8)

Then He tried to grasp the food with the mind, but He could not do so. Had He succeeded in grasping it with the mind, then everyone would be satisfied merely by thinking about food.

तच्छिश्नेनाजिघृक्षत्तन्नाशक्नोच्छिश्नेन ग्रहीतुं स यद्धैनच्छिश्नेनाग्रहैष्यद्विसृज्य हैवान्नमत्रप्स्यत् ॥ 9 ॥

Tachchhishnena Ajighrikshat Tannaashaknot Shishnena Graheetum Sa Yaddhainachchhishnena Agrahaishyadvisrijya Haivaannam Atrapsyat. (9)

Then He wanted to take the food in with the generative organ, but He could not do so. Had He been able to take it in with the generative organ, people would be satisfied merely by ejecting food.

तदपानेनाजिघृक्षत्तदावयत् सेषोऽन्नस्य ग्रहो यद्वायुरन्नायुर्वा एष यद्वायुः ॥ 10 ॥

Tadapaanenaajighrikshat Tadaavayat Seshoannasya Graho yadvaayaurannaayurvaa Esha Yadvaayuh. (10)

Then He wanted to catch it by apana, and He caught it. Therefore, it is apana which catches food, and apana is the main support of life by means of food.

स ईक्षत कथं न्विदं मदृते स्यादिति स ईक्षत कतरेण प्रपद्या इति। स ईक्षत
यदि वाचाभिव्याहृतं यदि प्राणेनाभिप्राणितं यदि चक्षुषा दृष्टं यदि श्रोत्रेण
श्रुतं यदि त्वचा स्पृष्टं यदि मनसा ध्यातं यद्यपानेनाभ्यपानितं यदि शिश्नेन
विसृष्टमथ कोऽहमिति ॥ 11 ॥

*Sa Eekshata Katham Nvidam Madrite Syaaditi Sa Eekshata
Katarena Prapadyaa Iti; Sa Eekshata Yadi Vaachaabhivyaahritam
Yadi Praanenaabhipraanitam Yadi Chakshushaa Drishtam Yadi
Shrotrena Shrutam Yadi Tvachaa Sprishtam Yadi Manasaa
Dhyaatam Yadyapaanenaabhyapaanitam Yadi Shishnena Visrishtam
Atha Koahamiti. (11)*

The Creator thought: How can this (the body, senses, etc.)
function without me? Then He asked Himself: By which of
the two ways (head or feet) shall I enter the body. Then He
thought: If speech speaks, the eye sees, the skin feels, the
mind thinks, apana digests and the generative organ ejects,
who then am I?

स एतमेव सीमानं विदार्यैतया द्वारा प्रापद्यत। सैषा विदृतिर्नाम द्वास्तदेतन्ना-
न्दनम्। तस्य त्रय आवसथास्त्रयः स्वप्नाः अयमावसथोऽयमावसथोऽ-
यमावसथ इति ॥ 12 ॥

*Sa Etameva Seemaanam Vidaaryaitayaa Dvaaraa Praapadyata;
Saishaa Vidritirnaama Dvaastadetannaandanam; Tasya Traya
Aavasathaastrayah Svapnaah, Ayamaavasathah Ayamaavasathah
Ayamaavasatha Iti. (12)*

Having made a cut in the skull, He entered the body through
that door. Vidriti, the place of joy, is the name of that door.
He has three residing places or three dream states. This,
and this, and this is the residing place.

स जातो भूतान्यभिव्यैख्यत् किमिहान्यं वावदिषदिति। स एतमेव पुरुषं ब्रह्म
ततममपश्यत् । इदमदर्शमिती ॥ 13 ॥

Sa Jaato Bhootaanyabhivyaikhyat Kimihaanyam Vaavadishaditi;
Sa Etameva Purusham Brahma Tatamam Apashyat;
Idamodarshamitee. (13)

Thus born, He named all things, and thought: Can I name
anything else? Then He realized this very being as Brahman,
the all-pervading, and with wonder said: I have realized
Him.

तस्मादिदन्द्रो नामेदन्द्रो ह वै नाम तनिदन्द्रं सन्तमिन्द्र इत्याचक्षते परोक्षेण
परोक्षप्रिया इव हि देवा: परोक्षप्रिया इव हि देवा: ॥ 14 ॥

Tasmaadidandro Naamedandro Ha Vai Naama Tanidandram
Santamindra Ityaachakshate Parokshena Parokshapriyaa Iva Hi
Devaah Parokshapriyaa Iva Hi Devaah. (14)

Therefore, His name is Idandra (one who has seen). Though
He is known as Idandra, one who is Idandra is mysteriously
called Indra. The Gods verily like the mysterious. The Gods
verily like the mysterious.

SECTION 2: PART I

पुरुषे ह वा अयमादितो गर्भो भवति। यदेतद्रेत: तदेतत् सर्वेभ्योऽङ्गेभ्यस्तेज:
सम्भूतमात्मन्येवात्मानं बिभर्ति तद्यदा स्त्रियां सिञ्चत्यथैनज्जनयति तदस्य
प्रथमं जन्म ॥ 1 ॥

*Purushe Ha Vaa Ayamaadito Garbho Bhavati; Yadetadretah
Tadetat Sarvebhyoangebhyastejah Sambhootamaatmanyeva
Aatmaanam Bibharti Tadyadaa Striyaam Sinchatyathainajjanayati
Tadasya Prathamam Janma. (1)*

In man, the soul enters in the form of seed. In this seed is
the essence assembled from all the limbs. Man retains this
essence of his self within his body. When he sheds the seed
in woman he generates it, and this is his first birth.

तत्स्त्रिया आत्मभूतं गच्छति। यथा स्वमङ्गं तथा। तस्मादेनां न हिनस्ति।
सास्यैतमात्मानमत्रगतं भावयति ॥ 2 ॥

*Tatstriyaa Aatmabhootam Gachchhati; Yathaa Svamanga Tathaa;
Tasmaadenaam Na Hinasti; Saasyaitamaatmaanam Atragatam
Bhaavayati. (2)*

The seed changes and becomes like her own limb and
therefore it does not hurt her. She protects this self given to
her by him.

सा भावयित्री भावयितव्या भवति। तं स्त्री गर्भं बिभर्ति। सोऽग्र एव कुमारं
जन्मनोऽग्रेधिभावयति। स यत्कुमारं जन्मनीऽग्रेधिभावयत्यात्मानमेव
तद्भावयत्येषां लोकानां संतत्या। एवं संतता हीमे लोकास्तदस्य द्वितीयं जन्म
॥ 3 ॥

*Saa Bhaavayitree Bhaavayitavyaa Bhavati; Tam Stree Garbham
Bibharti; Soagra Eva Kumaaram Janmanoagredhibhaavayati; Sa
Yatkumaaram Janmanoagredhibhaavayatyaa Aatmaanameva*

155

Tadbhaavayatyeshaam Lokaanaam Santatyaa; Evam Santataa Heeme Lokaastadasya Dviteeyam Janma. (3)

She, as its protector, has to be protected. The mother bears the child in her womb and the father takes care of the child before and after its birth as his own self, so that this world of progeny can go on without stopping. This birth of a soul is his second birth.

सोऽस्यायमात्मा पुण्येभ्य: प्रतिधीयते। अथास्यायमितर आत्मा कृतकृत्यो वयोगत: प्रैति। स इत: प्रयन्नेव पुनर्जायते तदस्य तृतीयं जन्म ॥ ४ ॥

Soasyaayamaatmaa Punyebhyah Pratidheeyate; Athaasyaayamitara Aatmaa Kritakrityo Vayogatah Praiti; Sa Itah Prayanneva Punarjaayate Tadasya Triteeyam Janma. (4)

The son, who is the very self of his father, is posted in his place to continue his holy deeds. Then the other self (the father), having fully completed his duties and become old, departs from the world and is born again. This is his third birth.

तदुक्तमृषिणा–
गर्भे नु सन्नन्वेषामवेदमहं देवानां जनिमानि विश्वा ।
शतं मा पुर आयसीररक्षन्नध: श्येनो जवसा निरदीयमिति ।
गर्भ एवैतच्छयानो वामदेव एवमुवाच ॥ ५ ॥

Taduktamrishinaa – Garbhe Nu Sannanveshaam Avedamaham Devaanaam Janimaani Vishvaa; Shatam Maa Pura Aaya-seerarakshannadhah Shyeno Javasaa Niradeeyamiti; Garbha Evaitachchhayaano Vaamadeva Evamuvaacha. (5)

This fact of the Highest Reality is stated by sage Vamadeva in the following Vedic verse: "While existing in the womb, I understood the births (of all the Gods). A hundred iron-strong bodies held me down, but I came out like a hawk, by force (merely through knowledge of the Self)." While in the mother's womb, Vamadeva asserted this fact.

स एवं विद्वानस्माच्छरीरभेदादूर्ध्व उत्क्रम्यामुष्मिन् स्वर्गे लोके सर्वान्कामानाप्त्वामृत: समभवत् समभवत् ॥ ६ ॥

Sa Evam Vidvaan Asmaachchhareerabhedaat Oordhva Utkram-yaamushmin Svarge Loke Sarvaan Kaamaan Aaptvaamritah Samabhavat Samabhavat. (6)

One who has known accordingly becomes one with Him, shining with the highest knowledge of the Self, after the fulfilment of all his desires here on Earth. He becomes immortal after the fall of the body in the world of the Self. Verily he becomes immortal.

कोऽयमात्मेति वयमुपास्महे। कतर: स आत्मा, येन वा पश्यति येन वा
शृणोति येन वा गन्धानाजिघ्रति येन वा वाचं व्याकरोति येन वा स्वादु
चास्वादु च विजानाति ॥ 1 ॥

*Koayamaatmeti Vayamupaasmahe; Katarah Sa Aatmaa, Yena Vaa
Pashyati Yena Vaa Shrinoti Yena Vaa Gandhaanaajighrati Yena
Vaa Vaacham Vyaakaroti Yena Vaa Svaadu Chaasvaadu Cha
Vijaanaati. (1)*

Who is He we adore as Atman? Is Atman the higher or lower
Brahman? Is Atman that through which one sees forms,
hears sound, smells odours, utters speech, and knows sweet
from sour?

यदेतद्‌हृदयं मनश्चैतत्‌। संज्ञानमाज्ञानं विज्ञानं प्रज्ञानं मेधा दृष्टिर्धृतिर्मतिर्मनीषा
जूति: स्मृति: संकल्प: क्रतुरसु: कामो वश इति सर्वाण्येवैतानि प्रज्ञानस्य
नामधेयानि भवन्ति ॥ 2 ॥

*Yadetaddhridayam Manashchaitat; Samjnaanamaajnaanam
Vijnaanam Prajnaanam Medhaa Drishtirdhritirmatirmaneeshaa
Jootih Smritih Sankalpah Kraturasuh Kaamo Vasha Iti
Sarvaanyevaitaani Prajnaanasya Naamadheyaani Bhavanti. (2)*

The heart and mind are but one, as That. Consciousness,
control, prudence, intelligence, retention, vision, steadiness,
thinking, genius, depression, memory, resolution, determination, vitality, attachment, love – all these are only the
names of consciousness.

एष ब्रह्मैष इन्द्र एष प्रजापतिरेते सर्वे देवा इमानि च पञ्च महाभूतानि पृथिवी
वायुराकाश आपो ज्योतींषीत्येतानीमानि च क्षुद्रमिश्राणीव बीजानीतराणि
चेतराणि चाण्डजानि च जारुजानि च स्वेदजानि चोद्भिज्जानि चाश्वा गाव:
पुरुषा हस्तिनो यत्किंचेदं प्राणि जङ्गमं च पत्रि च यच्च स्थावरं सर्वं
तत्प्रज्ञानेत्रम्‌। प्रज्ञाने प्रतिष्ठितं प्रज्ञानेत्रो लोक: प्रज्ञा प्रतिष्ठा प्रज्ञानं ब्रह्म ॥ 3 ॥

Esha Brahmaisha Indra Esha Prajaapatirete Sarve Devaa Imaani Cha Pancha Mahaabhootaani Prithivee Vaayuraakaasha Aapo Jyoteensheetyetaaneemaani Cha Kshudramishraaneeva Beeja-aneetaraani Chetaraani Chaandajaani Cha Jaarujaani Cha Svedajaani Chodbhijjaani Chaashvaa Gaavah Purushaa Hastino Yatkinchedam Praani Jangamam Cha Patatri Cha Yachcha Sthaavaram Sarvam Tatprajnaanetram. Prajnaane Pratishthitam Prajnaanetro Lokah Prajnaa Pratishthaa Prajnaanam Brahma.
(3)

Brahma, Indra, Prajapati and other Gods are this, and the five great elements: space, air, fire, earth and water, and light, and large and small creatures; born from egg, from womb, from sweat, and from shoot; horse and cow, man and elephant, and all living beings that walk, fly, or do not move – all these are directed by consciousness. The entire universe is based on consciousness. Therefore, consciousness is Brahman.

स एतेन प्रज्ञेनात्मनास्माल्लोकादुत्क्रम्यामुष्मिन्स्वर्गे लोके सर्वान् कामानाप्त्वामृतः समभवत्समभवत् ॥ 4 ॥

Sa Etena Prajnena Aatmanaa Smaallokaat Utkramya Amushmin Svarge Loke Sarvaan Kaamaanaaptvaa Amritah Samabhavat Samabhavat. (4)

One who has experienced Atman in this way, having gone beyond this world and having fulfilled all his desires in the world of bliss, attains immortality. Verily he attains immortality.

SHANTI PATH

ॐ वाङ् मे मनसि प्रतिष्ठिता मनो मे वाचि प्रतिष्ठितमाविरावीर्म एधि ।
वेदस्य म आणीस्थः श्रुतं मे मा प्रहासीः । अनेनाधीतेनाहोरात्रान्सं-दधाम्यृतं
वदिष्यामि । सत्यं वदिष्यामि तन्मामवतु । तद्वक्तारमवतु । अवतु मामवतु
वक्तारमवतु वक्तारम् ॥

ॐ शान्तिः शान्ति : शान्तिः

Om Vaan Me Manasi Pratishthitaa Mano Me Vaachi Pratishthitam
Aaviraaveerma Edhi; Vedasya Ma Aaneesthah Shrutam Me Maa
Prahaaseeh; Anenaadheetena Ahoraatraan Sandadhaamyritam
Vadishyaami; Satyam Vadishyaami Tanmaamavatu; Tadvak-
taaramavatu; Avatumaamavatu Vaktaaram Avatu Vaktaaram.

Om Shaantih Shaantih Shaantih.

Om. May my speech be fixed upon my mind and may my
mind be fixed upon my speech. O Self-luminous Brahman,
be Thou revealed to me. May both mind and speech make
me able to understand the truth of the Vedas. May the
Vedic truth be ever present in me. Day and night I shall
dedicate to this endeavour. I shall think the truth and I shall
speak the truth. May That (Brahman) protect me. May He
protect the teacher. May He protect me. May He protect the
teacher.

Om peace, peace, peace.

Shvetashvataropanishad

Shvestashvatara is not the real name of the Rishi, but it seems to be the honourable title which was given according to the custom in those days. Some split up this word as *shveta* – pure, *ashva* – senses, but according to others *shveta* means pure and *ashvatara* means mule. Either way, the figure of a great, enlightened sage comes before the eyes of the reader going through this short Upanishad of six chapters, having one hundred and thirteen verses (mantras).

No specific ideology or single philosophy is elaborated in this Upanishad, but a fine combination of philosophical, religious and other spiritual methods which seem to have been flowing at the time of its compilation. A portion of this Upanishad is given to the thoughts of Vedanta and its branches, some to Samkhya and Yoga, and some to jnana, bhakti and other such paths of spiritual life, which are all adjusted without the least conflict.

Those who adopt the path of their choice, as suggested, with sincerity and zeal, will cut the chain of the circle of birth and death.

SHANTI PATH

ॐ सह नाववतु। सह नौ भुनक्तु। सह वीर्यं करवावहै। तेजस्वि नावधीतमस्तु।
मा विद्विषावहै।

ॐ शान्ति: शान्ति: शान्ति:

Om Saha Naavavatu; Saha Nau Bhunaktu; Saha Veeryam
Karavaavahai; Tejasvinaavadheetamastu; Maa Vidvishaavahai.

Om Shaantih Shaantih Shaantih.

Om. May the Lord protect both teacher and disciple, and
may He cherish us both. May we work with full energy that
our study be perfect and give good results. May we never
feel ill will toward others.

Om peace, peace, peace.

CHAPTER I

हरि: ॐ ब्रह्मवादिनो वदन्ति-
किं कारणं ब्रह्म कुत: स्म जाता
जीवाम केन क्व च सम्प्रतिष्ठा: ।
अधिष्ठिता: केन सुखेतरेषु
वर्तामहे ब्रह्मविदो व्यवस्थाम् ॥ १ ॥

*Harih Om Brahmavaadino Vadanti – Kim Kaaranam Brahma
Kutah Sma Jaataa Jeevaama Kena Dva Cha Sampratishthaa;
Adhishthitaah Kena Sukhetareshu Vartaamahe Brahmavido
Vyavasthaam. (1)*

Some aspirants of Brahman, whilst discussing earnestly
amongst themselves, raised doubts regarding the mystery of
this creation. What is the reason for this creation? Why are
living beings born? Why do they survive? Where is their
abode? Under whose command do they live? Who controls
their suffering and happiness? Are there any rules to abide
by? Who knows the Brahman?

काल: स्वभावो नियतिर्यदृच्छा
भूतानि योनि: पुरुष इति चिन्त्या ।
संयोग एषां न त्वात्मभावा-
दात्माप्यनीश: सुखदु:खहेतो: ॥ २ ॥

*Kaalah Svavhaavo Niyatiryadrichchhaa Bhootaani Yonih Purusha
Iti Chintyaa; Samyoga Eshaam Na Twaatmabhaavaat Aatmaap-
yaneeshah Sukhadukhahetoh. (2)*

Neither time, nor nature, nor rules (law), nor will, nor
matter, nor energy, nor even a combination of all these, is
sufficient to consider as a cause, because they are all part
and parcel of the individual soul. Even the self is not master
of himself and not able to govern misery and happiness.

163

ते ध्यानयोगानुगता अपश्यन्
देवात्मशक्तिं स्वगुणैर्निगूढाम् ।
य: कारणानि निखिलानि तानि
कालात्मयुक्तान्यधितिष्ठत्येक: ॥ 3 ॥

*Te Dhyaanayogaanugataa Apashyan Devaatmashaktim
Svagunairnigoodhaam; Yah Kaaranaani Nikhilaani Taani
Kaalaatmayuktaani Adhistishthatyekah.* (3)

After starting the practice of meditation, they experienced
the Supreme Being hidden within as a self-shining power,
who is one without a second, who is the origin of the will,
emotions and intellect, who is the controller of all the
causes mentioned, starting with time and concluding with
the Self, but seeming to be limited due to everyone's
intellect.

तमेकनेमिं त्रिवृतं षोडशान्तं
शतार्धारं विंशतिप्रत्यराभि: ।
अष्टकै: षड्भिर्विश्वरूपैकपाशं
त्रिमार्गभेदं द्विनिमित्तैकमोहम् ॥ 4 ॥

*Tamekanemim Trivritam Shodashaantam Shataardhaaram
Vinshatipratyaraabhih; Ashtakaih Shadbhih Vishvaroopaikapaasham
Trimaargabhedam Dvinimittaikamoham.* (4)

We consider the Supreme Being as this universe, like a
wheel which has one circumference consisting of three tyres,
sixteen ends, fifty spokes, twenty counterspokes and six sets
of eight; one single but multifarious belt by which it is
driven in three separate directions; and its one delusion is
caused by two – happiness and misery.

पञ्चस्रोतोऽम्बुं पञ्चयोन्युग्रवक्रां
पञ्चप्राणोर्मिं पञ्चबुद्ध्यादिमूलाम् ।
पञ्चावर्तां पञ्चदुःखौघवेगां
पञ्चाशद्भेदां पञ्चपर्वामधीमः ॥ 5 ॥

Pancharotoambum Panchyonyugravakram Panchapraanormim Panchabuddhyadimoolaam; Panchaavartaam Panchaduhkhaughavegaam Panchaashadbhedaam Panchparvaamadheemah. (5)

We meditate on Him as a river of five streams, from five sources, fierce and crooked, whose waves are the five vital breaths, whose original source is the fivefold perception, with five whirlpools, an impetuous flood of five pains, divided into fifty kinds (of suffering) with five branches.

सर्वाजीवे सर्वसंस्थे बृहन्ते
अस्मिन् हंसो भ्राम्यते ब्रह्मचक्रे।
पृथगात्मानं प्रेरितारं च मत्वा
जुष्टस्ततस्तेनामृतत्वमेति ॥ 6 ॥

Sarvaajeeve Sarvasansthe Brihante Asmin Hanso Bhraamyate Brahmachakre; Prithagaatmaanam Preritaaram Cha Matvaa Jushtastatastena Amritatvameti. (6)

In this wheel of the universe all things live and rest. The travelling soul moves round with revolving force, considering his separate identity, but when he knows by himself harmony with the Supreme and is blessed by Him, he becomes immortal.

उद्गीतमेतत् परमं तु ब्रह्म
तस्मिंस्त्रयं सुप्रतिष्ठाक्षरं च ।
अत्रान्तरं ब्रह्मविदो विदित्वा
लीना ब्रह्मणि तत्परा योनिमुक्ताः ॥ 7 ॥

165

Udgeetametat Paramam Tu Brahma Tasminstrayam Supratish-
thaaksharam Cha Atraantaram Brahmavido Viditvaa Leenaa
Brahmani Tatparaa Yonimuktaah. (7)

This universe is clearly revealed by the Vedas as the Supreme Brahman, firmly upheld by the imperishable trio. Knowing this internal existence, knowers of the Vedas absolutely surrender themselves to Brahman and become free from the cycle of birth and death.

संयुक्तमेतत् क्षरमक्षरं च
व्यक्ताव्यक्तं भरते विश्वमीश: ।
अनीशश्चात्मा बध्यते भोक्तृभावा-
ज्ज्ञात्वा देवं मुच्यते सर्वपाशै: ॥ ८ ॥

Sanyuktametat Ksharamaksharam Cha Vyaktaavyaktam Bharate
Vishvameeshah Aneeshashcaatmaa Badhyate Bhoktibhaavaat
Jnaatvaa Devam Muchyate Sarvapaashaih. (8)

God upholds this universe, which is a union of the perishable and the imperishable, the clear and the unclear. As long as the self does not know God, he is bound and takes great pleasure in worldly affairs, but when He is known by the self, then he is free from all bondage.

ज्ञाज्ञौ द्वावजावीशनीशा-
वजा ह्येका भोक्तृभोग्यार्थयुक्ता ।
अनन्तश्चात्मा विश्वरूपो ह्यकर्ता
त्रयं यदा विन्दते ब्रह्ममेतत् ॥ ९ ॥

Jnaajnau Dvaavajaaveeshaneeshaav Ajaa Hyekaa Bhoktri-
bhogyaarthayukta; Anantashohaatmaa Vishvaroopo Hyakartaa
Trayam Yadaa Vindate Brahmametat. (9)

The conscious subject, the master, and the unconscious object, the dependant, both are unborn, and the third, who is busy keeping the relationship between these two, is also unborn. When the self realizes these as the Brahman, he becomes boundless, universal and free from all deeds.

क्षरं प्रधानममृताक्षरं हर:
क्षरात्मानावीशते देव एक: ।
तस्याभिध्यानाद् योजनात् तत्त्वभावाद्
भूयश्चान्ते विश्वमायानिवृति: ॥ 10 ॥

Ksharam Pradhaanam Amritaaksharam Harah Ksaharaat-
maanaaveeshate Deva Ekah; Tasyaabhidhyaanaad Yojanaat
Tattvabhaavaad Bhooyashchaante Vishvamaayaanivritih. (10)

Matter is perishable but God is imperishable and immortal. Perishable matter and individual souls are controlled by God only. When one meditates on Him, unites with Him and assimilates with Him, then at last he will be free from all illusions.

ज्ञात्वा देवं सर्वपाशापहानि:
क्षीणै: क्लेशैर्जन्ममृत्युप्रहाणि: ।
तस्याभिध्यानात् तृतीयं देहभेदे
विश्वैश्वर्यं केवल आप्तकाम: ॥ 11 ॥

Jnaatvaa Devam Sarvapaashaapahaanih Ksheenaih Kleshaih
Janmamrityupahaanih; Tasyaabhidhyaanaat Triteeyam Dehabhede
Vishvaishvaryam Kevala Aaptakaamah. (11)

Knowing God, all one's bondage will end and further births will cease. Whilst meditating on Him, his body consciousness will fall off and he will reach the third stage, the universal Lordship, when all his desires will be fulfilled and he will become One without a second.

एतद् ज्ञेयं नित्यमेवात्मसंस्थं
नात: परं वेदितव्यं हि किंचित् ।
भोक्ता भोग्यं प्रेरितारं च मत्वा
सर्वं प्रोक्तं त्रिविधं ब्रह्ममेतत् ॥ 12 ॥

Etad Jneyam Nityamevaatmasanstham Naatah Param Veditavyam Hi Kinchit; Bhoktaa Bhogyam Preritaaram Cha Matvaa Sarvam Proktam Trividham Brahmametat. (12)

This existing stage of knowing Brahman is always present in everyone's Self. There is nothing indeed to be known beyond That. The enjoyer, the enjoyed and the connecting power between the two, i.e. enjoyment – all are said to be the threefold aspect of Brahman.

वह्नेर्यथा योनिगतस्य मूर्तिर्न
दृश्यते नैव च लिङ्गनाश: ।
स भूय एवेन्धनयोनिगृह्य-
स्तद्वोभयं वै प्रणवेन देहे ॥ 13 ॥

Vahneryathaa Yonigatasya Moortirna Drishyate Naiva Cha Linganaashah; Sa Bhooya Evendhanayonigrihyah Tadvobhayam Vai Pranavena Dehe. (13)

Fire is not visible in a fire-stick, its original form, yet its subtle element is present in the source itself and can be obtained by striking it again. In the same way, the stage of Atman, before and after realization, is like that of the fire in the fire-stick. By meditating on the sound symbol Om, the Atman is revealed in the body, but actually it is there in a dormant state even before realization.

स्वदेहमरणिं कृत्वा प्रणवं चोत्तरारणिम् ।
ध्याननिर्मथनाभ्यासाद् देवं पश्येन्निगूढवत् ॥ 14 ॥

*Svadehamaranim Kritvaa Pranavam Chottaraaranim; Dhyaana-
nirmathanaabhyaasaad Devam Pashyennigoodhavat. (14)*

After making one's body the lower piece and the Pranava or
sound symbol the upper piece of wood, by the practice of
meditation one could reveal God as one obtains something
that is hidden.

तिलेषु तैलं दधनीव सर्पि-
राप: स्रोत:स्वरणीषु चाग्नि: ।
एवमात्माऽऽत्मनि गृह्यतेऽसौ
सत्येनैनं तपसा योऽनुपश्यति ॥ 15 ॥

*Tileshu Tailam Dadhaneeva Sarpih Aapah Srotahsvaraneeshu
Chaagnih; Evamaatmaa Aatmani Grihyateasau Satyenainam
Tapasaa Yoanupashyati. (15)*

Just as oil is in the whole sesame seed, butter in milk, water
in underground springs, fire in wood, so is the Self grasped
in one's own soul if one looks for Him with truthfulness and
austerity.

सर्वव्यापिनमात्मानं क्षीरे सर्पिरिवार्पितम् ।
आत्मविद्यातपोमूलं तद् ब्रह्मोपनिषत् परम्
तद् ब्रह्मोपनिषत् परम् ॥ 16 ॥

*Sarvavyaapinamaatmaanam Ksheere Sarpirivaarpitam;
Aatmavidyaatapomoolam Tad Brahmopanishat Param; Tad
Brahmopanishat Param. (16)*

The Self which pervades all things as butter is contained in
milk, which is the root of self-knowledge and austerity, That
is the Brahman and the destroyer of ignorance. That is the
Brahman and the destroyer of ignorance.

CHAPTER II

युञ्जान: प्रथमं मनस्तत्त्वाय सविता धिय: ।
अग्नेर्ज्योतिर्निचाय्य पृथिव्या अध्याभरत ॥ 1 ॥

Yunjaanah Prathamam Manastattvaaya Savitaa Dhiyah;
Agnerjyotirnichaayya Prithivyaa Adhayaabharata. (1)

Firstly, the mind and the senses are to be checked and
controlled in order to realize the eternal truth, and when
the light is discerned from the fire, the progressing soul is to
be brought out of the earth.

युक्तेन मनसा वयं देवस्य सवितु: सवे। सुवर्गेयाय शक्त्या ॥ 2 ॥

Yuktena Manasaa Vayam Devasya Savituh Save; Suvargeyaaya
Shaktyaa. (2)

We must control our mind to visualize that self-luminous
soul and shall try to attain the Supreme Bliss with full vigour.

युक्त्वाय मनसा देवान् सुवर्यतो धिया दिवम् ।
बृहज्ज्योति: करिष्यत: सविता प्रसुवाति तान् ॥ 3 ॥

Yuktvaaya Manasaa Devaan Suvaryato Dhiyaa Divam;
Brihajjyotih Karishyatah Savitaa Prasuvaati Taan. (3)

Keeping the extrovert tendency of the senses in order with
the help of the mind and intellect, the soul within keeps
them in the correct manner so as to see the self-luminous,
infinite light.

युञ्जते मन उत युञ्जते धियो
विप्रा विप्रस्य बृहतो विपश्चित: ।
वि होत्रा दधे वयुनाविदेक
इन्मही देवस्य सवितु: परिष्टुति: ॥ 4 ॥

Yunjate Mana Uta Yunjate Dhiyo Vipraa Viprasya Brihato Vipashchitah; Vi Hotraa Dadhe Vayunaavideka Inmahee Devasya Savituh Parishtutih. (4)

Such is the great glory of the great soul, who is all-pervading, infinite, all-knowing and self-luminous. Only a few wise men know this and adopt spiritual practices and strict discipline in life and meditation in order to control the multifarious activities of the intellect.

युजे वां ब्रह्म पूर्व्यं नमोभि-
विं श्लोक एतु पथ्येव सूरे: ।
श्रृण्वन्तु विश्वे अमृतस्य पुत्रा
आ ये धामानि दिव्यानि तस्थु: ॥ 5 ॥

Yuje Vaam Brahma Poorvyam Namobhirvi Shloka Etu Pathyeva Sooreh; Shrinvantu Vishve Amritasya Putraa Aa Ye Dhaamaani Divyaani Tasthuh. (5)

Adopting the way of the wise only, I assimilate you both (mind and intellect) in the ancient Brahman so as to prolong meditation. May the magnificent One reveal Himself. May the sons of eternal bliss, even though placed in the heavenly home, listen to me!

अग्निर्यत्राभिमथ्यते   वायुर्यत्राधिरुध्यते ।
सोमो यत्रातिरिच्यते तत्र संजायते मन: ॥ 6 ॥

Agniryatra Abhimathyate Vaayuryatra Adhirudhyate; Somo Yatra Atirichyate Tatra Sanjaayate Manah. (6)

Wherever the fire is stirred, the air is guided and the soma exceeds, there only the mind reaches the complete state.

सविता प्रसवेन जुषेत ब्रह्म पूर्व्यम् ।
तत्र योनिं कृणवसे न हि ते पूर्वमक्षिपत् ॥ 7 ॥

*Savitraa Prasavena Jusheta Brahma Poorvyam; Tatra Yonim
Krinavase Na Hi Te Poorvamakshipat. (7)*

After reaching that absolute state, the origin is demolished
and no more anxiety is needed about the results of previous
deeds. One should be fully devoted to Brahman, the Creator,
for the prior motive through the inherent soul.

त्रिरुन्नतं स्थाप्य समं शरीरं
        हृदीन्द्रियाणि मनसा संनिवेश्य ।
ब्रह्मोडुपेन प्रतरेत विद्वान्
        स्त्रोतांसि सर्वाणि भयावहानि ॥ 8 ॥

*Trirunnatam Sthaapya Samam Shareeram Hrideendriyaani
Manasa Sanniveshya; Brahmodupena Pratareta Vidvaan Srotaansi
Sarvaani Bhayaavahaani. (8)*

By keeping the body in a steady and straight pose, while
holding the chest, throat and head in line, and withdrawing
the senses and mind within the heart, one who knows this
will overcome all the terrible currents with the help of the
boat of Brahman.

प्राणान् प्रपीड्येह संयुक्तचेष्ट:
        क्षीणे प्राणे नासिकयोच्छ्वसीत ।
दुष्टाश्वयुक्तमिव वाहमेनं
        विद्वान् मनो धारयेताप्रमत्त: ॥ 9 ॥

*Praanaan Prapeedyeha Sanyuktacheshtah Ksheene Praane
Naasikayochchhvaseeta; Dushtaashvayuktamiva Vaahamenam
Vidvaan Mano Dhaarayetaapramattah. (9)*

Keeping the senses under command with great strength and adjusting their performance in the body, one should exhale through both nostrils until the vital force becomes mild and subtle. Then, one who knows this should hold the mind without hesitation, like reins fastened to restless horses.

समे शुचौ शर्कराग्निवालुका
विवर्जिते शब्दजलाश्रयादिभिः ।
मनोऽनुकूले न तु चक्षुपीडने
गुहानिवाताश्रयणे प्रयोजयेत् ॥ 10 ॥

Same Shuchau Sharkaraavahnivaalukaa Vivarjite Shabda-jalaashrayaadibhih; Manoanukoole Na Tu Chakshupeedane Guhaanivaataashrayane Prayojayet. (10)

One should practise his exercises with full concentration in a cave or a similar pure and clean place helpful for the purpose. It should be performed on level ground, having lovely and pleasing scenery, and one should avoid windy, dusty, noisy, smoky and damp places.

नीहारधूमार्कानिलानलानां
खद्योतविद्युत्स्फटिकशशीनाम् ।
एतानि रूपाणि पुरःसराणि
ब्रह्मण्यभिव्यक्तिकराणि योगे ॥ 11 ॥

Neehaaradhooma Arkaanilaanalaanaam Khadyotavidyutas-phasheenaam; Etaani Roopaani Purahsaraani Brahmani Abhivyaktikaraani Yoge. (11)

While doing yoga practice, visions like snow, smoke, sun, wind, fire, firefly, lightning, crystal and moon are visualized, then be sure that the revelation of Brahman is at hand.

पृथ्व्यप्तेजोऽनिलखे समुत्थिते
पञ्चात्मके योगुणे प्रवत्ते ।
न तस्य रोगो न जरा न मृत्यु:
प्राप्तस्य योगाग्निमयं शरीरम् ॥ 12 ॥

Prithvyaptejoanilakhe Samutthite Panchaatmake Yogagune
Pravritte; Na Tasya Rogo Na Jaraa Na Mrityuh Praaptasya
Yogaagnimayam Shareeram. (12)

When the fivefold elements of yoga come to the notice of a
yogi, while concentrating the mind on earth, water, light, air
and ether, then his gross body becomes the body made of the
fire of yoga and he is not affected by disease, old age or death.

लघुत्वमारोग्यमलोलुपत्वं
वर्णप्रसादं स्वरसौष्ठवं च ।
गन्ध: शुभो मूत्रपुरीषमल्पं
योगप्रवृत्तिं प्रथमां वदन्ति ॥ 13 ॥

Laghutvam   Aarogyam   Alolupatvam   Varnaprasaadam
Svarasaushthavam Cha; Gandhah Shubho Mootrapureeshamalpam
Yogapravrittim Prathamaam Vadanti. (13)

It is said that the foremost signs while practising yoga are
lightness of body, sound breath, thirstlessness, fairness of
complexion, a melodious voice, a pleasing odour and scanty
excretions.

यथैव बिम्बं मृदयोपलिप्तं
तेजोमयं भ्राजते तत् सुधान्तम् ।
तद्वाऽऽत्मतत्त्वं प्रसमीक्ष्य देही
एक: कृतार्थो भवते वीतशोक: ॥ 14 ॥

Yathaiva Bimbam Mridayopaliptam Tegomayam Bhraajate Tat
Sudhaantam; Tadvaa Aatmatattvam Prasameekshya Dehee Ekah
Kritaartho Bhavate Veetashokah. (14)

Just as a metal pot full of dust becomes shiny when cleaned, in the same way the embodied one, realizing the truth of Atman, becomes one and the same. He arrives at his destination and becomes free from sorrows.

यदाऽऽत्मतत्त्वेन तु ब्रह्मतत्त्वं
दीपोपमेनेह युक्त: प्रपश्येत् ।
अजं ध्रुवं सर्वतत्त्वैर्विशुद्धं
ज्ञात्वा देवं मुच्यते सर्वपाशै: ॥ 15 ॥

Yadaa Aatmatattvena Tu Brahmatattvam Deepopameneha Yuktah Prapashyet; Ajam Dhruvam Sarvatattvairvishuddham Jnaatvaa Devam Muchyate Sarvapaashaih. (15)

When a yogi reveals the truth of Brahman through his self in the body as a self-luminous reality, then, realizing the divineness as unborn, everlasting and free from all elements in nature (Prakriti), he is free from all sins.

एष ह देव: प्रदिषोऽनु सर्वा:
पूर्वो ह जात: स उ गर्भे अन्त: ।
स एव जात: स जनिष्यमाण:
प्रत्यङ् जनांस्तिष्ठति सर्वतोमुख: ॥ 16 ॥

Esha Ha Devah Pradishoanu Sarvaah Poorvo Ha Jaatah Sa U Garbhe Antah; Sa Eva Jaatah Sa Janishyamaanah Pratyam Janaanstishthati Sarvatomukhah. (16)

This divineness spreads in all directions as a whole. He is the first born, the Hiranyagarbha. He has entered into the womb. He alone is born and is to be born in the future. He is present in all living beings as the residing Self facing all sides.

यो देवो अग्नौ यो अप्सु यो विश्वं भुवनमाविवेश ।
य ओषधीषु यो वनस्पतिषु तस्मै देवाय नमो नमः ॥ 17 ॥

Yo Devo Agnau Yo Apsu Yo Vishvam Bhuvanam Aavivesha; Ya Oshadheeshu Yo Vanaspatishu Tasmai Devaaya Namo Namah. (17)

Salutations to that God who is in fire, in water, in plants, in trees and who is everywhere in this universe.

CHAPTER III

य एको जालवानीशत ईशनीभिः
सर्वाँ ँल्लोकानीशत ईशनीभिः।
य एवैक उद्भवे सम्भवे च
य एतद्विदुरमृतास्ते भवन्ति ॥ 1 ॥

Ya Eko Jaalavaaneeshata Eeshaneebhih Sarvaamllokaaneeshata Eeshaneebhih; Ya Evaika Udbhave Sambhave Cha Ya Etadviduramritaaste Bhavanti. (1)

That is the same Self who alone continues to be active at the time of the creation and dissolution of this world. He possesses innumerable powers and is visualized as the Divine Lord because of the mysterious power of Maya, which belongs to Him only. He protects and commands over all the worlds and the forces working therein. Those who are fully aware of this become immortal.

एको हि रुद्रो न द्वितीयाय तस्थुर्य
इमाँल्लोकानीशत ईशनीभिः।
प्रत्यङ् जनांस्तिष्ठति संचुकोचान्तकाले
संसृज्य विश्वा भुवनानि गोपाः ॥ 2 ॥

Eko Hi Rudro Na Dviteeyaaya Tashthurya Imaanllokaaneeshata Eeshaneebhih; Pratyan Jnanaanstishthati Sanchukochaantakaale Sansrijya Vishvaa Bhunanaani Gopaah. (2)

He is indeed the Rudra, the One without a second, who protects and controls these worlds by His own power. O men! He exists in the heart of every living being. After creating and maintaining these worlds, at the end He retracts them into Himself.

विश्वतश्चक्षुरुत विश्वतोमुखो
विश्वतोबाहुरुत विश्वतस्पात् ।
सं बाहुभ्यां धमति सं पतत्रै-
र्द्यावाभूमी जनयन् देव एक: ॥ 3 ॥

Vishvatashchakshuruta Vishvatomukho Vishvatobaahuruta Vishvataspaat; Sam Baahubhyaam Dhamati Sam Patatraih Dyaarvaabhoomee Janayam Deva Ekah. (3)

Although God, the creator of heaven and earth, is one and the same, yet He is really the possessor of all the eyes, faces, hands and feet in this universe. He guides them to perform their allotted works (according to their knowledge, their actions in past lives, and the inclinations of different living beings).

यो देवानां प्रभवश्चोद्भवश्च
विश्वाधिपो रुद्रो महर्षि: ।
हिरण्यगर्भं जनयामास पूर्वं
स नो बुद्ध्या शुभया संयुनक्तु ॥ 4 ॥

Yo Devaanaam Prabhavashcha Udbhavashcha Vishvaadhipo Rudro Maharshih; Hiranyagarbham Jananyaamaasa Poorvam Sa No Buddhyaa Shubhayaa Sanyunaktu. (4)

May He who is the creator and the supporter of the senses, who is the source of the Cosmic Soul, who bestows bliss and prudence on His devotees, destroying their sins and sorrows and giving punishment to wrongdoers, may He, the great prophet and the Lord of all, bestow on us auspicious thoughts.

या ते रुद्र शिवा तनूरघोरापापकाशिनी ।
तया नस्तनुवा शन्तमया गिरिशन्ताभिचाकशीहि ॥ 5 ॥

Yaa Te Rudra Shivaa Tanooraghoraapaapakaashinee; Tayaa Nastanuvaa Shantamayaa Girishantaabhichaakasheehi. (5)

O Lord who blesses all living beings by disclosing the Vedas with the intention of making us happy by your quiet and blissful Self, which shakes off our great fear and sin as well.

यामिषुं गिरिशन्त हस्ते बिभर्ष्यस्तवे ।
शिवां गिरित्र तां कुरु मा हिꣳसी: पुरुषं जगत् ॥ 6 ॥

Yaamishum Girishanta Haste Bibharshyastave; Shivaam Giritra Taam Kuru Maa Himseeh Purusham Jagat. (6)

O discloser of truth in the Vedas, make auspicious that arrow (Om) which is kept in your hand to aim at something. O protector of devotees, do not relinquish your quiet personal form which has created this universe.

तत: परं ब्रह्मपरं बृहन्तं
यथानिकायं सर्वभूतेषु गूढम् ।
विश्वस्यैकं परिवेष्टितार-
मीशं तं ज्ञात्वामृता भवन्ति ॥ 7 ॥

Tatah Param Brahmaparam Bhrihantam Yathaanikaayam Sarvabhooteshu Goodham; Vishvasyaikam Pariveshtitaaram Eesham Tam Jnaatvaamritaa Bhavanti. (7)

The infinite Supreme Brahman is higher than the personal Brahman hidden in all living beings according to their bodies and who, however, lives alone covering the whole universe. Realizing Him as the God, one attains immortality.

वेदाहमेतं पुरुषं महान्त-
मादित्यवर्णं तमस: परस्तात् ।
तमेव विदित्वाति मृत्युमेति
नान्य: पन्था विद्यतेऽयनाय ॥ 8 ॥

Vedaahmetam Purusham Mahaantam Aadityavarnam Tamasah Parastaat; Tameva Viditavaati Mrityumet Naanyah Panthaa Vidyateayanaaya. (8)

I (sage Shvetashvatara) have realized this Supreme Brahman, who is radiant like the sun above all darkness. One can cross over death only after realizing Him, as there is no other way to avoid the circle of birth and death.

यस्मात् परं नापरमस्ति किंचिद्
यस्मान्नाणीयो न ज्यायोऽस्ति कश्चित् ।
वृक्ष इव स्तब्धो दिवि तिष्ठत्येक-
स्तेनेदं पूर्णं पुरुषेण सर्वम् ॥ 9 ॥

Yasmaat Param Naaparamasti Kinchid Yasmaannaaneeyo Na Jyaayoasti Kashchit; Vriksha Iva Stabho Divi Tishthatyekah Tenedam Poornam Purushena Sarvam. (9)

There is none higher nor greater nor subtler than Him, standing like a firm tree rooted in his own glory, without a second and motionless. The whole of this universe is filled up by that Supreme Being.

ततो यदुत्तरतरं तदरूपमनामयम् ।
य एतद्विदुरमृतास्ते भवन्त्यथेतरे दुःखमेवापियन्ति ॥ 10 ॥

Tato Yaduttarataram Tadaroopamanaamayam; Ya Etadvidur-amritaaste Bhavantyathetare Duhkhamevaapiyanti. (10)

That Supreme Being is far more extensive than this world, without form and free from misery. Those who know this become immortal and others have to suffer the consequences.

सर्वाननशिरोग्रीवः   सर्वभूतगुहाशयः ।
सर्वव्यापी स भगवांस्तस्मात् सर्वगतः शिवः ॥ 11 ॥

*Sarvaananashirogreevah Sarvabhootaguhaashayah; Sarvavyaapee
Sa Bhagavaanstasmaat Sarvagatah Shivah. (11)*

Therefore, that Divine Lord, who is very kind and helpful, is
everywhere resting in the hearts of all living beings, utilizing
all the faces, hands and necks in this world.

महान् प्रभुर्वै पुरुषः सत्त्वस्यैष प्रवर्तकः ।
सुनिर्मलामिमां प्राप्तिमीशानो ज्योतिरव्ययः ॥ 12 ॥

*Mahaan Prabhurvai Purushah Sattvasyaisha Pravartakah;
Sunirmalaamimaam Praaptimeeshaano Jyotiravyayah. (12)*

This Self is indeed a very powerful Lord. He is the everlasting
light that keeps everything in order. He regulates the intellect
of all living beings in order to attain that extremely pure,
ultimate state (mukti).

अङ्गुष्ठमात्रः पुरुषोऽन्तरात्मा
सदा जनानां हृदये संनिविष्टः ।
हृदा मन्वीशो मनसाभिक्लृप्तो
य एतद्विदुरमृतास्ते भवन्ति ॥ 13 ॥

*Angushthamaatrah Purushoantaraatmaa Sadaa Janaanaam
Hridaye Sannivishtah; Hridaa Manveesho Manasaabhiklripto Ya
Etadviduramritaaste Bhavanti. (13)*

Taking the limited shape of a thumb, on account of intellect,
emotion, imagination and will, the Supreme Being rests in
the hearts of all living beings as their soul. Those who know
this attain immortality.

सहस्रशीर्षा पुरुषः सहस्राक्षः सहस्रपात् ।
स भूमिं विश्वतो वृत्वात्यतिष्ठद्दशाङ्गुलम् ॥ 14 ॥

*Sahasrasheershaa Purushah Sahasraakshah Sahasrapaat; Sa
Bhoomim Vishvato Vritvaatyatishthat Dashaangulam.* (14)

That Supreme Being has a thousand heads, eyes and feet
covering the whole universe from all directions and yet
remains above ten fingers (ten fingers here refers to the five
jnanendriyas and five karmendriyas).

पुरुष एवेदꣳ सर्वं यद्भूतं यच्च भव्यम् ।
उतामृतत्वस्येशानो यदन्नेनातिरोहति ॥ 15 ॥

*Purusha Evadam Sarvam Yadbhootam Yachcha Bhyavyam;
Utaamritatvasyeshaano Yadannenaatirohati.* (15)

This Supreme Being is nothing but is all that is, all that was
and all that will be. Even though He leaves His true nature
and assumes the shape of the objective universe, still He
continues to be the Lord of immortality.

सर्वतः पाणिपादं तत् सर्वतोऽक्षिशिरोमुखम् ।
सर्वतः श्रुतिमल्लोके सर्वमावृत्य तिष्ठति ॥ 16 ॥

*Sarvatah Paanipaadam Tat Sarvatoakshishiromukham; Sarvatah
Shrutimalloke Sarvamaavritya Tishthati.* (16)

Having hands and feet, eyes, heads, mouths and ears
everywhere, That remains throughout in this world.

सर्वेन्द्रियगुणाभासं सर्वेन्द्रियविवर्जितम् ।
सर्वस्य प्रभुमीशानं सर्वस्य शरणं बृहत् ॥ 17 ॥

*Sarvendriyagunaabhaasam Sarvendriyavivarjitam; Sarvasya
Prabhumeeshaanam Sarvasya Sharanam Brihat.* (17)

They know Him as lustrous by the activities of all the senses, nevertheless He remains without the senses as the Lord of all, the ruler of all, the protector of all and the friend of all.

नवद्वारे पुरे देही हᳵसो लेलायते बहि: ।
वशी सर्वस्य लोकस्य स्थावरस्य चरस्य च ॥ 18 ॥

Navadvaare Pure Dehee Hamso Lelaayate Bahih; Vashee Sarvasya Lokasya Sthaavarasya Charasya Cha. (18)

That is He who lives in the body, in the city of nine gates. He is the soul (swan) who goes in the outside world for merrymaking. He is the sovereign of the world, animate and inanimate.

अपाणिपादो जवनो ग्रहीता
पश्यत्यचक्षु: स शृणोत्यकर्ण: ।
स वेत्ति वेद्यं न च तस्यास्ति वेत्ता
तमाहुरग्रयं पुरुषं महान्तम् ॥ 19 ॥

Apaanipaado Javano Graheetaa Pashyatyachakshuh Sa Shirnotyakarnah; Sa Vetti Vedyam Na Cha Tasyaasti Vettaa Tamaahuragryam Purusham Mahaantam. (19)

He goes instantaneously and holds without hands and feet. He sees without eyes, hears without ears. He knows everything that is to be known, nevertheless there is nobody who knows Him. They say He is the chief, the extraordinary Supreme Being.

अणोरणीयान् महतो महीया-
नात्मा गुहायां निहितोऽस्य जन्तो: ।
तमक्रतुं पश्यति वीतशोको
धातु: प्रसादान्महिमानमीशम् ॥ 20 ॥

Anoranteeyaan Mahato Maheeryaan Aatmaa Guhaayaam Nihitoasya Jantoh; Tamakratum Pashyati Veetashoko Dhaatuh Prasaadaat Mahimaanameesham. (20)

This Atman is hidden in the heart of every living being. He is subtler than the subtlest and greater than the greatest. By the mercy of the Creator, one becomes free from sorrows and desires and then knows Him as the great Lord.

वेदाहमेतमजरं पुराणं
सर्वात्मानं   सर्वगतं विभुत्वात् ।
जन्मनिरोधं प्रवदन्ति यस्य
ब्रह्मवादिनो हि प्रवदन्ति नित्यम् ॥ 21 ॥

Vedaahametam Ajaram Puraanam Sarvaatmaanam Sarvagatam Vibhutvaat; Janmanirodham Pravadanti Yasya Brahmavaadino Hi Pravadanti Nityam. (21)

I know this imperishable, ancient and indwelling Self of all beings, whose existence is everywhere due to His all-pervading nature, and whom knowers of Brahman verily say to be always free from birth.

CHAPTER IV

य एकोऽवर्णो बहुधा शक्तियोगाद्
वर्णाननेकान् निहितार्थो दधाति ।
वि चैति चान्ते विश्वमादौ स देव:
स नो बुद्ध्या शुभया संयुनक्तु ॥ 1 ॥

*Ya Ekoavarno Bahundhaa Shaktiyogaad Varnaananekaan
Nihitaartho Dadhaati; Vi Chaiti Chaante Vishvamaadau Sa Devah
Sa No Buddhyaa Shubayaa Sanyunaktu. (1)*

Although that Supreme Being is colourless by Himself, yet
by His own power He creates innumerable colours in many
ways for His mysterious purpose and withdraws the whole
world into Himself at last. May that Divine Being bestow on
us auspicious thoughts.

तदेवाग्निस्तदादित्यस्तद्वायुस्तदु चन्द्रमा: ।
तदेव शुक्रं तद्ब्रह्म तदापस्तत् प्रजापति: ॥ 2 ॥

*Tadevaagnih Tadaadityah Tadvaayustadu Chandramaah; Tadeva
Shukram Tadbrahma Tadaapstat Prajaapatih. (2)*

That Itself is the fire, the sun, the air, the moon and also the
pure. That is the Brahman (Hiranyagarbha), the waters and
the Prajapati.

त्वं स्त्री त्वं पुमानसि कुमार त्वं उत वा कुमारी ।
त्वं जीर्णो दण्डेन वञ्चसि त्वं जातो भवसि विश्वतोमुख: ॥ 3 ॥

*Tvam Stree Tvam Pumaanasi Kumaara Tvam Uta Vaa Kumaaree;
Tvam Jeerno Dandena Vanchasi Tvam Jaato Bhavasi
Vishvatomukhah. (3)*

You are the woman, the man, the youth and the maiden
also. You are the old man who is shaky and using a stick for
support. You are born having turned your faces on all sides.

नील: पतङ्गो हरितो लोहिताक्ष-
स्तडिग्दर्भ ऋतव: समुद्रा: ।
अनादिमत्त्वं विभुत्वेन वर्तसे
यतो जातानि भुवनानि विश्वा ॥ 4 ॥

Neelah Patango Harito Lohitaakshah Tadigdarbha Ritavah
Samudraah; Anaadimattvam Vibhutvena Vartase Yato Jaataani
Bhuvanaani Vishvaa. (4)

You are the blue butterfly and the green parrot with red
eyes. You are the thundercloud, the seasons and the oceans.
You are everlasting and beyond all time and space. You are
He from whom all the world has come into existence.

अजामेकां लोहितशुक्लकृष्णां
बह्वी: प्रजा: सृजमानां सरूपा: ।
अजो ह्येको जुषमाणोऽनुशेते
जहात्येनां भुक्तभोगामजोऽन्य: ॥ 5 ॥

Ajaamekaam Lohitashuklarishnaam Bahveeh Prajaah Sri-
jamaanaam Saroopaah; Ajo Hyeko Jushamaanoanushete
Jahaatyenaam Bhuktabhogaamajoanyah. (5)

There is only one female (Prakriti) having red, white and
black colours. She is unborn and produces innumerable
products like herself. Besides her, another unborn male
(Purusha) also exists out of her affection, and leaves her
after having enjoyed her.

द्वा सुपर्णा सयुजा सखाया
समानं वृक्ष परिषस्व जाते ।
तयोरन्य: पिप्पलं स्वाद्वत्त्य-
नश्नन्नन्यो अभिचाकशीति ॥ 6 ॥

186

Dvaa Suparnaa Sayujaa Sakhaayaa Samaanam Vriksham Parishasva Jaate; Tayoranyah Pippalam Svaadvattyanah Ashnannanyo Abhichaakasheeti. (6)

Two birds having very fine feathers, united in firm friendship, rested on the same tree. One of them eats delicious fruits from the tree while the other looks on without eating.

समाने वृक्षे पुरुषो निमग्नो-
ऽनीशया शोचति मुह्यमान: ।
जुष्टं यदा पश्यत्यन्यमीश-
मस्य महिमानमिति वीतशोक: ॥ 7 ॥

Samaane Vrikshe Purusho Nimagnah Aneeshayaa Shochati Muhyamamaanah; Jushtam Yadaa Pashyatyanyameesham Asya Mahimaanamiti Veetashokah. (7)

While sitting on the same tree, one of them, the personal self (the Jiva), drowned in ignorance and delusion, regrets his powerlessness. However, when he sees the other, the Lord, worshipped by all and is convinced that all glory is due to Him only, then he becomes free from misery.

ऋचो अक्षरे परमे व्योमन्
यस्मिन् देवा अधि विश्वे निषेदु: ।
यस्तं न वेद किमृचा करिष्यति
य इत् तद् विदुस्त इमे समासते ॥ 8 ॥

Richo Akshare Parame Vyoman Yasmin Devaa Adhi Vishve Nisheduh; Yastam Na Veda Kimirichaa Karishyati Ya It Tad Vidusta Ime Samaasate. (8)

What will be the benefits of the Vedas to one who does not know that imperishable, greatest and ether-like invisible Being, where the various Gods and the Vedas dwell? Those who know That are satisfied.

छन्दांसि यज्ञाः क्रतवो व्रतानि
भूतं भव्यं यच्च वेदा वदन्ति ।
अस्मान्मायी सृजते विश्वमेतत्
तस्मिंश्चान्यो मायया संनिरुद्धः ॥ 9 ॥

Chhandaansi Yajnaah Kratavo Vrataani Bhootam Bhavyam Yachcha Vedaa Vadanti; Asmaanmaayee Srijate Vishvametat Tasmimshchaanyo Maayayaa Sanniruddhah. (9)

The Lord of Maya created the Vedas, offerings, spiritual practices, past and future religious rites, all that the Vedas revealed, the whole universe, including ourselves. The other (Jiva) again is confined by Maya in this, the world of creation.

मायां तु प्रकृतिं विद्यान्मायिनं तु महेश्वरम् ।
तस्यावयवभूतैस्तु व्याप्तं सर्वमिदं जगत् ॥ 10 ॥

Maayam Tu Prakritim Vidyaanmaayinam Tu Maheshvaram; Tasya Avayavabhootaistu Vyaaptam Sarvamidam Jagat. (10)

In that case, know that Nature is Maya and the controller of Maya is the great Lord. The whole universe is occupied by living beings, who are nothing but His parts.

यो योनिं योनिमधितिष्ठत्येको
यस्मिन्निदं स च विचैति सर्वम् ।
तमीशानं वरदं देवमीड्यं
निचाय्येमां शान्तिमत्यन्तमेति ॥ 11 ॥

Yo Yonim Yonimadhitishthatyeko Yasminnidam Sa Cha Vichaiti Sarvam; Tameeshaanam Varadam Devameedyam Nichaayyemaam Shaantimatyantameti. (11)

One attains everlasting peace after knowing that self-luminous adorable Lord, who gives His divine favour. Even though He seems to be one, yet He controls the manifold activities of Prakriti and in Him this universe merges and is seen in manifold shapes.

यो देवानां प्रभवश्चोद्भवश्च
विश्वाधिपो रुद्रो महर्षि: ।
हिरण्यगर्भं पश्यत जायमानं
स नो बुद्ध्या शुभया संयुनक्तु ॥ 12 ॥

Yo Devaanaam Prabhavah Cha Udbhavashcha Visvaadhipo Rudrom Maharshih; Hiranyagarbham Pashyata Jaayamaanam Sa No Buddhyaa Shubayaa Sanyunaktu. (12)

May He who is the creator of Gods, who observes the birth of the Cosmic Soul, who bestows the highest happiness and prudence on His devotees, demolishing their sins and sorrows and punishing all the rule-breakers – may He, the great sage and the Lord of all, provide us with auspicious thoughts.

यो देवानामधिपो यस्मिँल्लोका अधिश्रिता: ।
य ईशे अस्य द्विपदश्चतुष्पद: कस्मै देवाय हविषा विधेम ॥ 13 ॥

Yo Devaanaamadhipo Yasminllokaa Adhishritaah; Ya Eeshe Asya Dvipadashchatushpadah Kasmai Devaaya Havishaa Vidhema. (13)

Let us show our reverence with offerings to that Divine Being, who is full of bliss and is the Lord of the Gods, who rules over two-footed and four-footed beings and in whom the whole world exists.

सूक्ष्मातिसूक्ष्मं कलिलस्य मध्ये
विश्वस्य स्रष्टारमनेकरूपम् ।
विश्वस्यैकं परिवेष्टितारं
ज्ञात्वा शिवं शान्तिमत्यन्तमेति ॥ 14 ॥

Sookshmaatisookshmam Kalilasya Madhye Vishvasya Srashtaaramanekaroopam; Vishvasyaikam Pariveshtitaaram Jnaatvaa Shivam Shaantimatyantameti. (14)

One can attain everlasting peace when he knows that One who is full of bliss, subtler than the subtlest, who has projected this universe during time of confusion, taking different shapes, and who is the only one that encircles the universe.

स एव काले भुवनस्य गोप्ता
विश्वाधिप: सर्वभूतेषु गूढ: ।
यस्मिन् युक्ता ब्रह्मर्षयो देवताश्च
तमेवं ज्ञात्वा मृत्युपाशांश्छिनत्ति ॥ 15 ॥

Sa Eva Kaale Bhuvanasya Goptaa Vishvaadhipah Sarvabhooteshu Goodhah; Yasmin Yuktaa Brahmarshayo Devataashcha Tamevam Jnaatvaa Mrityupaashaanshchhinatti. (15)

He alone, the Lord of this universe, concealed in all living beings, is the protector of this universe at the right time. The great sages and the Gods merge in Him. Knowing Him in this way, one becomes free from the bondage of death.

घृतात् परं मण्डमिवातिसूक्ष्मं
ज्ञात्वा शिवं सर्वभूतेषु गूढम् ।
विश्वस्यैकं परिवेष्टितारं
ज्ञात्वा देवं मुच्यते सर्वपाशै: ॥ 16 ॥

Ghritaat Param Mandamivaatisookshmam Jnaatvaa Shivam Sarvabhooteshu Goodham; Vishvasyaikam Pariveshtitaaram Jnaatvaa Devam Muchyate Sarvapaashaih. (16)

One is relieved from all bondage after knowing that Supreme One, who is full of bliss, encircles the whole world, and conceals Himself in all living beings in an invisible part, like perfume in ghee.

एष देवो विश्वकर्मा महात्मा
सदा जनानां हृदये संनिविष्टः।
हृदा मनीषा मनसाभिक्लृप्तो
य एतद् विदुरमृतास्ते भवन्ति ॥ 17 ॥

Esha Devo Vishvakarmaa Mahaatmaa Sadaa Janaanaam Hridaye Sannivishtah; Hridaa Maneeshaa Manasaabhiklripto Ya Etad Viduramritaaste Bhavanti. (17)

This Divine Being, the creator and the all-pervading soul of this universe, resides in the heart of all living beings. Those who meditate on Him with heart, mind and intellect attain immortality.

यदातमस्तन्न दिवा न रात्रिर्न
सन्न चासच्छिव एव केवलः ।
तदक्षरं तत्सवितुर्वरेण्यं
प्रज्ञा च तस्मात् प्रसृता पुराणी ॥ 18 ॥

Yadaatamastanna Divaa Na Raatrih Na Sanna Chaasanchhiva Eva Kevalah; Tadaksharam Tadaksharam Tatsaviturvarenyam Prajnaa Cha Tasmaat Prasritaa Puraanee. (18)

When ignorance is removed there is no day or night, nor being or non-being. There remains that auspicious One only who is undecayable and deserving of being worshipped even by the Creator. From Him, the ancient wisdom (in the form of the Vedas) came.

नैनमूर्ध्वं न तिर्यञ्चं न मध्ये परिजग्रभत् ।
न तस्य प्रतिमा अस्ति यस्य नाम महद्यशः ॥ 19 ॥

Nainamoordhvam Na Tiryancham Na Madhye Parijagrabhat; Na Tasya Pratimaa Asti Yasya Naama Mahadyashah. (19)

There is no one who can hold Him up from above, across and in the middle, and also no one is identical to Him whose name is so renowned.

न संदृशे तिष्ठति रूपमस्य
न चक्षुषा पश्यति कश्चनैनम् ।
हृदा हृदिस्थं मनसा य एन-
मेवं विदुरमृतास्ते भवन्ति ॥ 20 ॥

Na Sandrishe Tishthati Roopamasya Na Chakshushaa Pashyati Kashchanainam; Hridaa Hiridistham Manasaa Ya Enam Evam Viduramritaaste Bhavanti. (20)

His figure does not come in the sphere of the senses. No one can see him with the naked eye. Those who know Him through intuition, stationed within the heart, attain immortality.

अजात इत्येवं कश्चिद् भीरु: प्रपद्यते ।
रुद्र यत्ते दक्षिणं मुखं तेन मां पाहि नित्यम् ॥ 21 ॥

Ajaata Ityevam Kashchid Bheeruh Prapadyate; Rudra Yatte Dakshinam Mukham Tena Maam Paahi Nityam. (21)

Some out of fear come to you, considering you to be unborn. O Rudra, help and protect me with your kind face forever.

मा नस्तोके तनये मा न आयुषि मा नो गोषु मा नो अश्वेषु रीरिष: ।
वीरान्मा नो रुद्र भामितो वधीर्हविष्मन्त: सदमित्त्वा हवामहे ॥ 22 ॥

Maa Nastoke Tanaye Maa Na Aayushi Maa No Goshu Maa No Ashveshu Reerishah; Veeraanmaa No Rudra Bhaamito Vadheerhavishmantah Sadamittvaa Havaamahe. (22)

Do not cause any harm to children, grandchildren and life, nor in regard to cows and horses. O Rudra, do not put our heroes to death by your wrath. We pray to you earnestly with offerings on all occasions.

CHAPTER V

द्वे अक्षरे ब्रह्मपरे त्वनन्ते
विद्याविद्ये निहिते यत्र गूढे ।
क्षरं त्वविद्या ह्यमृतं तु विद्या
विद्याविद्ये ईशते यस्तु सोऽन्यः ॥ १ ॥

Dve Akshare Brahmapare Tvanante Vidyaavidye Nihite Yatra Goodhe; Ksharam Tvavidyaa Hyamritam Tu Vidyaa Vidyaavidye Eeshate Yastu Soanyah. (1)

Ignorance take us to mortality and wisdom to eternity. Just the opposite is the Supreme Brahman who is decayless, eternal and secret. Again ignorance and prudence are within Him, who controls them both.

यो योनिं योनिमधितिष्ठत्येको
विश्वानि रूपाणि योनीश्च सर्वाः ।
ऋषिं प्रसूतं कपिलं यस्तमग्रे
ज्ञानैर्बिभर्ति जायमानं च पश्येत् ॥ २ ॥

Yo Yonim Yonimadhitishthatyeko Vishvaani Roopaani Yoneeshcha Sarvaah; Rishim Prasootam Kapilam Yastamagre Jnaanairbibharti Jaayamaanam Cha Pashyet. (2)

He is the one who governs nature in all respects and controls every being and their origin of production. He has seen the birth of the firstborn seer of golden colour (Hiranyagarbha) and supports him wisely.

एकैकं जालं बहुधा विकुर्व-
न्नस्मिन् क्षेत्रे संहरत्येष देवः ।
भूयः सृष्ट्वा पतयस्तथेशः
सर्वाधिपत्यं कुरुते महात्मा ॥ ३ ॥

*Ekaikam Jaalam Bahudhaa Vikurvan Asmin Kshetre Sanharatyesha
Devah; Bhooyah Srishtvaa Patayastatheshah Sarvaadhipatyam
Kurute Mahaatmaa. (3)*

Discriminating each group of beings into various forms, the
Supreme Being dissolves them into their respective sources
and again creating the same as before, the great soul grasps
and swings them all again.

सर्वा दिश ऊर्ध्वमधश्च तिर्यक्
    प्रकाशयन् भ्राजते यद्वनड्वान् ।
एवं स देवो भगवान् वरेण्यो
    योनिस्वभावानधितिष्ठत्येक: ॥ 4 ॥

*Sarvaa Disha Oordhvamadhashcha Tiryak Prakaashayan Bhraajate
Yadvanadvaan; Evam So Devo Bhagavaan Varenyo
Yonisvabhaavaan Adhitishthatyekah. (4)*

Just as the sun shines, reflecting light in every place upwards,
downwards and across, in the same way that adorable God,
the store of all virtues and greatness, regulates all as the
cause of creation.

यच्च स्वभावं पचति विश्वयोनि:
    पाच्यांश्च सर्वान् परिणामयेद् य: ।
सर्वमेतद् विश्वमधितिष्ठत्येको
    गुणांश्च सर्वान् विनियोजयेद् य: ॥ 5 ॥

*Yachcha Svabhaavam Pachati Vishvayonih Paachyaanshcha Sarvaan
Parinaamayed Yah; Sarvametad Vishvamadhistishthatyeko
Gunaanshcha Sarvaan Viniyojayed Yah. (5)*

He, who is the origin of this universe, conceives all things
out of His nature and develops those who are fit for perfection
according to their previous deeds and bestows them with

195

regard to their natural tendencies. In this manner He governs all the worlds.

तद् वेदगुह्योपनिषत्सु गूढं
तद् ब्रह्मा वेदते ब्रह्मयोनिम् ।
ये पूर्वदेवा ऋषयश्च तद्विदु-
स्ते तन्मया अमृता वै बभूवुः ॥ ६ ॥

Tad Vedaguhyopanishatsu Goodham Tad Brahmaa Vedate Brahma Yonim; Ye Poorva Devaa Rishayashcha Tadviduh Te Tanmayaa Amritaa Vai Babhoovuh. (6)

He seems to be hidden in the Upanishads, which are part and parcel of the Vedas. Hiranyagarbha knows Him as the origin of Himself and the Vedas. Those gods and great sages who recognized Him in bygone days became united with Him verily on attaining immortality.

गुणान्वयो यः फलकर्मकर्ता
कृतस्य तस्यैव स चोपभोक्ता ।
स विश्वरूपस्त्रिगुणस्त्रिवर्त्मा
प्राणाधिपः संचरति स्वकर्मभिः ॥ ७ ॥

Gunaanvayo Yah Phalakarmakartaa Kritasya Tasyaiva Sa Chopabhoktaa; Sa Vishvaroopah Trigunah Trivartmaa Praanaadhipah Sancharati Svakarmabhih. (7)

Only he who is attracted towards things from which pleasure is obtained works to harvest the fruits of his deeds and enjoys the same. Even though he is the master of the senses, yet he becomes limited by the three gunas, having several forms, and goes round the three paths as the consequence of his deeds.

अङ्गुष्ठमात्रो रवितुल्यरूप:
संकल्पाहंकारसमन्वितो य: ।
बुद्धेर्गुणेनामगुणेन चैव
आराग्रमात्रो ह्यपरोऽपि दृष्ट: ॥ 8 ॥

Angushthamaatro Ravitulyaroopah Sankalpa Ahankaarasamanvito Yah; Buddhergunena Aatmagunena Chaiva Aaraagramaatro Hyaparoapi Drishtah. (8)

He, the only one, is similar to the other, of the size of a thumb, who is pure, shining and everlasting like the sun, as minute as the point of a goad and connected with ego and sankalpa due to the restricted aspects of the intellect.

वालाग्रशतभागस्य शतधा कल्पितस्य च ।
भागो जीव: स विज्ञेय: स चानन्त्याय कल्पते ॥ 9 ॥

Vaalaagrashatabhaagasya Shatadhaa Kalpitasya Cha; Bhaago Jeevah Sa Vijneyah Sa Chaanantyaaya Kalpate. (9)

The personal soul is extremely minute, like a hair-point cut into parts and sub-parts a hundred times. Still He is capable of eternity, who is to be known.

नैव स्त्री न पुमानेष न चैवायं नपुंसक: ।
यद् यच्छरीरमादत्ते तेन तेन स युज्यते ॥ 10 ॥

Naiva Stree Na Pumaanesha Na Cahivaayam Napunsakah; Yad Yachchhareeramaadatte Tena Tena Say Yujate. (10)

He is not a female, nor a male, nor even a neuter. Whatever physical body he adopts is recognized with each of them.

संकल्पनस्पर्शनदृष्टिमोहै-
    ग्रासाम्बुवृष्ट्या चात्मविवृद्धिजन्म ।
कर्मानुगान्यनुक्रमेण   देही
    स्थानेषु   रूपाण्यभिसम्प्रपद्यते ॥ 11 ॥

Sankalpanasparshanadrishtimohaih Graasaambuvrishtyaa Chaatmavivriddhijanma; Karmaanugaani Anukramena Dehee Sthaaneshu Roopaani Abhisamprapadyate. (11)

Just as the gross body is nourished by ample food and water, so also the personal soul undertakes different forms in several places according to its deeds by means of desire, contact, sight and delusion.

स्थूलानि   सूक्ष्माणि बहूनि चैव
    रूपाणि देही स्वगुणैर्वृणोति ।
क्रियागुणैरात्मगुणैश्च तेषां
    संयोगहेतुरपरोऽपि   दृष्ट: ॥ 12 ॥

Sthoolaani Sookshmaani Bahooni Chaiva Roopaani Dehee Svagunairvrinoti; Kriyaagunaih Aatmagunaisheha Teshaam Sanyogaheturaparoapi Drishtah. (12)

This embodied Self selects gross, subtle and various forms, influenced by the qualities of the body, the mind and the senses, but the cause of this combination seems to be yet another.

अनाद्यनन्तं कलिलस्य मध्ये
    विश्वस्य स्रष्टारमनेकरूपम् ।
विश्वस्यैकं परिवेष्टितारं
    ज्ञात्वा देवं मुच्यते सर्वपाशै: ॥ 13 ॥

Anaadyanantam Kalilasya Madhye Vishvasya Srashtaaramaneka- roopam; Vishvasyaikam Pariveshtitaaram Jnaatvaa Devam Muchyate Sarvapaashaih. (13)

He has no beginning nor end, who has created this universe during the time of confusion, who has adopted various shapes and who alone has covered all things. Knowing Him, one is free from all bondage.

भावग्राह्यमनीडाख्यं   भावाभावकरं   शिवम् ।
कलासर्गकरं देवं ये विदुस्ते जहुस्तनुम् ॥ 14 ॥

Bhaavagraahyamaneedaakhyam Bhaavaabhaava Karam Shivam;
Kalaasargakaram Devam Ye Viduste Jahustanum. (14)

That Supreme Divine Being who has equally created life and matter, who is the origin of all arts and sciences, can be perceived by the pure and devoted mind. Revealing Him who is full of bliss, with name and without name, one becomes free from the circle of birth and death.

CHAPTER VI

स्वभावमेके कवयो   वदन्ति
     कालं तथान्ये परिमुह्यमाना: ।
देवस्यैष महिमा   तु लोके
     येनेदं भ्राम्यते ब्रह्मचक्रम् ॥ 1 ॥

Svabhaavameke Kavayo Vadanti Kaalam Tathaanye Parimuhyamaanaah; Devasyaisha Mahimaa Tu Loke Yenedam Bhraamyate Brahmachakram. (1)

Some perverted thinkers think that this wheel of Brahman revolves by the force of nature and others are of the opinion that time is the cause of its motion, but really it is the glory of God alone that is visible in this world.

येनावृतं नित्यमिदं हि सर्वं
     ज्ञ: कालकालो गुणी सर्वविद्य: ।
तेनेशितं कर्म विवर्तते ह
     पृथ्व्यप्तेजोऽनिलखानि चिन्त्यम् ॥ 2 ॥

Yenaavritam Nityamidam Hi Sarvam Jnah Kaalakaalo Gunee Sarvavidyah; Teneshitam Karma Vivartate Ha Prithvyapte-joanilakhaani Chintyam. (2)

That Supreme Divine Being, who is all-knowing and pure consciousness by itself, has covered this universe on all sides and is the owner of the gunas and the maker of time and rules over the actions (karma), which take several shapes, like earth, water, light, air and ether.

तत्कर्म कृत्वा विनिवर्त्य भूय-
     स्तत्त्वस्य तत्त्वेन समेत्य योगम् ।
एकेन द्वाभ्यां त्रिभिरष्टभिर्वा
     कालेन चैवात्मगुणैश्च   सूक्ष्मै: ॥ 3 ॥

Tatkarma Kritvaa Vinivartya Bhooyah Tattvasya Tattvena Sametya Yogam; Ekena Dvaabhyaam Tribhirashtabhirvaa Kaalena Chaivaatmagunaishcha Sookshmaih. (3)

After creating this universe and keeping it revolving, He keeps Himself aloof from it. He joins the principle of spirit together with the principle of matter in ratio with one (ignorance), with two (good and bad results of the deeds of past lives), with three (physical, subtle and causal) and with eight (five elements, mind, intellect and ego) by means of time and the natural tendencies of things.

आरभ्य कर्माणि गुणान्वितानि
   भावांश्च सर्वान् विनियोजयेद् यः ।
तेषामभावे कृतकर्मनाशः
   कर्मक्षये याति स तत्त्वतोऽन्यः ॥ ४ ॥

Aarabhya Karmaani Gunaanvitaani Bhaavaanshcha Sarvaan Viniyojayed Yah; Teshaamabhaave Kritakarmanaashah; Karmakshaye Yaati Sa Tattvatoanyah. (4)

After executing the work connected with the gunas and surrendering all of them to the Supreme Being, one becomes free from all deeds and of the circle of birth and death. All the results of the deeds vanish due to non-attachment.

आदिः स संयोगनिमित्तहेतुः
   परस्त्रिकालादकलोऽपि दृष्टः ।
तं विश्वरूपं भवभूतमीड्यं
   देवं स्वाचित्तस्थमुपास्य पूर्वम् ॥ ५ ॥

Aadih Sa Sanyoganimittahetuh Parastikaalaadakaloapi Drishtah; Tam Vishvaroopam Bhavabhootameedyam Devam Svaachittas-thamupaasya Poorvam. (5)

On account of prior meditation on that Supreme Worship-pable Being who resides in everyone's heart, visible as the universe, and who is the real origin of all beings, He reveals Himself in the form of the result caused by the union of spirit with matter, undivided and beyond the three divisions of time.

स वृक्षकालाकृतिभि: परोऽन्यो
यस्मात् प्रपञ्च: परिवर्ततेऽयम् ।
धर्मावहं पापनुदं भगेशं
ज्ञात्वात्मस्थममृतं   विश्वधाम ॥ 6 ॥

Sa Vrikshakaalaakritibhih Paroanyo Yasmaat Prapanchah Parivartateayam; Dharmaavaham Paapanudam Bhagesham Jnaatvaatmasthamamritam Vishvadhaama. (6)

Realizing Him, from whom this universe continues its cycle and dissolves in Him, who is the origin of all virtues, the destroyer of all sins, the owner of all excellent faculties, the Immortal, and the resting place of the universe, as stationed in one's own heart, He is observed as separate from and beyond the range of the tree of samsara, together with time and form.

तमीश्वराणां   परमं महेश्वरं
तं देवतानां परमं च दैवतम् ।
पतिं पतीनां परमं परस्ताद्
विदाम देवं भुवनेशमीड्यम् ॥ 7 ॥

Tameeshvaraanaam Paramam Maheshvaram Tam Devataanaam Parmam Cha Daivatam; Patim Pateenaam Paramam Parastaad Vidaama Devam Bhuvaneshameedhyam. (7)

May we reveal that excellent and worshippable owner of this universe, the Supreme Being, who is the highest Lord of all the Lords, the highest God of all the Gods, the highest ruler above all the rulers.

न तस्य कार्य करणं च विद्यते
न तत्समश्चाभ्यधिकश्च दृश्यत ।
परास्य शक्तिर्विधैव श्रूयते
स्वाभाविकी ज्ञानबलक्रिया च ॥ 8 ॥

Na Tasya Kaaryam Karanam Cha Vidyate Na Tatsamash-chaabhyadhikashcha Drishyate; Paraasya Shaktirvividhaiva Shroonyate Svaabhaavikee Jnaanabalakriyaa Cha. (8)

He, the Supreme Being, has no organs of action, nor anything to acquire for Himself. There is none in existence identical or superior to Him. His great power, which is said to be of several kinds, is explained in the Vedas and His knowledge, strength and action are stated as existing as the natural and permanent part of Himself.

न तस्य कश्चिद् पतिरस्ति लोके
न चेशिता नैव च तस्य लिङ्गम् ।
स कारणं करणाधिपाधिपो
न चास्य कश्चिज्जनिता न चाधिप: ॥ 9 ॥

Na Tasya Kaschid Patirasti Loke Na Cheshitaa Naiva Cha Tasya Lingam; Sa Kaaranam Karanaadhipaadhipo Na Chaasya Kashchijjanitaa na Chaadhipah. (9)

He has no owner in this world and none to command over Him also. He cannot be proved logically or by any signs. He is the cause of all and the controller of the controller of the sense organs. He has no lineage and none to be His Lord.

यस्तन्तुनाभ इव तन्तुभिः प्रधानजैः स्वभावतो देव एकः स्वमावृणोत् । स नो दधाह्ब्रह्माप्ययम् ॥ 10 ॥

Yastantunaabha Iva Tantubhih Pradhaanajaih Svabhaavato Deva Ekah Svamaavrinot; Sa No Dadhaahbrahmaapyayam. (10)

As a spider draws and withdraws the threads coming from its own self, so also the highest God, who instinctively overspreads Himself as part and parcel of Nature, may allow us to assimilate in Brahman.

एको देवः सर्वभूतेषु गूढः
सर्वव्यापी सर्वभूतान्तरात्मा ।
कर्माध्यक्षः सर्वभूताधिवासः
साक्षी चेता केवलो निर्गुणश्च ॥ 11 ॥

Eko Devah Sarvabhooteshu Goodhah Sarvavyaapee Sarvabhoota-antaraatmaa; Karmaadhyakshah Sarvabhootaadhivaasah Saakshee Chetaa Kevalo Nirgunashcha. (11)

The God who is the only one, hidden in all beings, all-pervading and the inner Self of all creatures, He controls all actions and all living beings dwell in Him. He is the witness and pure consciousness free from the three gunas of nature.

एको वशी निष्क्रियाणां बहूना-
मेकं बीजं बहुधा यः करोति ।
तमात्मस्थं येऽनुपश्यन्ति धीरा-
स्तेषां सुखं शाश्वतं नेतरेषाम् ॥ 12 ॥

Eko Vashee Nishkriyaanaam Bahoonaam Ekam Beejam Bahudhaa Yah Karoti; Tamaatmastham Yeanupashyanti Dheerah Teshaam Sukham Shaashvatam Netareshaam. (12)

The one controller of the many, inactive, who makes the one seed manifold. The wise who perceive Him as abiding in their self, to them belongs eternal happiness, not to others.

नित्यो नित्यानां चेतनश्चेतनाना-
मेको बहूनां यो विदधाति कामान् ।
तत् कारणं सांख्ययोगाधिगम्यं
ज्ञात्वा देवं मुच्यते सर्वपाशैः ॥ 13 ॥

Nityo Nityanaam Chetanashchetanaanaam Eko Bahoonaam Yo Vidadhaati Kaamaan; Tat Kaaraam Saankhyayogaadhigamyam Jnaatvaa Devam Muchyate Sarvapaashaih. (13)

He is everlasting among those who seem to be constant and intelligent, among all who are supposed to be intelligent (out of their developed organs of knowledge). He is single but fulfils the desires of the many. One becomes free from all bondage after knowing him, the cause of all, who is to be understood through the discipline of philosophy and yoga.

न तत्र सूर्यो भाति न चन्द्रतारकं
नेमा विद्युतो भान्ति कुतोऽयमग्निः ।
तमेव भान्तमनुभाति सर्वं
तस्य भासा सर्वमिदं विभाति ॥ 14 ॥

Na Tatra Sooryo Bhaati Na Chandrataarakam Nemaa Vidyuto Bhaanti Kutoayamagnih; Tameva Bhaantamanubhaati Sarvam Tasya Bhaasaa Sarvamidam Vibhaati. (14)

There the sun does not shine, nor the moon and the stars, nor lightning also. How then can this fire, which is seen by us, shine? When He shines, everything reflecting His light, the whole universe becomes bright with His light.

एको हँसो भुवनस्यास्य मध्ये
स एवाग्निः सलिले संनिविष्टः ।
तमेव विदित्वाति मृत्युमेति
नान्यः पन्था विद्यतेऽयनाय ॥ 15 ॥

*Eko Hamso Bhuvanasyaasya Madhye Sa Evaagnih Salile Sanni-
vishtah; Tameva Viditvaati Mrityumeti Naanyah Panthaa
Vidyateayanaaya.* (15)

He, the only one, destroyer of ignorance, is in the middle of
the whole world, who alone is the fire seated in the water.
After revealing Him, one crosses over death. There is no
other way for liberation.

स विश्वकृद् विश्वविदात्मयोनिर्ज्ञः-
कालकालो गुणी सर्वविद् यः ।
प्रधानक्षेत्रज्ञपतिर्गुणेशः
सँसारमोक्षस्थितिबन्धहेतुः ॥ 16 ॥

*Sa Vishvakrid Vishvavidaatmayonih Jnah Kaalakaalo Gunee
Sarvavid Yah; Pradhaanakshetrajnapatirgunaeshah Samsaara-
mokshasthitibandhahetuh.* (16)

He created all things and knows everything also. He is the
origin of Himself and the destroyer of time. He is the store
of all virtues and originator of all the sciences. He is the
supreme ruler of the gunas and keeps matter and spirit
under control. He is the cause of liberation from samsara
(birth and death circle) and of bondage, which follows its
continuation.

स तन्मयो ह्यमृतं ईशसंस्थो
ज्ञः सर्वगो भुवनस्यास्य गोप्ता ।
य ईशे अस्य जगतो नित्यमेव
नान्यो हेतुर्विद्यत ईशनाय ॥ 17 ॥

Sa Tanmayo Hyamritam Eeshasanstho Jnah Sarvago Bhuvanasyaasya Goptaa; Ya Eeshe Asya Jagato Nityameva Naanyo Heturvidyata Eeshanaaya. (17)

He is the soul of this universe, everlasting, and the supreme ruler. He is the all-knowing, the all pervading, the protector of the universe and the constant ruler. No one is so competent to conduct the affairs of this world continually.

यो ब्रह्माणं विदधाति पूर्वं
यो वै वेदांश्च प्रहिणोति तस्मै ।
तः ह देवमात्मबुद्धिप्रकाशं
मुमुक्षुर्वै शरणमहं प्रपद्ये ॥ 18 ॥

Yo Brahmaanam Vidadhaati Poorvam Yo Vai Vedaanshcha Prahinoti Tasmai; Tam Ha Devamaatmabuddhiprakaasham Mumukshurvai Sharanamaham Prapadye. (18)

निष्कलं निष्क्रियः शान्तं निरवद्यं निरञ्जनम् ।
अमृतस्य परः सेतुं दग्धेन्धनमिवानलम् ॥ 19 ॥

Nishkalam Nishkriyam Shaantam Niravadyam Niranjanam. Amritasya Param Setum Dagdhendhanamivaanalam. (19)

He, in the beginning of creation, created Brahma (Hiranyagarbha) and handed over the Vedas to him. He established the everlasting bridge. He, who is undivided, free from activities, quiet, without defect, spotless, and looks like the fire which has burnt up the fuel. Longing for salvation, I surrender myself to that radiant one, whose light turns the intelligence towards the Atman.

यदा   चर्मवदाकाशं वेष्टयिष्यन्ति मानवा: ।
तदा देवमविज्ञाय दु:खस्यान्तो भविष्यति ॥ 20 ॥

*Yadaa Charmavadaakaasham Veshtayishyanti Maanavaah; Tadaa
Devavijnaaya Duhkhasyaanto Bhavishyati. (20)*

Without revealing God, there will be no end to sorrow, even
though men shall wear (use) the sky like a skin.

तप:प्रभावाद् देवप्रसादाच्च ब्रह्म
ह   श्वेताश्वतरोऽथ विद्वान् ।
अत्याश्रमिभ्य: परमं पवित्रं
प्रोवाच सम्यगृषिसङ्घजुष्टम् ॥ 21 ॥

*Tapahprabhaavaad Devaprasaadaachcha Brahma Ha Shvetaash-
vataroatha Vidvaan; Atyaashramibhyah Paramam Pavitram
Provaacha Samyagrishisanghajushtam. (21)*

The sage Shvetashvatara, after realizing himself through
austerity and by the mercy of God, explained well to the self-
controlled sannyasins, the highest birth of the sublime,
sacred Brahman, adopted by all the seers.

वेदान्ते परमं गुह्यं पुराकल्पे प्रचोदितम् ।
नाप्रशान्ताय दातव्यं नापुत्रायाशिष्याय वा पुन: ॥ 22 ॥

*Vedaante Paramam Guhyam Puraakalpe Prachoditam;
Naaprashaantaaya Daatavyam Naaputraayaashishyaaya Vaa
Punah. (22)*

This supreme occult knowledge of Brahman, interpreted in
Vedanta as in ancient days, should not be imparted to the
restless one, or an unworthy son, or to a vile disciple.

यस्य देवे परा भक्तिर्यथा देवे तथा गुरौ ।
तस्यैते कथिता ह्यर्थाः प्रकाशन्ते महात्मनः ।
प्रकाशन्ते महात्मनः ॥ 23 ॥

Yasya Deve Paraa Bhaktiryathaa Deve Tathaa Gurau. Tasyaite Kathitaa Hyarthaah Prakaashante Mahaatmanah; Prakaashante Mahaatmanah. (23)

Then these supreme truths imparted to the most deserving high souls, who are greatly devoted to God as well as to the spiritual teacher (Guru), shine brightly. They shine brightly in those most deserving souls only.

SHANTI PATH

ॐ सह नाववतु। सह नौ भुनक्तु। सह वीर्यं करवावहै। तेजस्वि नावधीतमस्तु।
मा विद्विषावहै।

ॐ शान्ति: शान्ति: शान्ति:

Om Saha Naavavatu; Saha Nau Bhunaktu; Saha Veeryam Karavaavahai; Tejasvinaavadheetamastu; Maa Vidvishaavahai.

Om Shaantih Shaantih Shaantih.

Om. May the Lord protect both teacher and disciple, and may He cherish us both. May we work with full energy that our study be perfect and give good results. May we never feel ill will toward others.

Om peace, peace, peace.

Taittiriya Upanishad

This Upanishad consists of three chapters under the headings Shiksha-Valli, Brahmananda-Valli and Bhrigu-Valli. These are subdivided into thirty-one lessons of twelve, nine and ten respectively, in order to emphasize the fact, both directly and indirectly, to the seekers of Brahman, the Absolute Reality. All necessary instructions and definite advice are given to the pupils at the opening and also at the close of the session, in the form of a convocation message. This helps them to clearly understand the method of instruction from teacher to pupil, their education system, and the culture of the golden Vedic period.

In Shiksha-Valli, brief suggestions are given on the science of pronunciation, as well as different kinds of upasana (worship), by which pupils can purify their minds and sharpen their memories so that they may be able to ward off all odds and obstacles on the path of their study, and also in real life. These are given in a series for one to rest the mind upon and achieve calmness.

In subsequent chapters, the theory of the five koshas (sheaths) – i.e. annamaya, pranamaya, manomaya, vijnana-maya and anandamaya – has been introduced in detail. It demonstrates how the Absolute Reality (Brahman), which is Sat Chit Ananda, can be discovered through the self-experience of an individual. One cannot find the Supreme

211

merely by being told about Him. One has to know the way to Him also. Moreover, when the seeker knows the way, he has to follow it strictly until he reaches the goal. That goal is Brahman. One, who by constant meditation knows Brahman, attains the Supreme. Then, after realizing his Self, an individual experiences all joys at once.

SHANTI PATH

ॐ शं नो मित्रः शं वरुणः । शं नो भवत्वर्यमा । शं न इन्द्रो बृहस्पतिः । शं नो विष्णुरुरुक्रमः । नमो ब्रह्मणे । नमस्ते वायो । त्वमेव प्रत्यक्षं ब्रह्मासि । त्वामेव प्रत्यक्षं ब्रह्म वदिष्यामि । ऋतं वदिष्यामि । सत्यं वदिष्यामि । तन्मामवतु । तद्वक्तारमवतु । अवतु माम् । अवतु वक्तारम् ।

ॐ शान्तिः शान्तिः शान्तिः

*Om Sham No Mitrah Sham Varunah; Sham No Bhavatvaryamaa;
Sham Na Indro Brihaspatih; Sham No Vishnururukramah; Namo
Brahmane; Namaste Vaayo; Tvameva Pratyaksham Brahmaasi;
Tvaameva Pratyaksham Brahma Vadishyaami; Ritam Vadishyaami;
Satyam Vadishyaami; Tanmaamavatu; Tadvaktaaramavatu; Avatu
Maam; Avatu Vaktaaram.*

Om Shaantih Shaantih Shaantih.

May Mitra, Varuna, Aryama, Indra, Brihaspati and wide-
spreading Vishnu be gracious to us and bestow upon us
happiness and bliss. Salutation to Brahman. O Vayu,
salutation to you. You, verily, are the visible Brahman. I
shall speak of you alone as the direct Brahman. I shall call
you the Cosmic Law. I shall call you the Truth. May Brahman
protect me. May He protect the teacher. May Brahman
protect me, may He protect the teacher.

Om peace, peace, peace.

CHAPTER I: SHIKSHA VALLI

LESSON ONE

ॐ शं नो मित्र: शं वरुण: । शं नो भवत्वर्यमा । शं न इन्द्रो बृहस्पति: । शं
नो विष्णुरुरुक्रम: । नमो ब्रह्मणे । नमस्ते वायो । त्वमेव प्रत्यक्षं ब्रह्मासि।
त्वामेव प्रत्यक्षं ब्रह्म वदिष्यामि । ऋतं वदिष्यामि । सत्यं वदिष्यामि ।
तन्मामवतु । तद्वक्तारमवतु । अवतु माम् । अवतु वक्तारम् ।

ॐ शान्ति: शान्ति: शान्ति:

*Om Sham No Mitrah Sham Varunah; Sham No Bhavatvaryamaa;
Sham Na Indro Brihaspatih; Sham No Vishnururukramah; Namo
Brahmane; Namaste Vaayo; Tvameva Pratyaksham Brahmaasi;
Tvaameva Pratyaksham Brahma Vadishyaami; Ritam Vadishyaami;
Satyam Vadishyaami; Tanmaamavatu; Tadvaktaaramavatu; Avatu
Maam; Avatu Vaktaaram.*

Om Shaantih Shaantih Shaantih.

May Mitra, Varuna, Aryama, Indra, Brihaspati and wide-
spreading Vishnu be gracious to us and bestow upon us
happiness and bliss. Salutation to Brahman. O Vayu,
salutation to you. You, verily, are the visible Brahman. I
shall speak of you alone as the direct Brahman. I shall call
you the Cosmic Law. I shall call you the Truth. May Brahman
protect me. May He protect the teacher. May Brahman
protect me, may He protect the teacher.

Om peace, peace, peace.

LESSON TWO

शीक्षां व्याख्यास्यामः । वर्णः स्वरः । मात्रा बलम् । साम संतानः ।
इत्युक्तः शीक्षाध्यायः ।

*Sheekshaam Vyaakhyaasyaamah; Varnah Svarah; Maatraa Balam;
Saama Santaanah; Ityuktah Sheekshaadhyaayah.*

We shall now fully and clearly explain the science of
phonetics. It consists of alphabet, accent, quantity, force for
pronunciation, regulating the tone of voice, and the
conjunctions of the letters. In this way has been explained
the lesson on pronunciation.

LESSON THREE

सह नौ यशः सह नौ ब्रह्मवर्चसम् । अथातः सँहिताया उपनिषदं
व्याख्यास्यामः । पञ्चस्वधिकरणेषु । अधिलोकमधिज्यौतिषमधिविद्यमधि-
प्रजमध्यात्मम् । ता महासँहिता इत्याचक्षते । अथाधिलोकम् । पृथिवी
पूर्वरूपम् । द्यौरुत्तररूपम् । आकाशः संधिः । वायुः संधानम् । इत्यधिलोकम्
॥ 1 ॥

*Saha Nau Yashah Saha Nau Brahmavarchasam; Athaatah
Samhitaayaa Upanishadam Vyaakhyaasyaamah; Panchasvadhi-
karaneshu. Adhilokam Adhijyautisham Adhividyamadhiprajam
Adhyaatmam; Taa Mahaasamhitaa Ityaachakshate; Athaadhilokam;
Prithivee Poorva Roopam; Dyauruttararoopam; Aakaashah
Sandhih; Vaayuh Sandhaanam; Ityadhilokam.* (1)

May we both, teacher and pupil, obtain splendid reputation
and superiority born from spiritual knowledge and study
simultaneously.

Now we shall explain this divine teaching of conjunction
established on the five existing objects: universe, shining
things, learning, progeny and self. Meditation on these
objects is said to be the great combination. As regards the

universe, the earth is the first form, heaven is the last form, the sky is the junction and air is the joining link. One should meditate upon the universe considering this inner relation.

अथाधिज्यौतिषम् । अग्निः पूर्वरूपम् । आदित्य उत्तररूपम् । आपःसंधिः । वैद्युत: संधानम् । इत्यधिज्यौतिषम् ॥ 2 ॥

Athaadhijyautisham; Agnih Poorva Roopam; Aaditya Uttara-roopam; Aapah Sandhih; Vaidyutah Sandhaanam; Ityadhi-jyautisham. (2)

As regards the shining things, fire is the first form, the sun is the last form, water is the junction and lightning is the joining link. In this way one should meditate upon the shining things.

अथाधिविद्यम् । आचार्यः पूर्वरूपम् । अन्तेवास्युत्तररूपम् । विद्या संधिः । प्रवचन्ँ संधानम् । इत्यधिविद्यम् ॥ 3 ॥

Athaadhividyam; Aachaaryah Poorva Roopam; Antevaasyuttara-roopam; Vidyaa Sandhih; Pravachanam Sandhaanam; Ityadhividyam. (3)

Then, as regards learning, the teacher is the first form, the pupil is the last form, knowledge is the junction and instruction is the joining link. Thus, one should meditate upon learning.

अथाधिप्रजम् । माता पूर्वरूपम् । पितोत्तररूपम् । प्रजा संधिः । प्रजनन्ँ संधानम् इत्यधिप्रजम् ॥ 4 ॥

Athaadhiprajam; Maataa Poorva Roopam; Pitottara Roopam; Prajaasandhih; Prajananam Sandhaanam; Ityadhiprajam. (4)

Then, as regards progeny, the mother is the first form, the father is the last form, progeny is the junction and generation is the joining link. Thus, one should meditate upon progeny.

अथाध्यात्मम् । अधरा हनु: पूर्वरूपम् । उत्तराहनुरुत्तररूपम् । वाक् संधि: ।
जिह्वा संधानम् । इत्यध्यात्मम् ॥ 5 ॥

*Athaadhyaatmam; Adharaa Hanuh Poorva Roopam; Uttaraa-
hanuruttararoopam; Vaak Sandhih; Jihvaa Sandhaanam;
Ityadhyaatmam. (5)*

Then, as regards the self, the lower jaw is the first form, the
upper jaw is the last form, speech is the junction and the
tongue is the joining link. Thus, one should meditate upon
the self.

इतीमा महासँहिता य एवमेता महासँहिता व्याख्याता वेद । संधीयते प्रजया
पशुभि: । ब्रह्मवर्चसेनान्नाद्यन सुवर्गेण लोकेन ॥ 6 ॥

*Iteemaa Mahaasamhitaa Ya Evametaa Mahaasamhitaa
Vyaakhyaataa Veda; Sandheeyate Prajayaa Pashubhih; Brahma-
varchasenaannaadyena Suvargena Lokena. (6)*

These are called the great combinations. One who meditates
on these great conjunctions, as explained above, will obtain
progeny, wealth in cattle, the splendour of Brahma, food
and the like, and a favoured place in heaven.

LESSON FOUR

यश्छन्दसामृषभो विश्वरूप: । छन्दोभ्योऽध्यमृतात् सम्बभूव । स मेन्द्रो
मेधया स्पृणोतु । अमृतस्य देव धारणो भूयासम् । शरीरं मे विचर्षणम् ।
जिह्वा मे मधुमत्तमा। कर्णाभ्यां भूरि विश्रुवम् । ब्रह्मण: कोशोऽसि मेधया
पिहित: । श्रुतं मे गोपाय ॥ 1 ॥

*Yashchhandasaamrishabho Vishvaroopah; Chhandobhyoadhyamritaat
Sambabhoova; Sa Mendro Medhayaa Sprinotu; Amritasya Deva
Dhaarano Bhooyaasam; Shareeram Me Vicharshanam; Jihvaa Me
Madhumattamaa; Karnaabhyaam Bhoori Vishruvam; Brahmanah
Koshoasi Medhayaa Pihitah; Shrutam Me Gopaaya. (1)*

He, who is the most prominent in the hymns of the Vedas, who is all-pervading and whose widespread grandeur has sprung up from the sacred and immortal Vedas, may He – Om, that is Indra – the Supreme Lord, delight me with intelligence and mental power. O Lord, may I be the possessor of immortality, may my body be in good condition, may my speech be sweet to the highest degree, and may I hear much with my ears so that I may learn. You are the sheath of Brahman, covered by worldly intelligence. Guard my learning, which I acquired by hearing.

आवहन्ती वितन्वाना कुर्वाणाचीरमात्मनः । वासाँसि मम गावश्च। अन्नपाने च सर्वदा । ततो मे श्रियमावह । लोमशां पशुभिः सह स्वाहा ॥ 2 ॥

Aavahantee Vitanvaanaa; Kurvaanaa Cheeramaatmanah; Vaasaamsi Mama Gaavashcha; Annapaane Cha Sarvadaa; Tato Me Shriyamaavaha; Lomashaam Pashubhih Saha Svaahaa. (2)

O God, having gifted me with intelligence and fitness, grant me prosperity which will give me clothes, wool, cattle, food and drink, without delay, for all time. Svaha.

आ मायन्तु ब्रह्मचारिणः स्वाहा। विमायन्तु ब्रह्मचारिणः स्वाहा। प्रमायन्तु ब्रह्मचारिणः स्वाहा। दमायन्तु ब्रह्मचारिणः स्वाहा । शमायन्तु ब्रह्मचारिणः स्वाहा ॥ 3 ॥

Aa Maayantu Brahmachaarinah Svaahaa; Vimaayantu Brahma-chaarinah Svaahaa; Pramaayantu Brahmachaarinah Svaahaa; Damaayantu Brahmachaarinah Svaahaa; Shamaayantu Brahma-chaarinah Svaahaa. (3)

May students (brahmacharis) come to me from all corners. Svaha. May they come in large numbers from far off. May they be self-controlled and mentally calm.

यशो जनेऽसानि स्वाहा । श्रेयान् वस्यसोऽसानि स्वाहा । तं त्वा भग
प्रविशानि स्वाहा । स मा भग प्रविश स्वाहा । तस्मिन् सहस्रशाखे नि
भगाऽहं त्वयि मृजे स्वाहा ॥ ४ ॥

Yasho Janeasaani Svaahaa; Shreyaan Vasyasoasaani Svaahaa;
Tam Tvaa Bhaga Pravishaani Svaahaa; Sa Maa Bhaga Pravisha
Svaahaa; Tasmin Sahasrashaakhe Ni Bhagaaham Tvayi Mrije
Svaahaa. (4)

May I become popular among men. May I become superior
to the wealthy. Svaha. O Venerable Lord, may I enter into
Thee. Svaha. O Adorable Lord, may I purify my sins in Thy
all-pervading Self. Svaha.

यथाऽऽपः प्रवता यन्ति यथा मासा अहर्जरम् । एवं मां ब्रह्मचारिणो
धातरायन्तु सर्वतः स्वाहा । प्रतिवेशोऽसि प्र मा भाहि प्र मा पद्यस्व ॥ ५ ॥

Yathaa Aapah Pravataa Yanti Yathaa Maasaa Aharjaram; Evam
Maam Brahmachaarino Dhaataraayantu Sarvatah Svaahaa;
Prativeshoasi Pra Maa Bhaahi Pra Maa Padyasva. (5)

Just as water flows downwards, as the months are united
with the year, similarly, O Lord, the creator of all, may
students (brahmacharis) come to me from all directions.
Svaha. You are the resting place at hand, enlighten me and
take complete possession of me.

LESSON FIVE

भूर्भुवः सुवरिति वा एतास्तिस्रो व्याहृतयः । तासामु ह स्मैतां चतुर्थीं
माहाचमस्यः प्रवेदयते । मह इति । तद्ब्रह्म । स आत्मा । अङ्गान्यन्या
देवताः । भूरिति वा अयं लोकः । भुव इत्यन्तरिक्षम् । सुवरित्यसौ लोकः ।
मह इत्यादित्यः । आदित्येन वाव सर्वे लोका महीयन्ते ॥ १ ॥

Bhoorbhuvah Suvariti Vaa Etaastisro Vyaahritayah; Taasaamu
Ha Smaitaam Chaturtheem Maahaachamasyah Pravedayate; Maha

Iti; Tad Brahma; Sa Aatmaa; Angaanyanyaa Devataah; Bhooriti Vaa Ayam Lokah; Bhuva Ityantariksham; Suvarityasau Lokah; Maha Ityaadityah; Aadityena Vaava Sarve Lokaa Maheeyante. (1)

Bhuh, Bhuvah and Suvah, these, verily, are the three Vyahritis or mystical utterances, and the fourth one, Maha by name, which Mahachamasya visualized. That is Brahman. That is the Atman. Other gods are its limbs. What is known as Bhuh is, indeed, this world. What is called Bhuvah is the intermediate space. What is denoted as Suvah is heaven. What is known as Maha is the sun. Verily, through the sun all the world prospers.

भूरिति वा अग्निः । भुव इति वायुः । सुवरित्यादित्यः । मह इति चन्द्रमा । चन्द्रमसा वाव सर्वाणि ज्योतीꣳषि महीयन्ते । भूरिति वा ऋचः । भुव इति सामानि । सुवरिति यजूꣳषि । मह इति ब्रह्म । ब्रह्मणा वाव सर्वे वेदा महीयन्ते ॥ 2 ॥

Bhooriti Vaa Agnih; Bhuva Iti Vaayuh; Suvarityaadityah; Maha Iti Chandramaah; Chandramasaa Vaava Sarvaani Jyoteemshi Maheeyante; Bhooriti Vaa Richah; Bhuva Iti Saamaani; Suvariti Yajoomshi Maha Iti Brahma; Brahmanaa Vaava Sarve Vedaa Maheeyante. (2)

What is called Bhuh is indeed fire, Bhuvah is the air, Suvah is the sun, Maha is the moon, and through the moon all shine. Bhuh is the Rigveda, Bhuvah is the Samaveda, Suvah is the Yajurveda. Maha is Brahman (Om). Through Brahman (Om) verily all Vedas are magnified.

भूरिति वै प्राणः । भुव इत्यपानः । सुवरिति व्यानः । मह इत्यन्नम् । अन्नेन वाव सर्वे प्राणा महीयन्ते । ता वा एताश्चतस्रश्चतुर्धा । चतस्रश्चतस्रो व्याहृतयः । ता यो वेद । स वेद ब्रह्म । सर्वेऽस्मै देवा बलिमावहन्ति ॥ 3 ॥

Bhooriti Vai Praanah; Bhuva Ityapaanah; Suvariti Vyaanah; Maha Ityannam; Annena Vaava Sarve Praanaa Maheeyante;

Taa Vaa Etaashchatasrashchaturdhaa; Chatasrashchatasro Vyaahritayah; Taa Yo Veda; Sa Veda Brahma. Sarveasmai Devaa Balimaavahanti. (3)

Bhuh is indeed the air that is breathed in (prana). Bhuvah is the air that is breathed out (apana). Suvah is vital air that sustains life. Vyana is the retained breath. Maha is food and through food, verily, all animate beings are nourished. These indeed are the four Vyahritis, forming groups of four, become fourfold. One who meditates on them knows Brahman and the deities bring offerings to him.

LESSON SIX

स य एषोऽन्तर्हृदय आकाश: । तस्मिन्नयं पुरुषो मनोमय: । अमृतो हिरण्मय: ॥ 1 ॥

Sa Ya Eshoantarhridaya Aakaashah; Tasminnayam Purusho Manomayah; Amrito Hiranmayah. (1)

The bright space, familiar to all, is in the heart. Within that the intelligent, immortal and radiant soul (Purusha) exists who is realized and worshipped through meditation and knowledge.

अन्तरेण तालुके । य एष स्तन इवावलम्बते । सेन्द्रयोनि: । यत्रासौ केशान्तो विवर्तते । व्यपोह्य शीर्षकपाले । भूरित्यग्नौ प्रतिष्ठति । भुव इति वायौ। सुवरित्यादित्ये । मह इति ब्रह्मणि। ॥ 2 ॥

Antarena Taaluke; Ya Esha Stana Ivaavalambate, Sendrayonih; Yatraasau Keshaanto Vivartate; Vyapohya Sheershakapaale; Bhoorityagnau Pratishthati, Bhuva Iti Vaayau Suvarityaaditye; Maha Iti Brahmani. (2)

That which hangs down between the palates like a nipple, that is the birthplace of Indra; at the crown where the hair is made to part, separating the skull in the middle (Brahma yoni). In fire he rests as Bhuh, in air as Bhuvah, in the sun as Suvah, in Brahman as Maha.

आप्नोति स्वाराज्यम् । आप्नोति मनसस्पतिम् । वाक्पतिश्चक्षुष्पति: । श्रोत्रपतिर्विज्ञानपति: । एतत्ततो भवति ॥ 3 ॥

Aapnoti Svaaraajyam; Aapnoti Manasaspatim; Vaakpatish-chakshushpatih; Shrotrapatirvijnaanapatih; Etattato Bhavati. (3)

He attains self-rule. He becomes the lord of mind, the lord of speech, the lord of sight, the lord of hearing, the lord of intelligence; this and more he becomes.

आकाशशरीरं ब्रह्म । सत्यात्म प्राणारामं मनआनन्दम्। शान्ति समृद्ध ममृतम । इति प्राचीनयोग्योपास्स्व ॥ 4 ॥

Aakaashashareeram Brahma; Satyaatma Praanaaraamam Mana Aanandam; Shaantisamriddhamamritam; Iti Praacheena-yogyopaassva. (4)

After that he becomes imperishable and blissful Brahman, whose body is the space (akasha), which is associated with the gross and subtle, and truth is his real nature, whose sport is in vital force, whose mind is the source of delight, and who is bestowed with peace. In this way, O Prachinyogya, worship as stated above.

LESSON SEVEN

पृथिव्यन्तरिक्षं द्यौर्दिशोऽवान्तरदिश:।अग्निर्वायुरादित्यश्चन्द्रमा नक्षत्राणि। आप ओषधयो वनस्पतय आकाश आत्मा । इत्यधिभूतम् । अथाध्यात्मम् । प्राणो व्यानोऽपान उदान: समान: । चक्षु: श्रोत्रं मनो वाक् त्वक् ।चर्म माँ सँ स्नावास्थि मज्जा । एतदधिविधाय ऋषिरवोचत् । पाङ् क्तं वा इदँ सर्वम् । पाङ्क्तेनैव पाङ्क्तँ स्पृणोतीति ।

Prithivyantariksham Dyaurdishah Aavaantaradishah; Agnirvaa-yuraadityashchandramaa Nakshatraani; Aapa Oshadhayo Vanaspataya Aakaasha Aatmaa; Ityadhibhootam; Athaadhyaatmam; Praano Vyaanoapaana Udaanah Samaanah; Chakshuh Shrotram Mano Vaak Tvak; Charma Maam Sam Snaavaasthi Majjaa; Etadadhividhaaya Rishiravochat; Paanktam Vaa Idam Sarvam; Paanktenaiva Paanktam Sprinoteeti.

One should meditate upon the elements of which this whole universe is constructed, namely, earth, sky, heaven, the primary and intermediate quarters, fire, air, the sun, the moon, stars, water, herbs, trees, ether and the body. Then again one should meditate upon oneself, considering prana, vyana, apana, udana and samana, the organs of sight, hearing, thinking, speech and the sense of touch, and skin, flesh, muscles, bones and marrow. Having revealed thus by intuition, the seer proclaimed that the whole universe is based on verily this fivefold principle, and one set of five fulfils the other.

LESSON EIGHT

ओमिति ब्रह्म । ओमितीदँ सर्वम् । ओमित्येतदनुकृतिर्ह स्म वा अप्यो श्रावयेत्याश्रावयन्ति । ओमिति सामानि गायन्ति । ओँ॰ शोमिति । शस्त्राणि शँ सन्ति । ओमित्यध्वर्यूः प्रतिगरं प्रतिगृणाति । ओमिति ब्रह्मा प्रसौति । ओमित्यग्निहोत्रमनुजानाति । ओमिति ब्राह्मणः प्रवक्ष्यन्नाह ब्रह्मो-पाप्नवानीति । ब्रह्मैवोपाप्नोति ।

Omiti Brahma; Omiteedam Sarvam; Omityetadanukritirha Sma Vaa Apyo Shraavayetyaashraavayanti; Omiti Saamaani Gaayanti; Om Shomiti; Shastraani Shamsanti Omityadhvaryooh Pratigaram Pratigrinaati; Omiti Brahmaa Prasauti; Omityagnihotra-manujaanaati; Omiti Braahmanah Pravakshyannaaha Brahmopaapnavaaneeti; Brahmaivopaapnoti.

Om is Brahman. Om is all this universe, seen and imagined. It is the universal truth that Om is a term of compliance.

The priests doing sacrificial deeds direct the assistant with the word. Om makes the gods hear. They start singing Samas with Om. Chanting Om Shom in the beginning, the Hotra priests recite the shastras. The Adhvaryu addresses the Hotra priests with the word Om. Brahma makes the sacrifice in the proper way uttering Om. The sacrificers grant permission to offer oblations to the fire uttering Om. A Brahmana, before beginning to recite the Vedas, with a desire to become well-versed, chants Om. Verily, he attains Brahman.

LESSON NINE

ऋतं च स्वाध्यायप्रवचने च । सत्यं च स्वाध्यायप्रवचने च । तपश्च स्वाध्यायप्रवचने च । दमश्च स्वाध्यायप्रवचने च । शमश्च स्वाध्यायप्रवचने च । अग्नयश्च स्वाध्यायप्रवचने च । अग्निहोत्रं च स्वाध्यायप्रवचने च । अतिथयश्च स्वाध्यायप्रवचने च । मानुषं च स्वाध्यायप्रवचने च । प्रजा च स्वाध्यायप्रवचने च । प्रजनश्च स्वाध्यायप्रवचने च । प्रजातिश्च स्वाध्यायप्रवचने च । सत्यमिति सत्यवचा राथीतरः । तप इति तपोनित्यः पौरुशिष्टिः । स्वाध्यायप्रवचने एवेति नाको मौद्गल्यः । तद्धि तपस्तद्धि तपः ।

Ritam Cha Svaadhyaayapravachane Cha; Satyam Cha Svaadh-yaayapravachane Cha; Tapashcha Svaadhyaayapravachane Cha; Damashcha Svaadhyaayapravachane Cha; Shamashcha Svaadh-yaayapravachane Cha; Agnayashcha Svaadhyaayapravachane Cha; Agnihotram Cha Svaadhyaayapravachane Cha; Atithayashcha Svaadhyaayapravachane Cha; Maanusham Cha Svaadh-yaayapravachane Cha; Prajaa Cha Svaadhyaayapravachane Cha; Prajanashcha Svaadhyaayapravachane Cha; Prajaatishcha Svaadhyaayapravachane Cha; Satyamiti Satyavachaa Raatheetarah; Tapa Iti Taponityah Paurushishtih; Svaadhyaaya Pravachane Eveti Naako Maudgalyah; Taddhi Tapastaddhi Tapah.

Uprightness and learning and imparting Vedic knowledge as prescribed by the scriptures are to be practised. Truthfulness and learning and teaching are to be practised. Austerity and learning and teaching are to be adopted. Self-restraint and learning and teaching are to be practised. Calmness and learning and teaching are to be practised. Sacred fires are to be looked after and learning and teaching are to be practised. Offering oblations to the fire daily, morning and evening (Agnihotra) is to be performed, and learning and teaching are to be followed. Hospitality is to be observed and learning and teaching are to be carried on. Good and favourable behaviour for the welfare of human beings is to be adopted, and learning and teaching are to be practised. Bringing up the family and learning and teaching are to be carried on. A grandson is to be raised, and learning and teaching are to be practised.

Truthfulness alone is to be practised, says the sage Satyavacha of the line of Rathitara. Austerity is enough, thinks Taponitya, son of Purushishti. Naka, the son of Mudgala, emphasized learning and imparting Vedic knowledge. That, certainly, is penance; indeed, that is penance.

LESSON TEN

अहं वृक्षस्य रेरिवा । कीर्तिः पृष्ठं गिरेरिव । ऊर्ध्वपवित्रो वाजिनीव स्वमृतमस्मि । द्रविणꣳ सवर्चसम् । सुमेधा अमृतोक्षितः । इति त्रिशङ्कोर्वेदानुवचनम् ।

Aham Vrikshasya Rerivaa; Keertih Prishtham Girereiva; Oordhva Pavitro Vaajineeva Svamritamasmi; Dravinam Savarchasam; Sumedhaa Amritokshitah; Iti Trishankorvedaanuvachanam.

I am the stimulator of the tree of the universe. My fame is as high as the peak of the mountain. My source is pure

(Brahman). I am like the pure reality of the Self, as that is like the sun. I am the power, the wealth and the light of the divine intuition. I have realized the true knowledge, imperishable and immortal have I become. This was the declaration of Trishanku, the seer, after his Self-realization.

LESSON ELEVEN

वेदमनूच्याचार्योऽन्तेवासिनमनुशास्ति । सत्यं वद । धर्मं चर । स्वाध्यायान्मा प्रमद: । आचार्याय प्रियं धनमाहृत्य प्रजातन्तुं मा व्यवच्छेत्सी: । सत्यान्न प्रमदितव्यम् । धर्मान् न प्रमदितव्यम् । कुशलान्न प्रमदितव्यम् । भूत्यै न प्रमदितव्यम् । स्वाध्यायप्रवचनाभ्यां न प्रमदितव्यम् । देवपितृकार्याभ्यां न प्रमदितव्यम् ॥ 1 ॥

Vedamanoochyaachaaryoantevaasinamanushaasti; Satyam Vada; Dharmam Chara; Svaadhyaayaanmaa Pramadah; Aachaaryaaya Priyam Dhanamaahritya Prajaatantum Maa Vyavachchhetseeh; Satyaanna Pramaditavyam; Dharmaan Na Pramaditavyam; Kushalaanna Pramaditavyam; Bhootyai Na Pramaditavyam; Svaadhyaayapravachanaabhyaam Na Pramaditavyam; Devapitrikaaryaabhyaam Na Pramaditavyam. (1)

Having instructed in the Vedas, the teacher gives advice to the pupils. Speak the truth; keep to the rules of prescribed conduct; do not neglect study; offer to the teacher presents liked by him; be careful about the line of progeny; no negligence about Truth; no diversion from performing righteous duty; no carelessness about what is just and good; no carelessness about prosperity; no indifference towards study and imparting knowledge of the Vedas; do not be forgetful about duties towards the gods and the manes (forefathers).

मातृदेवो भव। पितृदेवो भव । आचार्चदेवो भव। अतिथिदेवो भव ।
यान्यनवद्यानि कर्माणि । तानि सेवितव्यानि । नो इतराणि । यान्यस्माकं
सुचरितानि । तानि त्वयोपास्यानि । नो इतराणि । ये के चास्मच्छ्रेयाः सो
ब्राह्मणाः । तेषां त्वयाऽऽसनेन प्रश्वसितव्यम् । श्रद्धया देयम् ।
अश्रद्धयादेयम् । श्रिया देयम् । ह्रिया देयम् । भिया देयम् । संविदा देयम्
॥ 2 ॥

Maatridevo Bhava; Pitridevo Bhava; Aachaaryadevo Bhava;
Atithidevo Bhava; Yaanyanavadyaani Karmaani; Taani
Sevitavyaani; No Itaraani; Yaanyasmaakam Sucharitaani; Taani
Tvayopaasyaani; No Itaraani; Ye Ke Chaasmachchhreyaamso
Braahmanaah; Teshaam Tvayaa Aasanena Prashvasitavyam;
Shraddhayaa Deyam; Ashraddhayaa Deyam; Shriyaa Deyam;
Hriyaa Deyam; Bhiyaa Deyam; Samvidaa Deyam. (2)

Treat your mother like a god; worship your father as a god; think your teacher to be a god; behave with your guest like a god; do not perform blameworthy acts but restore the others; commendable actions are to be followed, not others; pay due respect to those who are superior and praiseworthy among us by offering a seat and other necessities; presents are to be offered gladly, willingly and full of faith; never offer unwilling, dishonourable or faithless gifts; the presents are to be offered in plenty with modesty and fear; the presents are to be with sympathy.

अथ यदि ते कर्मविचिकित्सा वा वृत्तविचिकित्सा वा स्यात् । ये तत्र
ब्राह्मणाः सम्मर्शिनः । युक्ता आयुक्ताः । अलूक्षा धर्मकामाः स्युः । यथा
ते तत्र वर्तेरन् । युक्ता आयुक्ताः । अलूक्षा धर्मकामाः स्युः । यथा ते तत्र
वर्तेरन् । तथा तत्र वर्तेथाः । अथाभ्याख्यातेषु । ये तत्र ब्राह्मणाः
सम्मर्शिनः । युक्ता आयुक्ताः । अलूक्षा । धर्मकामाः स्युः । यथा ते तेषु
वर्तेरन् । तथा तेषु वर्तेथाः । एष आदिशः । एष उपदेशः । एषा
वेदोपनिषत् । एतदनुशासनम् । एवमुपासितव्यम् । एवमुचैतदुपास्यम् ॥ 3 ॥

Atha Yadi Te Karmavichikitsaa Vaa Vrittavichikitsaa Vaa Syaat;
Ye Tatra Braahmanaah Sammarshinah; Yuktaa Aayuktaah.
Alookshaa Dharmakaamaah Syuh; Yathaa Te Tatra Varteran;
Tathaa Tatra Vartethaah; Athaabhyaakhyaateshu; Ye Tatra
Braahmanaah Sammarshinah; Yuktaa Aayuktaah; Alookshaa
Dharmakaamaah Syuh; Yathaa Te Teshu Varteran; Tathaa Teshu
Vartethaah; Esha Aadeshah; Esha Upadeshah; Eshaa Vedopanishat;
Etadanushaasanam; Evamupaasitavyam; Evamuchaitadupaasyam.
(3)

Then, if there is any doubt in the mind in respect to rites
and duties and conduct in life, act exactly as Brahmans do
who happen to be present there and who are able to judge
impartially, who are more experienced, independent in view,
gentle by nature and well-versed and lovers of law; regarding
such matters, you have to act accordingly. In the same way,
with those who are wrongly accused of crimes, behave with
them according to the way of the Brahmans who happen to
be present there, who are gentle, independent, experienced
and prudent. That is the direction, that is the advice, that is
the secret instruction of the Vedas. These are verily the
commandments. One must practise them throughout life
in the way stated above, and not otherwise.

LESSON TWELVE

ॐ शं नो मित्र: शं वरुण: । शं नो भवत्वर्यमा । शं न इन्द्रो बृहस्पति: ।
शं नो विष्णुरुरुक्रम: । नमो ब्रह्मणे । नमस्ते वायो । त्वमेव प्रत्यक्षं
ब्रह्मासि । त्वामेव प्रत्यक्षं ब्रह्मावादिषम् । ऋतमवादिषम् । सत्यमवादिषम्
तन्मामावीत् तद्वक्तारमावीत् । आवीन्माम् । आवीद्वक्तारम् ।

ॐ शांति: शांति: शांति:

Om Sham No Mitrah Sham Varunah; Sham No Bhavatvaryamaa;
Sham Na Indro Brihaspatih; Sham No Vishnururukramah; Namo
Brahmane; Namaste Vaayo; Tvameva Pratyaksham Brahmaasi;

228

Tvameva Pratyaksham Brahmaavaadisham; Tvaameva Pratyak-
sham Brahma Vadishyaam; Ritamavaadisham; Satyamavaadisham.
Tanmaamaaveet. Tadvaktaaramaaveet; Aaveenmaam Aaveed-
vaktaaram.

Om Shaantih Shaantih Shaantih.

May Mitra, Varuna, Aryana, Indra, Brihaspati and wide-
spreading Vishnu be gracious to us and bestow upon us
happiness and bliss. Salutation to Brahman, O Vayu,
salutation to you. You, verily, are the visible Brahman. I
spoke of you alone as the direct Brahman. I spoke of you
alone as the manifested Brahman. I spoke of you as the
Cosmic Law. I spoke of you as the Truth. He (Brahman)
protected me. He protected the teacher. He protected me,
He protected the teacher.

Om peace, peace, peace.

SHANTI PATH

ॐ सह नाववतु । सह नौ भुनक्तु । सह वीर्यं करवावहै। तेजस्वि नावधीतमस्तु । मा विद्विषावहै।

ॐ शान्ति: शान्ति: शान्ति:

Om Saha Naavavatu; Saha Nau Bhunaktu; Saha Veeryam Karavaavahai; Tejasvi Naavadheetamastu; Maa Vidvishaavahai.

Om Shaantih Shaantih Shaantih.

Om. May He protect us both (teacher and pupil) together. May He cherish us both together. May we work together with full energy. May our study be perfect and achieve good results. May we never have ill will towards others.

Om peace, peace, peace.

CHAPTER II: BRAHMANANDA VALLI

LESSON ONE

ब्रह्मविदाप्नोति परम् । तदेषाभ्युक्ता ॥ 1 ॥

Brahmavidaapnoti Param; Tadeshaabhyuktaa. (1)

One who realizes Brahman attains the Supreme; in this context it has been proclaimed.

सत्यं ज्ञानमनन्तं ब्रह्म । यो वेद निहित गुहायां परमं व्योमन् । सोऽश्नुते सर्वान् कामान् सह ब्रह्मणा विपश्चितेति ॥ 2 ॥

Satyam Jnaanamanantam Brahma; Yo Veda Nihita Guhaayaam Parame Vyoman; Soashnute Sarvaan Kaamaan Saha Brahmanaa Vipashchiteti. (2)

Brahman is truth, knowledge and boundless. One who realizes that Brahman as resting in the intellect, in the highest space, in the cave of the heart, fulfils all desires, as Brahman is all-knowing.

तस्माद्वा एतस्मादात्मन आकाश: सम्भूत: । आकाशाद्वायु: । वायोरग्नि: । अग्नेराप: । अद्भ्य: पृथिवी । पृथिव्या ओषधय: । ओषधीभ्योऽन्नम् । अन्नात्पुरुष: । स वा एष पुरुषोऽन्नरसमय: । तस्येदमेव शिर: । अयं दक्षिण: पक्ष: । अयमुत्तर: पक्ष: । अयमात्मा । इदं पुच्छं प्रतिष्ठा । तदप्येष श्लोको भवति ॥ 3 ॥

Tasmaadvaa Etasmaadaatmana Aakaashah Sambhootah; Aakaashaadvaayuh; Vaayoragnih; Agneraapah; Adbhyah Prithivee; Prithivyaa Oshadhayah; Oshadheebhyoannam; Annaatpurushah; Sa Vaa Esha Purushoannarasamayah; Tasyedameva Shirah; Ayam Dakshinah Pakshah; Ayamuttarah Pakshah; Ayam Aatmaa; Idam Puchchham Pratishthaa; Tadapyesha Shloko Bhavati. (3)

From that very Atman (Self), which has been referred to as Brahman, ether came into existence; from ether, air; from air, fire; from fire, water; from water, the earth; from the earth, herbs; from herbs, food; and from food was born man. Man, as he is, is the yield of the essence of food indeed. This, verily, is his head, his right side, his left side, his trunk, his self and the hind part forming the basis. There is a verse explaining the same fact.

LESSON TWO

अन्नाद्वै प्रजाः प्रजायन्ते । याः काश्च पृथिवीꣳ श्रिताः । अथो अन्नेनैव जीवन्ति । अथैनदपि यन्त्यन्ततः । अन्नꣳ हि भूतानां ज्येष्ठम् । तस्मात्सर्वौषधमुच्यते । सर्वं वै तेऽन्नमाप्नुवन्ति येऽन्नं ब्रह्मोपासते । अन्नꣳ हि भूतानां ज्येष्ठम् । तस्मात्सर्वौषधमुच्यते । अन्नाद्भूतानि जायन्ते । जातान्यन्नेन वर्धन्ते । अद्यतेऽत्ति च भूतानि । तस्मादन्नं तदुच्यत इति ॥ १ ॥

Annaadvai Prajaah Prajaayante; Yaah Kaashcha Prithiveem Shritaah; Atho Annenaiva Jeevanti; Athainadapi Yantyantatah; Annam Hi Bhootaanaam Jyeshtham; Tasmaatsarvaushadha-muchyate; Sarvam Vai Teannamaapnuvanti Yeannam Brahmopaasate; Annam Hi Bhootaanaam Jyeshtham; Tasmaatsarvaushadhamuchyate; Annaadbhootaani Jaayante; Jaataanyannena Vardhante; Adyateatti Cha Bhootaani; Tasmaadannam Taduchyata Iti. (1)

Whatsoever living beings live on this earth, truly they are born from food, also they remain alive on food alone, and in the same way they return into it at the end. Food is verily the first among all that is created; therefore, it is said to be the medicine for all. One who meditates on food as Brahman surely obtains all food. Verily, food is the first among all, hence it is the universal remedy. All creatures are born from food, they grow by food. All beings consume it and are consumed by it, hence it is regarded as food.

तस्माद्वा एतस्मादन्नरसमयादन्योऽन्तर आत्मा प्राणमय: । तेनैष पूर्ण: । स
वा एष पुरुषविध एव । तस्य पुरुषविधतामन्वयं पुरुषविध: । तस्य प्राण
एव शिर: । व्यानो दक्षिण: पक्ष: । अपान उत्तर: पक्ष: । आकाश आत्मा ।
पृथिवी पुच्छं प्रतिष्ठा । तदप्येष श्लोको भवति ॥ 2 ॥

*Tasmaadvaa Etasmaadannarasamayaat Anyoantara Aatmaa
Praanamayah; Tenaisha Poornah; Sa Vaa Esha Purushavidha
Eva; Tasya Purushavidhataam Anvayam Purushavidhah; Tasya
Praana Eva Shirah; Vyaano Dakshinah Pakshah; Apaana Uttarah
Pakshah; Aakaasha Aatmaa; Prithivee Puchcham Pratishthaa;
Tadapyesha Shloko Bhavati. (2)*

Verily, besides this, which is made of the essence of food,
there is the other inner Self, comprised of vital air (energy)
with which this Self is filled. Really this Self is exactly like the
form of a person. That earlier Self, having taken the form of
a person, accordingly this Self is also the shape of a person.
Of this, prana, indeed, is the head, vyana is the right side,
apana is the left side, space is the Self and earth is the support
and foundation. There is the following verse about it.

LESSON THREE

प्राणं देवा अनु प्राणन्ति । मनुष्या: पशवश्च ये । प्राणो हि भूतानामायु: ।
तस्मात्सर्वायुषमुच्यते । सर्वमेव त आयुर्यन्ति ये प्राणं ब्रह्मोपासते । प्राणो हि
भूतानामायु: । तस्मात्सर्वायुषमुच्यत इति । तस्यैष एव शारीर आत्मा य:
पूर्वस्य ॥ 1 ॥

*Praanam Devaa Anu Praananti; Manushyaah Pashavashcha Ye;
Praano Hi Bhootaanaamaayuh; Tasmaatsarvaayushamuchyate;
Sarvameva Ta Aayuryanti Ye Praanam Brahmopaasate; Praano
Hi Bhootaanaamaayuh; Tasmaatsarvaayushamuchyata Iti;
Tasyaisha Eva Shaareera Aatmaa Yah Poorvasya. (1)*

Whatsoever gods, men or animals exist, all depend on prana
(vital force) for their lives. Really, prana is the vital force of

all creatures; therefore, it is regarded as the universal life. Those who worship prana as Brahman surely attain the full span of life. Prana is the life of all living beings; therefore, it is called the life of all. The embodied Self of the earlier one is this one, indeed.

तस्माद्वा एतस्मात्प्राणमयादन्योऽन्तर आत्मा मनोमयः । तेनैष पूर्णः । स वा एष पुरुषविध एव। तस्य पुरुषविधतामन्वय पुरुषविधः । तस्य यजुरेव शिरः । ऋग्दक्षिणः पक्षः । सामोत्तरः पक्षः । आदेश आत्मा । अथर्वाङ्गिरसः पुच्छं प्रतिष्ठा । तदप्येष श्लोको भवति ॥ 2 ॥

Tasmaadvaa Etasmaatpraanamayaat Anyoantara Aatmaa Manomayah; Tenaisha Poornah; Sa Vaa Esha Purushavidha Eva; Tasya Purushavidhataam Anvayam Purushavidhah; Tasya Yajureva Shirah; Rig Dakshinah Pakshah; Saamottarah Pakshah; Aadesha Aatmaa; Atharvaangirasah Puchchham Pratishthaa; Tadpyesha Shloko Bhavati. (2)

As for that former Self comprised of prana, there is another Self consisting of mind within, by which this inner Self is filled. That Self comprised of mind is also like the shape of a person according to the other ones, being in the form of a person. Of this, Yajus is the head, Rik is his right side, Sama is his left side, the Brahman portion (injunctive part) is his trunk, and the hymns of the Atharva Veda are his support and foundation. There is the following verse about it.

LESSON FOUR

यतो वाचो निवर्तन्ते । अप्राप्य मनसा सह । आनन्दं ब्रह्मणो विद्वान् । न बिभेति कदाचनेति । तस्यैष एव शारीर आत्मा यः पूर्वस्य ॥ 1 ॥

Yato Vaacho Nivartante; Apraapya Manasaa Saha; Aanandam Brahmano Vidvaan; Na Bibheti Kadaachaneti; Tasyaisha Eva Shaareera Aatmaa Yah Poorvasya. (1)

Where all speech along with mind retreat, being unable to reach, one who knows the bliss of the Brahman parts with fear forever. Verily, this one is the embodied Self of the former.

तस्माद्वा एतस्मान्मनोमयादन्योऽन्तर आत्मा विज्ञानमयस्तेनैष पूर्ण: । स वा एष पुरुषविध एव । तस्य पुरुषविधतामन्वयं पुरुषविध: । तस्य श्रद्धैव शिर: । ऋतं दक्षिण: पक्ष: । सत्यमुत्तर: पक्ष: । योग आत्मा । मह: पुच्छं प्रतिष्ठा । तदप्येष श्लोको भवति ॥ 2 ॥

Tasmaadvaa Etasmaanmanomayaat Anyoantara Aatmaa Vijnaanamayastenaisha Poornah; Sa Vaa Esha Purushavidha Eva; Tasya Purushavidhataam Anvayam Purushavidhah; Tasya Shraddhaiva Shirah; Ritam Dakshinah Pakshah; Satyamuttarah Pakshah; Yoga Aatmaa; Mahah Puchchham Pratishthaa; Tadapyesha Shloko Bhavati. (2)

Separate from that Self comprised of mind, there is another inner self consisting of intelligence by which this one is filled. This one is also like the shape of a person according to the other ones. Surely, faith is his head, righteousness is his right wing, truth is his left wing, Yoga is his trunk and Maha is his support and foundation. There is the following verse about it.

LESSON FIVE

विज्ञानं यज्ञं तनुते । कर्माणि तनुतेऽपि च । विज्ञानं देवा: सर्वे । ब्रह्म ज्येष्ठमुपासते । विज्ञानं ब्रह्म चेद्वेद । तस्माच्चेन्न प्रमाद्यति । शरीरे पाप्मनो हित्वा । सर्वान्कामान्समश्नुत इति । तस्यैष एव शारीर आत्मा य: पूर्वस्य ॥ 1 ॥

Vijnaanam Yajnam Tanute; Karmaani Tanuteapi Cha; Vijnaanam Devaah Sarve; Brahma Jyeshthamupaasate; Vijnaanam Brahma Chedveda; Tasmaachchenna Pramaadyati; Shareere Paapmano

Hitvaa; Sarvaankaamaansamashnuta Iti; Tasyaisha Eva Shaareera Aatmaa Yah Poorvasya. (1)

The knowledge performs the sacrifice and fulfils the various deeds as well. All gods worship this, the first born, as Brahman. If one realizes knowledge as Brahman and contemplates on Him as Brahman, never inattentive about it, he is freed from all sins in the body and enjoys all desires. Verily, this one is the embodied Self of the former.

तस्माद्वा एतस्माद्विज्ञानमयादन्योऽन्तर आत्माऽऽनन्दमयः । तेनैष पूर्णः । स वा एष पुरुषविध एव । तस्य पुरुषविधतामन्वयं पुरुषविधः । तस्य प्रियमेव शिरः । मोदो दक्षिणः पक्षः । प्रमोद उत्तरः पक्षः । आनन्द आत्मा । ब्रह्म पुच्छं प्रतिष्ठा । तदप्येष श्लोको भवति ॥ 2 ॥

Tasmaadvaa Etasmaadvijnaanamayaat Anyoantara Aatmaa Aanandamayah; Tenaisha Poornah; Sa Vaa Esha Purushavidha Eva; Tasya Purushavidhataamanvayam Purushavidhah; Tasya Priyameva Shirah; Modo Dakshinah Pakshah; Pramoda Uttarah Pakshah; Aananda Aatmaa; Brahma Puchchham Pratishthaa; Tadapyesha Shloko Bhavati. (2)

The other one (earlier), within this Self, is also comprised of bliss. Really, this one also is like the form of a person according to the earlier one. Verily, love is his head, joy is his right wing, delight is his left wing, bliss is his trunk, and Brahman is his support and foundation. There is the following verse about it.

LESSON SIX

असन्नेव स भवति । असद्ब्रह्मेति वेद चेत् । अस्ति ब्रह्मेति चेद्वेद । सन्तमेनं ततो विदुरिति ॥ 1 ॥

Asanneva Sa Bhavati; Asadbrahmeti Veda Chet; Asti Brahmeti Chedveda; Santamenam Tato Viduriti. (1)

If a man thinks Brahman is an unreal one, truly, he himself becomes unreal. If he knows Brahman as the real one, then the wise will consider him right and correct in that knowledge.

तस्यैष एव शारीर आत्मा यः पूर्वस्य ॥ 2 ॥

Tasyaisha Eva Shaareera Aatmaa Yah Poorvasya. (2)

This is indeed the embodied soul of the former.

अथातोऽनुप्रश्नाः । उताविद्वानमुं लोकं प्रेत्य कश्चन गच्छती। आहो विद्वानमुं लोकं प्रेत्य कश्चित्समश्नुता उ ॥ 3 ॥

Athaatoanuprashnaah; Utaavidvaanamum Lokam Pretya Kashchana Gachchhatee; Aaho Vidvaanamum Lokam Pretya Kashchitsamashnutaa U. (3)

Now, therefore, the questions (regarding the lessons taught before) are raised. Does one ignorant about Brahman attain Him after departing from this world? Or does one enlightened about Brahman attain Him after leaving this world?

सोऽकामयत । बहु स्यां प्रजायेयेति । स तपोऽतप्यत । स तपस्तप्त्वा इदᳬ सर्वमसृजत यदिदं किं च । तत्सृष्ट्वा तदेवानुप्राविशत् । तदनुप्रविश्य सच्च त्यच्चाभवत् । निरुक्तं चानिरुक्तं च । निलयनं चानिलयनं च । विज्ञानं चाविज्ञानं च । सत्यं चानृतं च सत्यमभवत् । यदिदं किं च । तत्सत्यमित्याचक्षते । तदप्येष श्लोको भवति ॥ 4 ॥

Soakaamayata; Bahu Syaam Prajaayeyeyeti; Sa Tapoatapyata; Sa Tapastaptvaa Idam Sarvamasrijata Yadidam Kim Cha; Tatsrishtvaa Tadevaanupraavishat; Tadanupravishya Sachcha Tyachchaabhavat; Niruktam Chaaniruktam Cha; Nilayanam Chaanilayanam Cha; Vijnaanam Chaavijnaanam Cha; Satyam Chaanritam Cha Satyamabhavat; Yadidam Kim Cha; Tatsatyamityaachakshate; Tadapyesha Shloko Bhavati. (4)

He, the Self (Atman) desired: May I become numerous, let me be born. He brooded over himself. That Brahman, having created, entered into the very thing and having entered, then He became the formed and formless, defined and undefined, supported and unsupported, conscious and unconscious, the real and the unreal. Whatever there is, He became that reality. For this reason the sages say that all is real, the Brahman. There is the following verse about it.

LESSON SEVEN

असद्वा इदमग्र आसीत् ततो वै सदजायत । तदात्मान ्ँ स्वयमकुरुत । तस्मात्तत्सुकृतमुच्यत इति ॥ 1 ॥

Asadvaa Idamagra Aaseet Tato Vai Sadajaayata; Tadaatmaanam Svayamakuruta; Tasmaat Tatsukritamuchyata Iti. (1)

In the beginning all this was indeed the unmanifested Brahman. From that the manifested sprang up. That Brahman created himself by the self. Therefore, he is called the self-made.

यद्वै तत्सुकृतं रसो वै स: । रस ्ँ ह्येवायं लब्ध्वाऽऽनन्दी भवति । को ह्येवान्यात्क: प्राण्याद् यदेष आकाश आनन्दो न स्यात् । एष ह्येवानन्दयाति ॥ 2 ॥

Yadvai Tatsukritam Raso Vai Sah; Rasam Hyevaayam Labdhvaa Aanandee Bhavati; Ko Hyevaanyaat Kah Praanyaad Yadesha Aakaasha Aanando Na Syaat; Esha Hyevaanandayaati. (2)

He who is known as self-made is truly the source of joy. Whosoever comes into association with that source of joy becomes blessed. Who, indeed, will breathe in and breathe out if this bliss be not in the ether? He is the cause of that blessedness.

यदा ह्येवैष एतस्मिन्नदृश्येऽनात्म्येऽनिरुक्तेऽनिलयनेऽभयं प्रतिष्ठां विन्दते।
अथ सोऽभयं गतो भवति ॥ 3 ॥

*Yadaa Hyevaisha Etasminnadrishyeanaatmyeanirukteanilayanea-
bhayam Pratishthaam Vindate; Atha Soabhayam Gato Bhavati. (3)*

When an aspirant is firmly established in that invisible,
selfless, unutterable, supportless Brahman he becomes
fearless.

यदा ह्येवैष एतस्मिन्नुदरमन्तरं कुरुते। अथ तस्य भयं भवति । तत्त्वेव भयं
विदुषो मन्वानस्य । तदप्येष श्लोको भवति ॥ 4 ॥

*Yadaa Hyevaisha Etasminnudaramantaram Kurute; Atha Tasya
Bhayam Bhavati Tattveva Bhayam Vidusho Manvaanasya;
Tadapyesha Shloko Bhavati. (4)*

And whenever he creates the smallest difference in that
state, then he is engrossed in fear. That is why even a wise
man has fear when he is not reflective. There is the following
verse about that.

LESSON EIGHT

भीषास्माद्वातः पवते । भीषोदेति सूर्यः । भीषास्मादग्निश्चेन्द्रश्च मृत्युर्धावति
पञ्चम इति ।

*Bheesha Asmaadvaatah Pavate; Bheeshodeti Sooryah; Bheeshaa
Asmaadagnishchendrashcha Mrityurdhaavati Panchama Iti.*

सैषाऽऽनन्दस्य मीसाँसा भवति । युवा स्यात्साधुयुवाध्यायक आशिष्ठो
द्रढिष्ठो बलिष्ठस्तस्येयं पृथिवी सर्वा वित्तस्य पूर्णा स्यात् । स एको मानुष
आनन्दः ।

*Saishaa Aanandasya Meemaamsaa Bhavati; Yuvaa Syaatsaadhu
Yuvaadhyaayaka Aashishtho Dradhishtho Balishthah Tasyeyam*

239

Prithivee Sarvaa Vittasya Poornaa Syaat. Sa Eko Maanusha Aanandah.

ते ये शतं मानुषा आनन्दा: । स एको मनुष्यगन्धर्वाणामानन्द: । श्रोत्रियस्य चाकामहतस्य ।

Te Ye Shatam Maanushaa Aanandaah; Sa Eko Manushya-gandharvaanaamaanandah; Shrotriyasya Chaakaamahatasya.

ते ये शतं मनुष्यगन्धर्वाणामानन्द: । स एको देवगन्धर्वाणामानन्द: । श्रोत्रियस्य चाकामहतस्य।

Te Ye Shatam Manushyagandharvaanaamaanandah; Sa Eko Devagandharvaanaamaanandah Shrotriyasya Chaakaamahatasya.

ते ये शतं देवगन्धर्वाणामानन्द: । स एक: पितृणां चिरलोकलोकानामानन्द: । श्रोत्रियस्य चाकामहतस्य ।

Te Ye Shatam Devagandharvaanaamaanandah; Shrotriyasya Chaakaamahatasya.

ते ये शतं पितृणां चिरलोकलोकानामानन्दा: । स एक आजानजानां देवानामानन्द: । श्रोत्रियस्य चाकामहतस्य ।

Te Ye Shatam Pitrinaam Chiralokalokaanaamaanandaah; Sa Eka Aajaanajaanaam Devaanaamaanandah; Shrotriyasya Chaakaa-mahatasya.

ते ये शतमाजानजानां देवानामानन्द: । स एक: कर्मदेवानां देवानामानन्द:। ये कर्मणा देवानपियन्ति । श्रोत्रियस्य चाकामहतस्य ।

Te Ye Shatamaajaanajaanaam Devaanaamaanandaah; Sa Ekah Karmadevaanaam Devaanaamaanandah; Ye Karmanaa Devaanapiyanti; Shrotriyasya Chaakaamahatasya.

ते ये शतं कर्मदेवानां देवानामानन्दा: । स एको देवानामानन्द: । श्रोत्रियस्य चाकामहतस्य ।

Te Ye Shatam Karmadevaanaam Devaanaamaanandaah; Sa Eko Devaanaamaanandah; Shrotriyasya Chaakaamahatasya.

ते ये शतं देवानामानन्द: । स एक इन्द्रस्यानन्द: । श्रोत्रियस्य चाकामहतस्य ।

Te Ye Shatam Devaanaamaanandaah; Sa Eka Indrasyaanandah; Shrotriyasya Chaakaamahatasya.

ते ये शतमिन्द्रस्यानन्दा: । स एको बृहस्पतेरानन्द: । श्रोत्रियस्य चाकामहतस्य ।

Te Ye Shatamindrasyaanandaah; Sa Eko Brihaspateraanandah; Shrotriyasya Chaakaamahatasya.

ते ये शतं बृहस्पतेरानन्दा: । स एक: प्रजापतेरानन्द: । श्रोत्रियस्य चाकामहतस्य ।

Te Ye Shatam Brihaspateraanandaah; Sa Ekah Prajaapater- aanandah; Shrotriyasya Chaakaamahatasya.

ते ये शतं प्रजापतेरानन्दा: । स एको ब्रह्मण आनन्द: । श्रोत्रियस्य चाकामहतस्य ।

Te Ye Shatam Prajaapateraanandaah; Sa Eko Brahmana Aanandah Shrotriyasya Chaakaamahatasya.

स यश्चायं पुरुषे यश्चासावादित्ये स एक: । स य एवंविदस्माल्लोकात्प्रेत्य। एतमन्नमयमात्मानमुपसंक्रामति । एवं प्राणमयमात्मानमुपसंक्रामति । एतं मनोमयमात्मानमुपसंक्रामति । एतं विज्ञानमयमात्मानमुपसंक्रामति । एतमानन्दमयमात्मानमुपसंक्रामति । तदप्येष श्लोको भवति।

Sa Yashchaayam Purushe Yashchaasaavaaditye Sa Ekah; Sa Ya Evamvidasmaallokaat Pretya; Etamannamayam Aatmaanamu-

pasankraamati; Etam Praanamayamaatmaanam Upasankraamati;
Etam Manomayamaatmaanamupasankraamati; Etam Vijnaana-
mayamaatmaanamupasankraamati; Etamaanandamayamaatmaa-
namupasankraamati; Tadapyesha Shloko Bhavati.

Out of fear for him the wind blows, through fear of him the
sun rises, through fear of him Agni, also Indra and Death,
the fifth, run thus.

This then is the scrutiny of that bliss. Take for granted
that there is a youth, a noble youth, in the prime of his age,
good, learned, well-built and alert, and suppose the entire
earth, full of all riches, belongs to him. This will be regarded
as one unit of human joy. One hundred such units of
human joy make a single unit of a joy which the Man-
Gandharvas possess. The enlightened and desireless sages
also possess the same joy. One hundred such units of joy
which the Man-Gandharvas possess make the joy of the
Divine-Gandharvas. One hundred such units of joy which
the Divine-Gandharvas possess make the joy of the Manes,
whose world is everlasting. One hundred such units of joy
which the Manes possess make the joy of heaven-born Gods.
One hundred such units of joy which the heaven-born Gods
possess make the joy of those who have become Gods by
their deeds; one hundred such units of joy which those who
have become Gods by their deeds make the joy of the eternal
Gods. One hundred such units of joy of the highest Gods
make the joy of Indra. One hundred such units of joy of
Indra make the joy of Brihaspati. One hundred such units
of joy make the joy of Prajapati. One hundred such units of
the joy of Prajapati make the bliss of Brahman.

The fully enlightened and desireless sages possess all
these measures, separately and collectively. This bliss in the
human being and in the sun are the same. One who knows,
as explained above, attains thus after departing from this
world and crosses over the annamaya, pranamaya, mano-

maya, vijnanamaya and anandamaya selves. There is the following verse regarding that.

LESSON NINE

यतो वाचो निवर्तन्ते अप्राप्य मनसा सह । आनन्दं ब्रह्मणो विद्वान् न विभेति कुतश्चनेति ॥ 1 ॥

Yato Vaacho Nivartante Apraapya Manasaa Saha; Aanandam Brahmano Vidvaan Na Vibheti Kutashchaneti. (1)

That from which all speech returns, together with the mind, failing to reach Him. Knowing that bliss of Brahman, the enlightened man does not fear.

एतꣳह वाव न तपति । किमहꣳ साधु नाकरवम् । किमहं पापमकरवमिति। स य एवं विद्वानेते आत्मानꣳ स्पृणुते । उभे ह्येवैष एते आत्मानꣳ स्पृणुते । य एवं वेद । इत्युपनिषत् ॥ 2 ॥

Etam Ha Vaava Na Tapati; Kimaham Saadhu Naakaravam; Kimaham Paapamakaravamiti; Sa Ya Evam Vidvaanete Aatmaanam Sprinute; Ubhe Hyevaisha Ete Aatmaanam Sprinute; Ya Evam Veda. Ityupanishat. (2)

Verily, to him the thought: Why have I not done good deeds? Why have I done bad deeds? does not, of course, cause distress. One who is enlightened as stated above keeps himself aloof and considers both with the Supreme Self. This is the secret instruction.

CHAPTER III: BHRIGU VALLI

LESSON ONE

भृगुर्वै वारुणिः वरुणं पितरमुपससार अधीहि भगवो ब्रह्मोति । तस्मा एतत्प्रोवाच । अन्नं प्राणं चक्षुः श्रोत्रं मनो वाचमिति । तꣳ होवाच । यतो वा इमानि भूतानि जायन्ते येन जातानि जीवन्ति । यत्प्रयन्त्यभिसंविशन्ति । तद्विजिज्ञासस्व । तद् ब्रह्मोति । स तपोऽतप्यत । स तपस्तप्त्वा ।

Bhrigurvai Vaarunih Varunam Pitaramupasasaara Adheehi Bhagavo Brahmeti; Tasmaa Etat Provaacha; Annam Praanam Chakshuh Shrotram Mano Vaachamiti; Tam Hovaacha; Yato Vaa Imaani Bhootaani Jaayante Yena Jaataani Jeevanti; Yat Prayantyabhisanvishanti; Tad Vijijnaasasva. Tad Brahmeti; Sa Tapoatapyata; Sa Tapastaptvaa.

The famous Bhrigu Varuni came to his father Varuna with a request: Revered Sir, teach me about Brahman. To him, Varuna taught food, vital force, sight, hearing, mind and speech, as a means to know Brahman. Further, Varuna said: Strive for that from where all living beings are born, where they live after being born, and where they ultimately dissolve. That is Brahman. Bhrigu started Tapas. He, having performed austerity,

LESSON TWO

अन्नं ब्रह्मोति व्यजानात् । अन्नाद्ध्येव खल्विमानि भूतानि जायन्ते । अन्नेन जातानि जीवन्ति। अन्नं प्रयन्त्यभिसंविशन्तीति । तद्विज्ञाय पुनरेव वरुणं पितरमुपससार । अधीहि भगवो ब्रह्मोति । तꣳ होवाच । तपसा ब्रह्म विजिज्ञासस्व । तपो ब्रह्मोति । स तपोऽतप्यत । स तपस्तप्त्वा ।

Annam Brahmeti Vyajaanaat; Annaaddhyeva Khalvimaani Bhootaani Jaayante; Annena Jaataani Jeevanti; Annam Prayantyabhisanvishanteeti; Tadvijnaaya Punareva Varunam

244

Pitaramupasasaara; Adheehi Bhagavo Brahmeti; Tam Hovaacha; Tapasaa Brahma Vijijnaasasva; Tapo Brahmeti; Sa Tapoatapyata; Sa Tapastaptvaa.

– came to know that food is Brahman, because from food indeed all these living beings are born and having been born, they live by food and at the end they enter into food again. Having understood thoroughly the reality of food, he again approached Varuna, his father, requesting: Revered Sir, teach me Brahman. To him, Varuna said: Strive for that Brahman through Tapas. Tapas is Brahman. Bhrigu started Tapas. He, having performed austerity,

LESSON THREE

प्राणो ब्रह्मेति व्यजानात् । प्राणाद्ध्येव खल्विमानि भूतानि जायन्ते । प्राणेन जातानि जीवन्ति । प्राणं प्रयन्त्यभिसंविशन्तीति । तद्विज्ञाय पुनरेव वरुणं पितरमुपससार । अधीहि भगवो ब्रह्मेति । तᳵ होवाच । तपसा ब्रह्म विजिज्ञासस्व । तपो ब्रह्मेति । स तपोऽतप्यत । स तपस्तप्त्वा ।

Praano Brahmeti Vyajaanaat. Praanaaddhyeva Khalvimaani Bhootaani Jaayante. Praanena Jaataani Jeevanti. Praanam Prayantyabhisanvishanteeti Tadvijnaaya Punareva Varunam Pitaramupasasaara. Adheehi Bhagavo Brahmeti. Tam Hovaacha. Tapasaa Brahma Vijijnaasasva. Tapo Brahmeti. Sa Tapoatapyata. Sa Tapastaptvaa.

– came to know that prana is Brahman, because from prana, indeed, all living beings are born and having been born, they remain alive by prana and at the end they merge into prana again. Having understood thoroughly the reality of prana, he again approached Varuna, his father, requesting: Revered Sir, teach me Brahman. To him, Varuna said: Strive for that Brahman through Tapas. Tapas is Brahman. Bhrigu started Tapas. He, having performed austerity,

LESSON FOUR

मनो ब्रह्मेति व्यजानात् । मनसो ह्येव खल्विमानि भूतानि जायन्ते। मनसा जातानि जीवन्ति । मन: प्रयन्त्यभिसंविशन्तीति । तद्विज्ञाय पुनरेव वरुणं पितरमुपससार । अधीहि भगवो ब्रह्मेति । त॰ होवाच । तपसा ब्रह्म विजिज्ञासस्व । तपो ब्रह्मेति । स तपोऽतप्यत । स तपस्तप्त्वा ।

Mano Brahmeti Vyajaanaat; Manaso Hyeva Khalvimaani Bhootaani Jaayante; Manasaa Jaataani Jeevanti; Manah Prayantyabhisanvishanteeti; Tadvijnaaya Punareva Varunam Pitaramupasasaara; Adheehi Bhagavo Brahmeti; Tam Hovaacha; Tapasaa Brahma Vijijnaasasva; Tapo Brahmeti; Sa Tapoatapyata; Sa Tapastaptvaa.

– came to know that mind is Brahman, because from mind, indeed, all living beings are born and having been born, they remain alive by mind and at the end they absorb into mind again. Having understood thoroughly the reality of mind, he again approached Varuna, his father, requesting: Revered Sir, teach me Brahman. To him, Varuna said: Strive for that Brahman through Tapas. Tapas is Brahman. Bhrigu started Tapas. He, having performed austerity,

LESSON FIVE

विज्ञानं ब्रह्मेति व्यजानात् । विज्ञानाद्ध्येव खल्विमानि भूतानि जायन्ते । विज्ञानेन जातानि जीवन्ति । विज्ञानं प्रयन्त्यभिसंविशन्तीति । तद्विज्ञाय पुनरेव वरुणं पितरमुपससार । अधीहि भगवो ब्रह्मेति । त॰ होवाच । तपसा ब्रह्म विजिज्ञासस्व । तपो ब्रह्मेति । स तपोऽतप्यत । स तपस्तप्त्वा ।

Vijnaanam Brahmeti Vyajaanaat; Vijnaanaaddhyeva Khalvimaani Bhootaani Jaayante; Vijnaanena Jaataani; Jeevanti; Vijnaanam Prayantyabhisanvishanteeti; Tadvijnaaya Punareva Varunam Pitaramupasasaara; Adheehi Bhagavo Brahmeti; Tam Hovaacha;

Tapasaa Brahma Vijijnaasasva; Tapo Brahmeti; Sa Tapoatapyata; Sa Tapastaptvaa.

– came to know that vijnana (knowledge) is Brahman, because from vijnana, indeed, all living beings here are born and having been born, they remain alive by vijnana and at last they merge into vijnana again. Having understood thoroughly the reality of vijnana, he again approached Varuna, his father, requesting: Revered Sir, teach me Brahman. To him, Varuna said: Strive for that Brahman through Tapas. Tapas is Brahman. Bhrigu started Tapas. He, having performed austerity,

LESSON SIX

आनन्दो ब्रह्मेति व्यजानात् । आनन्दाद्ध्येव खल्विमानि भूतानि जायन्ते । आनन्देन जातानि जीवन्ति । आनन्दं प्रयन्त्यभिसंविशन्तीति । सैषा भार्गवी वारुणी विद्या परमे व्योमन् प्रतिष्ठिता । स य एवं वेद प्रतितिष्ठति । अन्नवानन्नादो भवति । महान् भवति प्रजया पशुभिर्ब्रह्मवर्चसेन । महान् कीर्त्या ।

Aanando Brahmeti Vyajaanaat; Aanandaaddhyeva Khalvimaani Bhootaani Jaayante; Aanandena Jaataani Jeevanti; Aanandam Prayantyabhisanvishanteeti; Saishaa Bhaargavee Vaarunee Vidyaa Parame Vyoman Pratishthitaa; Sa Ya Evam Veda Pratitishthati; Annavaanannaado Bhavati; Mahaan Bhavati Prajayaa Pashubhirbrahmavarchasena; Mahaan Keertyaa.

– came to know that bliss is Brahman, because from bliss, indeed, all living beings here are born and having been born, they remain alive by bliss and at last they merge into bliss again. This knowledge, taught by Varuna and realized by Bhrigu, ends in the highest bliss, established in the cavity of the heart. One who grasps this becomes firmly established, he becomes the possessor and eater of food. He becomes great in progeny, in cattle and the shining of sacred wisdom, and great in glory.

LESSON SEVEN

अन्नं न निन्द्यात् । तद्व्रतम् । प्राणो वा अन्नम् । शरीरमन्त्रादम् । प्राणे शरीरं प्रतिष्ठितम् । शरीरे प्राणः प्रतिष्ठितः । तदेतदन्नमन्ने प्रतिष्ठितम् । स य एतदन्नमन्ने प्रतिष्ठितं वेद प्रतितिष्ठति । अन्नवानन्नादो भवति। महान् भवति प्रजया पशुभिर्ब्रह्मवर्चसेन । महान् कीर्त्या ।

Annam Na Nindyaat; Tad Vratam; Praano Vaa Annam; Shareeramannaadam; Praane Shareeram Pratishthitam; Shareere Praanah Pratishthitah; Tadetadannamanne Pratishthitam; Sa Ya Etadannamaane Pratishthitam Veda Pratitishthati; Anna-vaanannaado Bhavati; Mahaan Bhavati Prajayaa Pashubhir-brahmavarchasena; Mahaan Keertyaa.

One should not find fault with food. This sacred rule should be followed. Vital force (life breath) is indeed food. The body is the consumer of food. The body is dependent upon the life breath and the life breath depends upon the body. Therefore, food is dependent on food. Thus, one who knows that food is dependent on food becomes firmly established. He becomes the possessor and enjoyer of food. Similarly, he becomes great in progeny, in cattle and the shining of sacred wisdom and great in glory.

LESSON EIGHT

अन्नं न परिचक्षीत । तद् व्रतम् । आपो वा अन्नम् । ज्योतिरन्नादम् । अप्सु ज्योतिः प्रतिष्ठितम् । ज्योतिष्याप: प्रतिष्ठिता: । तदेतदन्नमन्ने प्रतिष्ठितम् । सय एतदन्नमन्ने प्रतिष्ठितं वेद प्रतितिष्ठति । अन्नवानन्नादो भवति । महान् भवति प्रजया पशुभिर्ब्रह्मवर्चसेन । महान् कीर्त्या ।

Annam Na Parichaksheeta; Tad Vratam; Aapo Vaa Annam;
Jyotirannaadam; Apsu Jyotih Pratishthitam; Jyotishyaapah
Pratishthitaah; Tadetadannamanne Pratishthitam; Sa Ya
Etadannamanne Pratishthitam Veda Pratitishthati;
Annavaanannaado Bhavati; Mahaan Bhavati Prajayaa
Pashubhirbrahmavarchasena; Mahaan Keertyaa.

One should not disregard food. This sacred rule should be
followed. Water indeed is food. Fire is the consumer of food.
Fire is dependent upon water and water is dependent on
fire. Therefore, food is dependent upon food. One who
knows that food is dependent upon food becomes firmly
established. He becomes a possessor and enjoyer of food.
Similarly, he becomes great in progeny, in cattle and the
shining of sacred wisdom and great in glory.

LESSON NINE

अन्नं बहु कुर्वीत । तद् व्रतम् । पृथिवी वा अन्नम् । आकाशोऽन्नाद: ।
पृथिव्यामाकाश: प्रतिष्ठित: । आकाशे पृथिवी प्रतिष्ठिता। तदेतदन्नमन्ने
प्रतिष्ठितम् । स य एतदन्नमन्ने प्रतिष्ठितं वेद प्रतितिष्ठति । अन्नवानन्नादो
भवति । महान् भवति प्रजया पशुभिर्ब्रह्मवर्चसेन । महान् कीर्त्या ।

Annam Bahu Kurveeta; Tad Vratam; Prithivee Vaa Annam;
Aakaashoannaadah; Prithivyaamaakaashah Pratishthitah; Aakaashe
Prithivee Pratishthitaa; Tadetadannamanne Pratishthitam; Sa Ya
Etadannamanne Pratishthitam Veda Pratitishthati; Annavaanan-
naado Bhavati; Mahaan Bhavati Prajayaa Pashubhir-
brahmavarchasena; Mahaan Keertyaa.

One should produce plenty of food. This sacred rule should
be followed. The earth, indeed, is food. Space is the consumer
of food. The space is dependent on earth and the earth is
dependent upon space. Therefore, food is dependent upon
food. One who knows that food is dependent on food
becomes firmly established. He becomes a possessor and

enjoyer of food. Similarly, he becomes great in progeny, in cattle and the shining of sacred wisdom and great in glory.

LESSON TEN

न कंचन वसतौ प्रत्याचक्षीत । तद् व्रतम् । तस्माद्यया कया च विधया बह्वन्नं प्राप्नुयात् । आराध्यस्मा अन्नमित्याचक्षते । एतद्वै मुखतोऽन्न ़ राद्धम् । मुखतोऽस्मा अन्न ़ राध्यते । एतद्वै मध्यतोऽन्न ़ राद्धम् । मध्यतोऽस्मा अन्न ़ राध्यते एतद्वा अन्ततोऽन्न ़ राद्धम् । अन्ततोऽस्मा अन्न ़ राध्यते । य एवं वेद ॥ 1 ॥

Na Kanchana Vasatau Pratyaachaksheeta; Tad Vratam; Tasmaadyayaa Kayaa Cha Vidhayaa Bahvannam Praapnuyaat; Aaraadhyasmaa Annamityaachakshate; Etad Vai Mukhatoannam Raaddham; Mukhatoasmaa Annam Raadhyate. Etad Vai Madhyatoannam Raddham Madhyatoasmaa Annam Raadhyate Etad Vaa Antatoannam Raddham; Antatoasmaa Annam Raadhyate;. Ya Evam Veda. (1)

An aspirant should not turn back anyone who comes to his residence. This sacred rule should be followed. Therefore, he should collect plenty of food, by all means whatsoever. They (householders) should say that the food is ready for the guest. The food which is cooked and offered in the best possible way returns to the giver in exactly the same manner; if given in the medium way, it returns in the medium way, and if offered in the lowest way, it returns to the giver in the lowest way. One who knows this, as explained, obtains the results stated above.

क्षेम इति वाचि । योगक्षेम इति प्राणापानयो: । कर्मेति हस्तयो: । गतिरिति पादयो: । विमुक्तिरिति पायौ । इति मानुषी: समाज्ञा: । अथ दैवी: । तृप्तिरिति वृष्टौ । बलमिति विद्युति । यश इति पशुषु । ज्योतिरिति नक्षत्रेषु। प्रजातिरमृतमानन्द इत्युपस्थे । सर्वमित्याकाशे ॥ 2 ॥

Kshema Iti Vaachi; Yogakshema Iti Praanaapaanayoh; Karmeti Hastayoh; Gatiriti Paadayoh; Vimuktiriti Paayau; Iti Maanusheeh Samaajnaah; Atha Daiveeh; Triptiriti Vrishtau; Balamiti Vidyuti; Yasha Iti Pashushu; Jyotiriti Nakshatreshu; Prajaatiramrita-maananda Ityupasthe; Sarvamityaakaashe. (2)

One should meditate on Brahman as preservation in speech, as acquisition and preservation in prana and apana, as work in the hands, as motion in the feet and evacuation in the anus. These meditations pertain to man.

Then the following refer to the gods. One should meditate on Brahman as gratification in rain, as vigour in lightning, as fame in animals, as light in the stars, as procreation, immortality and joy in the generative organs, and as all in space.

तत्प्रतिष्ठेत्युपासीत । प्रतिष्ठावान् भवति । तन्मह इत्युपासीत । महान् भवति । तन्मन इत्युपासीत । मानवान् भवति । तन्नम इत्युपासीत । नम्यन्तेऽस्मै कामा: । तद् ब्रह्मेत्युपासीत । ब्रह्मवान् भवति । तद् ब्रह्मण: परिमर इत्युपासीत । पर्यणं म्रियन्ते द्विषन्त: सपत्ना: । परियेऽप्रिया भ्रातृव्या: ॥ 3 ॥

Tatpratishthetyupaaseet; Pratishthaavaan Bhavati; Tanmaha Ityupaaseeta; Mahaan Bhavati; Tanmana Ityupaaseeta; Maanavaan Bhavati; Tannama Ityupaaseeta; Namyanteasmai Kaamaah; Tad Brahmetyupaaseeta; Brahmavaan Bhavati; Tad Brahmanah Parimara Ityupaaseeta; Paryenam Mriyante Dvishantah Sapatnaah Pariyeapriyaa Bhraatrivyaah. (3)

One should meditate on Him as the basis of all, thereby one becomes well-based. One should meditate on Him as greatness, thereby one becomes great. One should meditate on Him as mind, then one becomes mindful. One should meditate on Him as bowing down in homage, thereby all desired objects bow down before him. One should meditate on Him as the highest God, thereby one possesses supremacy.

One should meditate on Him as destructive power, thereby all his hateful opponents and enemies surrounding him die.

स यश्चायं पुरुषे यश्चासावादित्ये स एक: । स य एवंवित् । अस्माल्लोकात्प्रेत्य । एतमन्नमयमयमात्मानमुपसंक्रम्य । एतं प्राणमयमात्मानमुपसंक्रम्य । एतं मनोमयमात्मानमुपसंक्रम्य । एतं विज्ञानमयमात्मानमुपसंक्रम्य । एतमानन्दमयमात्मानमुपसंक्रम्य । इमाँल्लोकान्कामान्नी कामरूप्यनुसंचरन् । एतत्साम गायन्नास्ते ।।४।।

Sa Yashchaayam Purushe Yashchaasaavaaditye Sa Ekah; Sa Ya Evamvit; Asmaallokaat Pretya; Etam Annamayamaatmaanam-upasankramya; Etam Praanamayamaatmaanamupasankramya; Etam Manomayam Aatmaanamupasankramya; Etam Vijnaana-mayamaatmaanamupasankramya; Etamaanandamayam-aatmaanam Upasankramya; Imaanllokaan Kaamaannee Kaamaroopyanusancharan; Etat Saama Gaayannaaste. (4)

He who is here in person and He who is yonder in the sun are One. He who knows this, on departing from this world transcends that self which consists of food, transcends that self which consists of life, transcends that self which consists of mind, transcends that self which consists of under-standing, transcends that self which consists of bliss, goes up and down these worlds, eating the food he desires, assuming the form he desires. He sits singing this chant:

हावु हावु हावु । अहमन्नमहमन्नमहमन्नम् । अहमन्नादोऽहमन्नादोऽहमन्नाद: । अहꣳश्लोककृदहꣳ श्लोककृदहꣳश्लोककृत् । अहमस्मि प्रथमजा ऋतास्य । पूर्वं देवेभ्योऽमृतस्य नाभायि । यो मा ददाति स इदेव मा ३ व: । अहमन्नमन्नमदन्तमाद्मि । अहं विश्वं भुवनमभ्यभवाम् । सुवर्ण ज्योति: । य एवं वेद । इत्युपनिषत् ।।५।।

Haavu Haavu Haavu; Ahamannamahamannamahamannam; Ahamannaado Ahamannaado Ahamannaadah; Aham-shlokakridaham Shlokakridaham Shlokakrit; Ahamasmi

252

Prathamajaa Ritaa Asya; Poorvam Devebhyo Amritasya Naabhaayi; Yo Maa Dadaati Sa Ideva Maa 3 Vaah; Ahamannaman- namadantamaadmi; Aham Vishvam Bhuvanamabhyabhavaam; Suvarna Jyotih; Ya Evam Veda; Ityupanishat. (5)

O Wonderful, O Wonderful, O Wonderful. I am food, I am food, I am food. I am the food eater, I am the food eater, I am the food eater. I am the combining agent, I am the combining agent, I am the combining agent. I am the firstborn of the world order, earlier than the gods, in the centre of immortality. Whosoever gives me, he surely does save thus. I, who am food, eat the eater of food. I have overcome the whole world. I am brilliant like the sun. He who knows this, such is the secret doctrine.

SHANTI PATH

ॐ शं नो मित्र: शं वरुण: । शं नो भवत्वर्यमा । शं न इन्द्रो बृहस्पति: । शं नो विष्णुरुरुक्रम:। नमो ब्रह्मणे। नमस्ते वायो । त्वमेव प्रत्यक्षं ब्रह्मासि। त्वामेव प्रत्यक्षं ब्रह्म वदिष्यामि । ऋतं वदिष्यामि । सत्यं वदिष्यामि । तन्मामवतु । तद्वक्तारमवतु । अवतु माम् । अवतु वक्तारम् ।

ॐ शान्ति: शान्ति: शान्ति:

Om Sham No Mitrah Sham Varunah; Sham No Bhavatvaryamaa; Sham Na Indro Brihaspatih; Sham No Vishnururukramah; Namo Brahmane; Namaste Vaayo; Tvameva Pratyaksham Brahmaasi; Tvaameva Pratyaksham Brahma Vadishyaami; Ritam Vadishyaami; Satyam Vadishyaami; Tanmaamavatu; Tadvaktaaramavatu; Avatu Maam; Avatu Vaktaaram.

Om Shaantih Shaantih Shaantih.

May Mitra, Varuna, Aryama, Indra, Brihaspati and wide-spreading Vishnu be gracious to us and bestow upon us happiness and bliss. Salutation to Brahman. O Vayu, salutation to you. You, verily, are the visible Brahman. I shall speak of you alone as the direct Brahman. I shall call you the Cosmic Law. I shall call you the Truth. May Brahman protect me. May He protect the teacher. May Brahman protect me, may He protect the teacher.

Om peace, peace, peace.

Notes